ISDN For Dummies® 2nd Edition

W9-AZI-470

Cheat Sheet

Telco Numbers and URLs

Ameritech	24-hour voice/fax-back system: 800-832-6328
	Home ISDN service: 800-419-5400
	Business ISDN service: 800-417-9888
	World Wide Web: http://www.ameritech.com/products/data/isdn/index.html
Bell Atlantic	ISDN InfoSpeed Solutions Center: 800-204-7332
	Small business: 800-843-2255
	TeleProducts: 800-221-0845
	World Wide Web: http://www.bell-atl.com/
BellSouth	ISDN individual line service: 800-858-9413
	World Wide Web: http://www.bell.bellsouth.com/
Cincinnati Bell	513-566-3282
GTE	24-hour menu-driven voice/fax-back system: 800-888-8799
	Voice: 214-718-5608
	World Wide Web: http://wcn.gte.com/
Nevada Bell	Small businesses: 702-334-4811
	Large businesses: 702-688-7100
NYNEX New York	24-hour, menu-driven voice/fax-back system: 800-438-4736
	Voice: 914-644-5152
	World Wide Web: http://www.nynex.com/
NYNEX New England	24-hour, menu-driven voice/fax-back system: 800-438-4736
	ISDN Service Center: 800-650-4736
	World Wide Web: http://www.nynex.com/
Pacific Bell	24-hour voice/fax-back system: 800-995-0345
	ISDN Service Center: 800-472-4736
	World Wide Web: http://www.pacbell.com/

Rochester Telephone	716-777-1234
Southwestern Bell	Austin: 800-792-4736
	Dallas: 214-268-1403
	South Houston: 713-567-4300
	North Houston: 713-537-3930
	ISDN DigiLine Service: 800-792-4736 x 500
	World Wide Web: http://www.sbc.com/
US West	24-hour voice/fax-back system: 800-728-4929
	Voice: 800-246-5226
	World Wide Web: http://www.uswest.com/

Eight Steps to ISDN Service

1. Check ISDN availability in your area.

2. Determine your ISDN line configuration options.

3. Figure out what ISDN service will cost you.

4. Develop your ISDN equipment and wiring plan.

5. Assemble your ISDN equipment provisioning information.

6. Shop for your ISDN Internet service provider.

7. Order your ISDN service.

8. Set up your ISDN devices.

...For Dummies: #1 Computer Book Series for Beginners

ISDN ISP Checklist

- ✔ Make sure that you don't have to pay any telephone usage charges beyond a local call.

- ✔ Figure out how much time you spend online and compare charges based on that.

- ✔ Determine whether your ISP is overloaded by asking about the customer-to-CPE ratio, which should be between 8-to-1 and 12-to-1.

- ✔ Make sure that an ISP offers telephone support with a staff that knows about ISDN and different ISDN devices.

- ✔ Shop around for the best total ISDN package pricing plan for your needs.

- ✔ Find out what ISDN remote-access devices the ISP supports or has experience working with.

- ✔ Analyze your ISDN Internet access options. Talk to your friends and associates and talk to several ISPs.

- ✔ Check whether the ISP offers compression. Remember a 4-to-1 compression rate can mean up to a 512 Kbps data communications rate.

ISDN CPE Vendor Web Sites

- ✔ 3Com Corporation: `http://www.3com.com`

- ✔ ADTRAN: `http://www.adtran.com`

- ✔ Alpha Telecom: `http://iquest.com/~ati_usa`

- ✔ Angia Communications: `http://www.angia.com`

- ✔ Ascend Communications: `http://www.ascend.com`

- ✔ Bay Networks: `http://www.baynetworks.com`

- ✔ Cisco Systems: `http://www.cisco.com`

- ✔ Diamond Multimedia: `http://www.diamondmm.com`

- ✔ Eicon Technology: `http://www.eicon.com`

- ✔ E-Tech Research: `http://www.e-tech.com`

- ✔ Farallon Computing: `http://www.farallon.com`

- ✔ Intel: `http://www.intel.com`

- ✔ Motorola: `http://www.motorola.com`

- ✔ PicturePhone Direct: `http://www.picturephone.com`

- ✔ PictureTel Corporation: `http://www.picturetel.com`

- ✔ Tone Commander: `http://www.halcyon.com/tcs`

- ✔ U.S. Robotics: `http://www.usr.com`

- ✔ WINNOV: `http://www.winnov.com`

ISDN

FOR

DUMMIES®

2ND EDITION

ISDN FOR DUMMIES®

2ND EDITION

by David Angell

IDG Books Worldwide, Inc.
An International Data Group Company

Foster City, CA ♦ Chicago, IL ♦ Indianapolis, IN ♦ Southlake, TX

ISDN For Dummies,® 2nd Edition

Published by
IDG Books Worldwide, Inc.
An International Data Group Company
919 E. Hillsdale Blvd.
Suite 400
Foster City, CA 94404
http://www.idgbooks.com (IDG Books Worldwide Web site)
http://www.dummies.com (Dummies Press Web site)

Library of Congress Catalog Card No.: 96-79267

ISBN: 0-7645-0064-3

Printed in the United States of America

10 9 8 7 6 5 4 3 2 1

2O/RT/RR/ZW/IN

Distributed in the United States by IDG Books Worldwide, Inc.

Distributed by Macmillan Canada for Canada; by Contemporanea de Ediciones for Venezuela; by Distribuidora Cuspide for Argentina; by CITEC for Brazil; by Ediciones ZETA S.C.R. Ltda. for Peru; by Editorial Limusa SA for Mexico; by Transworld Publishers Limited in the United Kingdom and Europe; by Academic Bookshop for Egypt; by Levant Distributors S.A.R.L. for Lebanon; by Al Jassim for Saudi Arabia; by Simron Pty. Ltd. for South Africa; by Pustak Mahal for India; by The Computer Bookshop for India; by Toppan Company Ltd. for Japan; by Addison Wesley Publishing Company for Korea; by Longman Singapore Publishers Ltd. for Singapore, Malaysia, Thailand, and Indonesia; by Unalis Corporation for Taiwan; by WS Computer Publishing Company, Inc. for the Philippines; by WoodsLane Pty. Ltd. for Australia; by WoodsLane Enterprises Ltd. for New Zealand. Authorized Sales Agent: Anthony Rudkin Associates for the Middle East and North Africa.

For general information on IDG Books Worldwide's books in the U.S., please call our Consumer Customer Service department at 800-762-2974. For reseller information, including discounts and premium sales, please call our Reseller Customer Service department at 800-434-3422.

For information on where to purchase IDG Books Worldwide's books outside the U.S., please contact our International Sales department at 415-655-3172 or fax 415-655-3295.

For information on foreign language translations, please contact our Foreign & Subsidiary Rights department at 415-655-3021 or fax 415-655-3281.

For sales inquiries and special prices for bulk quantities, please contact our Sales department at 415-655-3200 or write to the address above.

For information on using IDG Books Worldwide's books in the classroom or for ordering examination copies, please contact our Educational Sales department at 800-434-2086 or fax 817-251-8174.

For press review copies, author interviews, or other publicity information, please contact our Public Relations department at 415-655-3000 or fax 415-655-3299.

For authorization to photocopy items for corporate, personal, or educational use, please contact Copyright Clearance Center, 222 Rosewood Drive, Danvers, MA 01923, or fax 508-750-4470.

is a trademark under exclusive license to IDG Books Worldwide, Inc., from International Data Group, Inc.

About the Author

David Angell

David Angell has authored or coauthored 15 books on a wide range of computer topics. He is a principal in angell.com (`www.angell.com`), a technical communications firm based in Boston, Massachusetts. David is a frequent contributor to *Internet World* and other computer-related magazines. You can contact David via e-mail at `david@angell.com`.

ABOUT IDG BOOKS WORLDWIDE

Welcome to the world of IDG Books Worldwide.

IDG Books Worldwide, Inc., is a subsidiary of International Data Group, the world's largest publisher of computer-related information and the leading global provider of information services on information technology. IDG was founded more than 25 years ago and now employs more than 8,500 people worldwide. IDG publishes more than 275 computer publications in over 75 countries (see listing below). More than 60 million people read one or more IDG publications each month.

Launched in 1990, IDG Books Worldwide is today the #1 publisher of best-selling computer books in the United States. We are proud to have received eight awards from the Computer Press Association in recognition of editorial excellence and three from *Computer Currents*' First Annual Readers' Choice Awards. Our best-selling *...For Dummies*® series has more than 30 million copies in print with translations in 30 languages. IDG Books Worldwide, through a joint venture with IDG's Hi-Tech Beijing, became the first U.S. publisher to publish a computer book in the People's Republic of China. In record time, IDG Books Worldwide has become the first choice for millions of readers around the world who want to learn how to better manage their businesses.

Our mission is simple: Every one of our books is designed to bring extra value and skill-building instructions to the reader. Our books are written by experts who understand and care about our readers. The knowledge base of our editorial staff comes from years of experience in publishing, education, and journalism — experience we use to produce books for the '90s. In short, we care about books, so we attract the best people. We devote special attention to details such as audience, interior design, use of icons, and illustrations. And because we use an efficient process of authoring, editing, and desktop publishing our books electronically, we can spend more time ensuring superior content and spend less time on the technicalities of making books.

You can count on our commitment to deliver high-quality books at competitive prices on topics you want to read about. At IDG Books Worldwide, we continue in the IDG tradition of delivering quality for more than 25 years. You'll find no better book on a subject than one from IDG Books Worldwide.

IDG BOOKS WORLDWIDE

John J. Kilcullen

John Kilcullen
President and CEO
IDG Books Worldwide, Inc.

WINNER
*Eighth Annual
Computer Press
Awards ≥1992*

WINNER
*Ninth Annual
Computer Press
Awards ≥1993*

WINNER
*Tenth Annual
Computer Press
Awards ≥1994*

WINNER
*Eleventh Annual
Computer Press
Awards ≥1995*

IDG Books Worldwide, Inc., is a subsidiary of International Data Group, the world's largest publisher of computer-related information and the leading global provider of information services on information technology. International Data Group publishes over 275 computer publications in over 75 countries. Sixty million people read one or more International Data Group publications each month. International Data Group's publications include: **ARGENTINA:** Buyer's Guide, Computerworld Argentina, PC World Argentina; **AUSTRALIA:** Australian Macworld, Australian PC World, Australian Reseller News, Computerworld, IT Casebook, Network World, Publish, Webmaster; **AUSTRIA:** Computerwelt Österreich, Networks Austria, PC Tip Austria; **BANGLADESH:** PC World Bangladesh; **BELARUS:** PC World Belarus; **BELGIUM:** Data News; **BRAZIL:** Annuario de Informatica, Computerworld, Connections, Macworld, PC Player, PC World, Publish, Reseller News, Supergamepower; **BULGARIA:** Computerworld Bulgaria, Network World Bulgaria, PC & MacWorld Bulgaria; **CANADA:** CIO Canada, Client/Server World, ComputerWorld Canada, InfoWorld Canada, NetworkWorld Canada, WebWorld; **CHILE:** Computerworld Chile, PC World Chile; **COLOMBIA:** Computerworld Colombia, PC World Colombia; **COSTA RICA:** PC World Centro America; **THE CZECH AND SLOVAK REPUBLICS:** Computerworld Czechoslovakia, Macworld Czech Republic, PC World Czechoslovakia; **DENMARK:** Communications World Danmark, Computerworld Danmark, Macworld Danmark, PC World Danmark, Techworld Denmark; **DOMINICAN REPUBLIC:** PC World Republica Dominicana; **ECUADOR:** PC World Ecuador; **EGYPT:** Computerworld Middle East, PC World Middle East; **EL SALVADOR:** PC World Centro America; **FINLAND:** MikroPC, Tietoverkko, Tietoviikko; **FRANCE:** Distributique, Hebdo, Info PC, Le Monde Informatique, Macworld, Reseaux & Telecoms, WebMaster France; **GERMANY:** Computer Partner, Computerwoche, Computerwoche Extra, Computerwoche FOCUS, Global Online, Macwelt, PC Welt; **GREECE:** Amiga Computing, GamePro Greece, Multimedia World; **GUATEMALA:** PC World Centro America; **HONDURAS:** PC World Centro America; **HONG KONG:** Computerworld Hong Kong, PC World Hong Kong, Publish in Asia; **HUNGARY:** ABCD CD-ROM, Computerworld Szamitastechnika, Internetto online Magazine, PC World Hungary, PC-X Magazin Hungary; **ICELAND:** Tolvuheimur PC World Island; **INDIA:** Information Communications World, Information Systems Computerworld, PC World India, Publish in Asia; **INDONESIA:** InfoKomputer PC World, Komputek Computerworld, Publish in Asia; **IRELAND:** ComputerScope, PC Live!; **ISRAEL:** Macworld Israel, People & Computers/Computerworld; **ITALY:** Computerworld Italia, Macworld Italia, Networking Italia, PC World Italia; **JAPAN:** DTP World, Macworld Japan, Nikkei Personal Computing, OS/2 World Japan, SunWorld Japan, Windows NT World, Windows World Japan; **KENYA:** PC World East African; **KOREA:** Hi-Tech Information, Macworld Korea, PC World Korea; **MACEDONIA:** PC World Macedonia; **MALAYSIA:** Computerworld Malaysia, PC World Malaysia, Publish in Asia; **MALTA:** PC World Malta; **MEXICO:** Computerworld Mexico, PC World Mexico; **MYANMAR:** PC World Myanmar; **NETHERLANDS:** Computer! Totaal, LAN Internetworking Magazine, LAN World Buyers Guide, Macworld Netherlands, Net, WebWereld; **NEW ZEALAND:** Absolute Beginners Guide and Plain & Simple Series, Computer Buyer, Computer Industry Directory, Computerworld New Zealand, MTB, Network World, PC World New Zealand; **NICARAGUA:** PC World Centro America; **NORWAY:** Computerworld Norge, CW Rapport, Datamagasinet, Financial Rapport, Kursguide Norge, Macworld Norge, Multimediaworld Norge, PC World Ekspress Norge, PC World Nettverk, PC World Norge, PC World ProduktGuide Norge; **PAKISTAN:** Computerworld Pakistan; **PANAMA:** PC World Panama; **PEOPLE'S REPUBLIC OF CHINA:** China Computer Users, China Computerworld, China InfoWorld, China Telecom World Weekly, Computer & Communication, Electronic Design China, Electronics Today, Electronics Weekly, Game Software, PC World China, Popular Computer Week, Software Weekly, Software World, Telecom World; **PERU:** Computerworld Peru, PC World Profesional Peru, PC World SoHo Peru; **PHILIPPINES:** Click!, Computerworld Philippines, PC World Philippines, Publish in Asia; **POLAND:** Computerworld Poland, Computerworld Special Report Poland, Cyber, Macworld Poland, Networld Poland, PC World Komputer; **PORTUGAL:** Cerebro/PC World, Computerworld/Correio Informático, Dealer World Portugal, Mac*In/PC*In Portugal, Multimedia World; **PUERTO RICO:** PC World Puerto Rico; **ROMANIA:** Computerworld Romania, PC World Romania, Telecom Romania; **RUSSIA:** Computerworld Russia, Mir PK, Publish, Seti; **SINGAPORE:** Computerworld Singapore, PC World Singapore, Publish in Asia; **SLOVENIA:** Monitor; **SOUTH AFRICA:** Computing SA, Network SA, Software World SA; **SPAIN:** Communicaciones World España, Computerworld España, Dealer World España, Macworld España, PC World España, PC World Espana; **SRI LANKA:** Infolink PC World; **SWEDEN:** CAP&Design, Computer Sweden, Corporate Computing Sweden, Internetworld Sweden, it branschen, Macworld Sweden, MikroDatorn, Nätverk & Kommunikation, PC World Sweden, PCaktiv, Windows World Sweden; **SWITZERLAND:** Computerworld Schweiz, Macworld Schweiz, PCtip; **TAIWAN:** Computerworld Taiwan, Macworld Taiwan, NEW ViSiON/Publish, PC World Taiwan, Windows World Taiwan; **THAILAND:** Publish in Asia, Thai Computerworld; **TURKEY:** Computerworld Turkiye, Macworld Turkiye, Network World Turkiye, PC World Turkiye; **UKRAINE:** Computerworld Kiev, Multimedia World Ukraine, PC World Ukraine; **UNITED KINGDOM:** Acorn User UK, Amiga Action UK, Amiga Computing UK, Apple Talk UK, Computing, Macworld, Parents and Computers UK, PC Advisor, PC Home, PSX Pro, The WEB; **UNITED STATES:** Cable in the Classroom, CIO Magazine, Computerworld, DOS World, Federal Computer Week, GamePro Magazine, InfoWorld, I-Way, Macworld, Network World, PC Games, PC World, Publish, Video Event, THE WEB Magazine, and WebMaster; online webzines: JavaWorld, NetscapeWorld, and SunWorld Online; **URUGUAY:** InfoWorld Uruguay; **VENEZUELA:** Computerworld Venezuela, PC World Venezuela; and **VIETNAM:** PC World Vietnam.   10/22/96

Dedication

To the love of my life, Joanne Angell

Author's Acknowledgments

My journey to digital enlightenment via ISDN is the result of the generous help and support of many people along the way. These people created a thousand points of light that helped illuminate the path to ISDN conversion.

First and foremost, I want to thank Gareth Hancock at IDG Books, and my agent, Matt Wagner at Waterside Productions, for making this second edition happen.

On the technical side, a special thanks to my technical editor Anita Freeman at Pacific Bell. She has been a constant source of enlightenment for me through the first and second editions of this book. I'd also like thank Mark Phillips at ZipNet for going beyond the call of duty. His expertise in ISDN Internet access and routers was invaluable. Likewise, a special thanks to ZipNet for providing the ISDN access accounts for this project.

I would like to express my thanks also to Susan Pink, the project editor for this book.

Last but not least, my thanks to the following people and companies for providing essential support for this project. Bob Larribeau at the California ISDN User's Group; John Pecoraro at NetManage; Jeremy Goldstein and Dave Webber at PicturePhone Direct; Jon Jackson at Intel; Leslie Conway and Bill Moon at ADTRAN; Peg Berry, Kevin Flanagan, and Amy Slater at PictureTel; Jonathan Gaines at The Internet Access Company; Lisa Volmar and Sandy Golding at Motorola; Sid Sung, Nancy Keene, and John Sevigne at Alpha Telecom; Jennifer Wade at 3Com; Paul Stout at Angia Communications; Burt Forbes and Celene Cohen at Ascend Communications; Mark Bryne-Quinn and Matthew Dolbren at Cabletron Systems; Michael Hakkert and Ed Alcoff at Cisco Systems; Mark Franklin at Connectix Corporation; Paul Corning and Joan Huang at Diamond Multimedia; Amal Abed at Farallon Computing; Dickson Wong and Charles Nieman at Trancell Systems; Mike Beltrano, Beth Dempsey, and David Bachta at U.S. Robotics; Don Moulder at Vendors ISDN Association; Debbie Golden at ZipNet; Tracy Specht at White Pine Software; Frank Guerrero and David Somers at WINNOV; Jonathan Chang at NETGEAR; Peter Gieger at Eicon; Rich White at Best Communications; Ernie Himsl at Lava Computer MFG; and Dan Kegel, Webmaster of Dan Kegel's ISDN Page Web site.

Publisher's Acknowledgments

We're proud of this book; please send us your comments about it by using the Reader Response Card at the back of the book or by e-mailing us at feedback/dummies@idgbooks.com. Some of the people who helped bring this book to market include the following:

Acquisitions, Development, and Editorial

Project Editor: Susan Pink

Assistant Acquisitions Editor: Gareth Hancock

Product Development Manager:
Mary Bednarek

Permissions Editor: Joyce Pepple

Technical Editors: Anita Freeman,
Charles Ledbetter

Editorial Manager: Mary C. Corder

Editorial Assistant: Chris H. Collins

Production

Project Coordinator: Regina Snyder

Layout and Graphics: Angela F. Hunckler,
E. Shawn Aylsworth, Brett Black,
Cameron Booker, J. Tyler Connor,
Maridee Ennis, Todd Klemme,
Jane Martin, Drew Moore,
Elizabeth Cardenas-Nelson, Mark Owens,
Michael Sullivan,

Proofreaders: Rachel Garvey, Carrie Voorhis,
Karen York

Indexer: Sharon Hilgenberg

Special Help

Suzanne Packer, Lead Copy Editor

General and Administrative

IDG Books Worldwide, Inc.: John Kilcullen, President and CEO; Steven Berkowitz,
COO and Publisher

Dummies, Inc.: Milissa Koloski, Executive Vice President and Publisher

Dummies Technology Press and Dummies Editorial: Diane Graves Steele, Vice President and
Associate Publisher; Judith A. Taylor, Brand Manager

Dummies Trade Press: Kathleen A. Welton, Vice President and Publisher; Stacy S. Collins,
Brand Manager

IDG Books Production for Dummies Press: Beth Jenkins, Production Director; Cindy L. Phipps,
Supervisor of Project Coordination; Kathie S. Schutte, Supervisor of Page Layout; Shelley Lea,
Supervisor of Graphics and Design; Debbie J. Gates, Production Systems Specialist,
Tony Augsburger, Reprint Coordinator; Leslie Popplewell, Media Archive Coordinator

Dummies Packaging and Book Design: Patti Sandez, Packaging Assistant; Kavish+Kavish,
Cover Design

◆

The publisher would like to give special thanks to Patrick J. McGovern,
without whom this book would not have been possible.

◆

Contents at a Glance

Cartoons at a Glance

By Rich Tennant • Fax: 508-546-7747 • E-mail: the5wave@tiac.net

page 7

page 319

page 233

page 352

page 99

Table of Contents

· ·

Introduction

● ●

*W*hile you've been clunking around cyberspace using a modem over a plain old telephone line, telephone companies have been building a new digital telecommunications network called Integrated Services Digital Network — ISDN for short. Digital communications isn't new. What is new is that the rest of us can now afford to tap into high-speed digital communications for as little as $25 per month. The telephone wires you use now for regular telephone service are the same conduit for ISDN.

What ISDN delivers is data communications at speeds up to seven times faster than today's modem — even without compression. With compression, ISDN can transmit data at speeds up to 512 Kbps. Imagine cruising the Internet at speeds that make the World Wide Web come alive, telecommuting in the fast lane, or grabbing multimedia files in a flash.

But wait, there's more! ISDN is like a Swiss army knife. You can use it to conduct virtual meetings via desktop video conferencing. You can even do two things at once. For example, you can be talking to someone on the telephone while surfing the World Wide Web — both on a single line. ISDN changes everything, so it's time to get rewired for your digital future.

About This Book

ISDN For Dummies, 2nd Edition, makes your conversion from the bucolic world of analog communications to digital communications via ISDN a smooth one. You'll find that this guide serves two distinct purposes. The first is to make you an educated consumer of ISDN services and products. The second is to give you hands-on experience working with ISDN to perform a variety of real-world applications.

ISDN For Dummies, 2nd Edition, boils down a heavy stockpot of technical gobbledygook into a light broth of the essentials you need to master ISDN's powerful capabilities. Using this guide, you'll find out how to

- ✔ Grasp the Zen of ISDN to understand how it works
- ✔ Get ISDN service from your telephone company

- ✔ Set up your ISDN connection to get the most from it
- ✔ Develop your own ISDN implementation game plan
- ✔ Equip yourself with the right ISDN equipment
- ✔ Surf the Internet and World Wide Web via ISDN
- ✔ Telecommute to your office LAN via ISDN
- ✔ Conduct video conferences from your desktop via ISDN
- ✔ Save money getting and using ISDN
- ✔ Understand the jargon of ISDN
- ✔ Install, manage, and use your own ISDN equipment

Who Are You?

In writing this book, I make some assumptions about who you are and what you are seeking from ISDN. Even if only one of the following describes why you're looking into ISDN, you're a candidate for this book:

- ✔ You've heard about ISDN but don't have a clue as to what it's all about.
- ✔ You're using a PC running Microsoft Windows 95 or Windows NT 4.0, and you know how to navigate Windows and how to insert an adapter board in your PC.
- ✔ You're searching for a faster ride when you surf the World Wide Web.
- ✔ You want to telecommute by connecting to your office network from home.
- ✔ You're tired of waiting so long to download and upload files.
- ✔ You'd like to explore new ways to extend your reach (using desktop video conferencing, for example) so that you can collaborate with others without added travel.
- ✔ You're on the lookout for new ways to gain a competitive advantage in today's business environment.
- ✔ You'd like to connect your office LAN to the Internet so that everyone on your network has high-speed, easy access to the Net.

How to Use This Book

To understand ISDN essentials, read the five chapters in Part I, "Getting Started with ISDN." All digital roads begin from Part I. From there, you go on to a hands-on exploration of specific ISDN applications — from Internet access to desktop video conferencing. You'll be able to experience the entire process of installing, setting up, and using the leading ISDN devices for these applications.

How This Book Is Organized

ISDN For Dummies, 2nd Edition, has four parts that present the material in a steady progression of what you need to know at the time you need to know it. After building a foundation of ISDN fundamentals in the first part, the book goes on to working with specific ISDN applications, such as remote access and desktop video conferencing. Each part is self contained but also interconnected to every other part, which is the natural order of ISDN.

Part I: Getting Started with ISDN

Part I lays the foundation for working and playing in the ISDN realm. In concise terms, you get the essentials to become an educated consumer and user of ISDN. This part explains the benefits and pitfalls of ISDN, and how it works. You learn how to order and configure your ISDN connection, as well as what equipment you need for each type of ISDN application. You also learn the essentials for creating your own blueprint for getting the most from your ISDN service.

Part II: Internet Surfing and Telecommuting the ISDN Way

Remote access is the bread and butter of ISDN service. In Part II, you find out how to harness ISDN for remote access, including how to connect your PC or LAN to the Internet or to another network for telecommuting. This part focuses on ISDN remote-access options and sorts through them to help you choose the right solution. It guides you through developing a plan that gives you the most flexibility in your remote-access capabilities. You take a walkthrough of leading ISDN devices — from single-user ISDN modems to ISDN routers for connecting a local area network — to discover what they can do for you and how they work.

Part III: Face to Face via Desktop Video Conferencing

Part III exposes you to one of the most exciting ISDN applications, desktop video conferencing. For as little as $500, you can collaborate with geographically dispersed people via real-time video as well as share applications. Desktop video-conferencing systems use a video camera, video capture board, ISDN adapter, and software to turn your PC into a visual communications medium. You find out how video conferencing can increase your productivity and cut your travel and meeting costs. To help you get a feel for this visual medium, you work with three leading desktop video-conferencing systems.

Part IV: The Part of Tens

"The Part of Tens," as its name implies, provides you with tens upon tens of valuable resource nuggets. Much of this information enhances and supports topics covered in previous chapters. You can find information on ways to save money getting ISDN, a bird's-eye view of the process for getting up and running with ISDN, sources of more help with ISDN, and guidelines for choosing an ISDN Internet service provider.

Appendixes

As a bonus, *ISDN For Dummies,* 2nd Edition, includes a tariff summary of what ISDN costs from the major telephone companies in the U.S. Check out Appendix A to see what your telephone company charges for BRI ISDN service. But wait, there's more! You also get extensive references to leading ISDN equipment vendors, ISDN Internet service providers, ISDN resources, and more.

Glossary

Finally, the glossary defines all the lingo and jargon of ISDN that you're likely to come across as you walk toward the digital enlightenment of ISDN.

Icons Used in This Book

Several icons are used throughout this book. These icons illuminate important, useful, or just interesting tidbits of knowledge. Here's what they look like and what they denote.

This icon identifies interesting but nonessential information. I use this icon to provide you with the sort of technical background information that people who ask "why?" need. You can skip them if you like.

If you're looking for tips and tricks that will save you aggravation and money, here's where you'll find them.

Watch out! ISDN may be the road to digital enlightenment, but the road has numerous pitfalls and hairpin turns. This icon points out these problems, and tells you how to avoid them or how to solve them.

These icons mark a special point of interest that is related to the topic at hand. They can denote where to find more information in the book (think of these references as manual hyperlinks that give you access to important information) or mark tales of my own ISDN experiences. Whatever the information, it will enrich your ISDN learning experience.

Where to Go from Here

That's all you need to know to get started on your journey to digital enlighten- ment via ISDN. *ISDN For Dummies,* 2nd Edition, will be your guide as you walk toward the digital light. Use it to illuminate what ISDN is all about and harness its digital power. Let's get started with the first step.

Part I
Getting Started
with ISDN

The 5th Wave — By Rich Tennant

IN A DISPLAY OF PERVERSE BRILLIANCE, CARL THE REPAIRMAN MISTAKES A ROOM HUMIDIFIER FOR A MID-RANGE COMPUTER BUT MANAGES TO TIE IT INTO THE NETWORK ANYWAY.

In this part . . .

The foundation is laid for working in the ISDN realm. In concise terms, you get the essentials to become an educated consumer and user of ISDN. You find out what ISDN delivers, how it works, how you connect to it, and what ISDN equipment and application options are available. You discover how to put it all together into a game plan to get the most bang for the buck from your ISDN service.

After you complete the boot camp of ISDN communications, you'll be ready to roll up your sleeves and get down to work using ISDN for Internet access, telecommuting, and desktop video conferencing.

Chapter 1

We're Not in Analog Anymore, Toto

In This Chapter

▶ Learning why the bucolic analog communications era will become history

▶ Entering the next stage in data communications via ISDN

▶ Discovering what ISDN can do for your Internet access and telecommuting

▶ Understanding why ISDN is not plug and play — yet

*T*urn on your answering machine, turn off your modem, and take a little time to become acquainted with your digital communications future. In case you haven't noticed, you live in the digital age. Images, sounds, videos, and just about any other form of information are widely available in digital form. Yet, the system millions of us use to transmit this data continues to clunk along using technology that has been around for almost 100 years: the telephone system. That is, until now. You're about to enter the age of digital communications via ISDN, or Integrated Services Digital Network. What ISDN delivers is nothing short of a communications revolution for the rest of us.

Life in the Bucolic Analog Communications Era

The ubiquitous telephone system we all use today transmits the human voice using the analog device known as the telephone. This analog system transforms sound into electrical signals. The telephone network contains amplifiers along the way to boost those signals for long distances from telephone company switching centers. This voice-based system is called *POTS* in telecommunications circles, which stands for *plain old telephone service*.

With the advent of the fax and computers, we started to use the telephone system as a data communications link. And the rapid ascent of the Internet has created even more demand for expanded data communications. These combined factors are dramatically affecting the makeup of communications over the telephone system. Data communications now account for more than 50 percent of all the traffic going over the POTS network.

Digital communications primer

Digital means data based on the binary number system, which uses only 0 and 1 to represent all information. By manipulating electronic on and off switches, computers manage information in any form. Digital communications is the exchange of information sent in binary form instead of a series of analog signals.

The common measurement of data transmission speeds is *bits per second (bps)*. The term *bit* is a contraction of *binary digit,* the smallest unit

of digital information. It takes 8 bits to make up a byte, which is also the equivalent of a single character. The term *Kbps* stands for *kilobits per second,* which is a thousand bits per second. In real terms, however, a kilobit is actually 1,024 bits.

The term *Mbps* stands for *megabits per second,* which is a million bits per second. The term *MB* stands for *megabytes,* which is a million bytes. This digital measurement is typically used with files and data storage.

The modem is the current staple for data communications over the analog telephone system for most PC users. Modems have continued to get faster, with 28.8 Kbps modems in common use today and 57.6 Kbps modems over the horizon. Today's modems, however, are coming up against the inherent data speed limits of POTS technology. Simply put, POTS wasn't designed for digital communications.

In the analog world, you use the telephone for voice, a fax to send documents, and a modem to connect to the Internet. If you have only one POTS line, you can perform only one task at a time. To conduct multiple tasks at the same time, you must have a separate analog line for each device. Figure 1-1 shows a typical POTS line setup for a small business or work-at-home scenario. This bucolic analog communication age in which we all grew up is in its twilight years.

Figure 1-1:
To use a telephone, fax, and PC at the same time, each device requires a separate line in the typical analog layout.

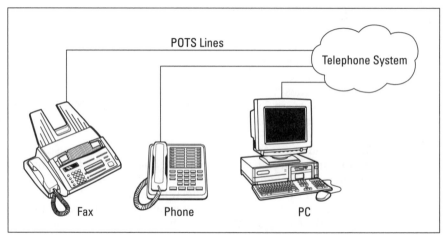

Bandwidth isn't the girth of a heavy-metal band

The capacity of any data communications line is a function of its range of frequencies for carrying information, which is called *passband*. Bandwidth is the width of the passband, that is, the difference between the highest and lowest frequencies in a given range. For example, the human voice produces sounds in the passband of 50 Hz to 15,000 Hz (15 kilohertz or 15 kHz). That translates to a bandwidth of 14,950 Hz (15,000 Hz minus 50 Hz). In this case, Hertz (Hz) is not a car rental agency but a unit of frequency measurement for a waveform cycle.

GUI gets stuck in the modem bottleneck

The world of PC computing has changed from a barren, text-only environment to a rich, graphical, multimedia realm. Microsoft Windows (Windows 95 and Windows NT) dominates the PC platform. As software becomes easier and more powerful, file sizes become bigger and bigger. Windows application file sizes are now in megabytes instead of kilobytes. The migration to easier and more powerful computing comes at a price. The price is the urgent need for more data communications capacity, called *bandwidth,* than can be supplied by POTS and modems. As multimedia makes more demands on file sizes, all those bits can't squeak through a POTS line and modem.

Enter the wacky World Wide Web

The World Wide Web is synonymous with the Internet. The Web has evolved from just a graphical system for still images and text into a full-blown multimedia system. A new generation of multimedia applications is quickly becoming standard, such as ShockWave for video, Real Audio for voice, Java applets for downloadable programs, and VRML *(Virtual Reality Modeling Language)* for virtual reality worlds. Figures 1-2, 1-3, and 1-4 show the interactive interfaces of today's Web. To operate at speeds that don't put you to sleep, these new technologies demand more bandwidth.

For Web users who want to be full participants on the Web, the modem is becoming a serious barrier. In the modern *GUI (graphical user interface)* and multimedia computing environment, vast amounts of data, including image, sound, and video files, are transferred to the user. Squeezing this large amount of information through a modem and POTS telephone line just doesn't cut it.

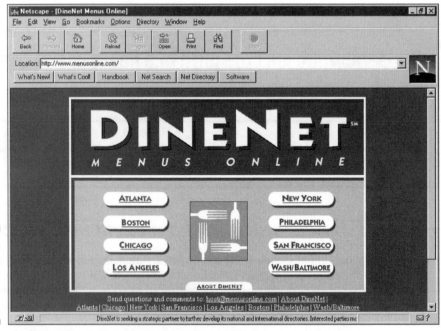

Figure 1-2:
A Web site
with
graphics
and text.

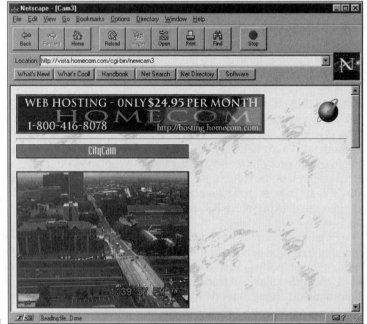

Figure 1-3:
A Java
applet is
downloaded
for
execution
on your PC.

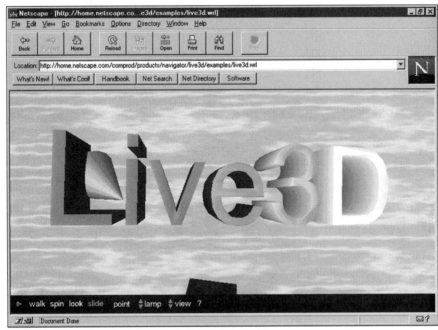

Figure 1-4:
A 3-D Web site based on VRML.

And the bandwidth played on

In popular telecommunications and networking lingo, *bandwidth* means data transmission capacity. The higher the bandwidth supported by a channel, the more data it can pass through in a given amount of time. All the whiz-bang technology of graphical and multimedia computing demands more bandwidth to function at a reasonable pace. Sure, you can send a huge file over an analog line using a 14.4 Kbps modem, but it's not economically viable because of the transfer time and connection charges. You can transfer that same file in a fraction of the time through a digital line. Figure 1-5 shows a comparison of modem and ISDN speeds.

The bandwidth of a connection affects the data transfer rate for not only file transfers but also real-time images, sounds, or videos via the Internet or between your home PC or laptop and the office LAN. The bottom line is that the more bandwidth a communications link has, the more sophisticated the applications it can support, such as video conferencing.

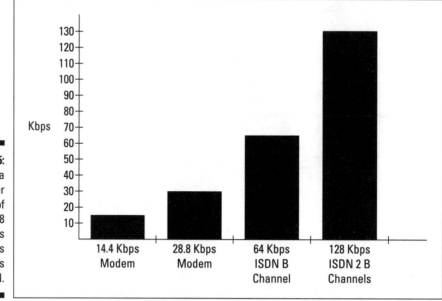

A compressing situation

Typically, modem vendors promote raw data transfer speeds based on rates that include data compression. So a 14.4 Kbps modem transferring data with 4 to 1 compression delivers data at 57.6 Kbps. On paper, this looks great, but compression rates vary depending on the data file format you are transferring. For example, a graphic file typically will compress a lot more than a text-only file. ISDN supports compression, so you can reach data transfer speeds of up to 512 Kbps. Typically, data transmission over compressed links works out to about a 2 to 1 compression ratio given a good mix of graphics, text, and audio files.

Other factors besides compression affect data transmission speeds. Even the fastest connection in the world to the Internet is only as good as the traffic congestion across the Internet. Remember that data goes from a server through the Net to your ISP's network and then down to your computer.

Walk toward the Digital Light

For individuals and small businesses, POTS — the lowest level in the data communications food chain — was the only game in town. To make the move up the food chain to faster digital communications was prohibitively expensive. Now ISDN delivers digital data communications power — up to 128 Kbps — at prices that a growing number of us can afford.

For the first time, an affordable, digital Internet or telecommuting link has caught up with our data-intensive computing needs. And the telephone company pipes ISDN service into your home or office just like regular POTS lines.

ISDN, or Integrated Services Digital Network, is the next step in the evolution of data communications from analog to digital. The telecommunications industry has taken a simple concept and made it complex. The following should help make sense of the ISDN acronym:

- ✓ **Integrated** means that various data and voice services can be combined to travel over an ISDN line simultaneously.
- ✓ **Services** refer to all the services ISDN supports, such as bearer services, supplementary voice services, and signaling services. The bearer services are the bread-and-butter of ISDN.
- ✓ **Digital** is the heart and soul of ISDN. It's about using strings of ones and zeros to transmit data in its natural format instead of converting it to go over a voice grade telephone line.
- ✓ **Network** represents the telephone company as one giant network.

ISDN benefits in a nutshell

ISDN is an integrated voice and data network that offers an impressive collection of benefits. Here are the specifics of what ISDN offers in practical terms:

- ✓ ISDN delivers data at speeds up to 128 Kbps without compression. With standard 4-1 compression, you can reach speeds of up to 512 Kbps, depending on the type of data being transferred.
- ✓ ISDN is an affordable and cost-effective service. Basic ISDN service costs an average of $35 to $50 per month.
- ✓ ISDN uses the same telephone wiring as POTS. You don't need new wiring to handle ISDN service in most homes and businesses.
- ✓ ISDN lets you perform more than one communications task at the same time. You can speak on the telephone while surfing the Internet (at 64 Kbps) using the same single ISDN line.
- ✓ ISDN handles all types of information, including voice, text, images, sounds, and video.

✔ ISDN lets you connect up to eight devices on a single line. You can get multiple telephone numbers, with each number routed to a specific device.

✔ ISDN is part of the ubiquitous analog telephone system, so you can communicate with ISDN users as well as people connected to the larger POTS universe.

✔ ISDN enables you to not only connect and use your existing analog devices, such as telephones, faxes, and modems, but also switch to digital data transmission overdrive when you need it.

✔ ISDN offers greater reliability. AT&T estimates that a POTS connection has a reliability rate of 75 percent, and a digital connection, 99 percent.

Where did ISDN come from?

The implementation of ISDN by the telephone companies has taken a long time to come of age. With several false starts along the way, ISDN's march to the mainstream has left in its wake a path littered with the disillusioned. Many early adapters became followers of the ISDN acronym It Still Does Nothing. But ISDN's full implementation was inevitable because the march towards a digital telephone network has been going on for years.

For the last few decades, the telephone companies have been converting from analog to digital. The digital system uses computers to perform switching tasks that route calls. The introduction of digital switches allowed the telephone network to operate more efficiently and allowed telephone companies to offer new communications services to customers. You're already familiar with many of these services, such as call waiting, call forwarding, and conference calling.

At the same time that the telephone companies were going digital, the interface to you and the rest of the world remained POTS to maintain compatibility with the huge consumer analog equipment infrastructure as well as for political and economic reasons. This last link between the telephone company and customers finally delivers ISDN to the rest of us.

The Web puts the fire under ISDN demand

Like so many areas of computing, the Internet is the driving force behind the rebirth of ISDN. Before the Internet exploded on the scene, ISDN languished as a solution in search of a problem. Even in the early text-only days of the Internet, the demand for more bandwidth wasn't on most users' minds. The World Wide Web changed everything. Millions of PC users were looking for a faster way to surf the multimedia Web and download stuff. ISDN began looking like a good solution.

In the rush to get ISDN service, the fast-paced PC world crashed head-on with the slow, bureaucratic structure of the regulated telephone industry, a complete lack of easy-to-use equipment, and other barriers. As a result, the early days of ISDN service were a minefield. The good news is that this situation has dramatically improved.

Where is ISDN going?

By the end of 1996, most telephone companies expect to have 85 to 95 percent of their lines capable of handling ISDN. Most large metropolitan areas in the U.S. are already ISDN-ready. According to the Yankee Group Inc., a technology consulting firm based in Boston, ISDN use in 1996 will grow to nearly three times what it was in 1995, reaching 1.5 million lines. Most telephone companies are beefing up their ISDN ordering and support services to streamline the process of establishing ISDN service.

A Telecommunications Act

A big factor affecting the deployment and pricing of ISDN is the new competitive environment of digital communications. The Telecommunications Act of 1996 removed many of the laws and restrictions governing the broadcast, cable, telecommunications, and computer industries. Congress left the future direction of these industries in the hands of competition.

The bill gives the telecommunications industry its first big injection of competition since the government broke up AT&T in 1984. Before 1984, AT&T was the telephone company for most of the United States. The 1996 act promises to spread competition to all domestic telephone markets. It establishes ground rules for long distance and local telephone companies to compete in one another's traditional markets. Competition already has driven the Bells to plan mergers — including the combination of Bell South (SBS Communications) and Pacific Bell (Pacific Telesis), as well as Bell Atlantic and NYNEX. These mergers are subject to regulatory approvals.

Competition generated by the breakup of AT&T has driven down long-distance rates by 40 percent in the past 12 years. It's hopeful that this trend will hit the local telephone companies that provide ISDN service. It takes time to fully open local markets to competition, however, because federal and state regulators are just now starting to write the rules that will govern that competition.

Computer industry pushes ISDN service

Compared to the telecommunications industry, the computer industry is more adaptive and responsive to end users. A new generation of ISDN equipment vendors from the ranks of the PC industry is affecting ISDN service. Through a trade group called the Vendors ISDN Association (VIA), leading ISDN equipment vendors are working with each other and the telecommunications industry to make establishing an ISDN line easier.

Many ISDN equipment vendors offer customer service groups as an alternative to telephone company service centers to help customers get up and running with ISDN service. These organizations typically provide help through the entire process of getting your ISDN connection through your local telephone company.

Additionally, Microsoft Windows NT and 95 have added ISDN support that didn't exist in Windows 3.11 to make connecting via ISDN easier.

The threat of competing technologies

Another factor affecting the 11th hour push of ISDN service by telephone companies and ISDN equipment vendors is the looming threat of ISDN alternatives. Emerging technologies, including direct broadcast satellite, cable modem, and Asymmetric Digital Subscriber Line (ADSL) promise to deliver faster and cheaper connections than ISDN. However, these alternative technologies won't be widely available for several years. Until then, ISDN is the best choice for high-speed connections to the Internet or telecommuting.

What ISDN Can Do for You

Right now, PC users find ISDN attractive because of what it does for Internet access and telecommuting (also referred to as the *virtual office*). These two applications will continue to dominate the ISDN landscape for the next few years. Of course, you can use your ISDN line also to connect your analog equipment for voice, fax, or modem communications. But the bottom line on ISDN service is its data communications capabilities.

You may want to use your ISDN line as a second line for modem and fax communications. You typically won't want to use an ISDN line for your primary voice line.

In the future, ISDN may provide a conduit for all kinds of new voice and data services that aren't feasible with POTS. For example, ISDN can support sophisticated digital voice services that can turn a desktop telephone into a PBX (private branch exchange) system. Other potential uses of ISDN service are for alarm systems, utility meter reading, energy management, and other services that operate in the background to monitor your home or business.

Are you a candidate for ISDN?

ISDN offers the kind of power that will support the activities of a broad range of people, including Internet users, telecommuters, self-employed home workers, consultants, contract workers, business executives, researchers, and customer service representatives.

Companies and other organizations of all sizes can use the power of ISDN to conduct business more efficiently. ISDN is a great bandwidth matchup for the needs of the SOHO (Small Office/Home Office) market. Large companies are also candidates for ISDN as an inexpensive way to connect branch offices to regional offices or headquarters. ISDN also provides fast access to a company's networks for systems administrators.

Are you a candidate for ISDN service? You are if you

✔ Work at home as a telecommuter and need to connect to your company's corporate network

✔ Operate a home-based business

✔ Regularly send and receive large files (such as image, video, or sound files) over the Internet or another network

✔ Surf the Web regularly for work and play

✔ Collaborate with geographically dispersed people and travel frequently to attend meetings

Telecommuting (or working in your bunny slippers)

Telecommuters are employees who work from home part time or full time during normal business hours. Telecommuting is a rapidly emerging trend as companies downsize, people seek different working options, and environmental and social changes converge. As the virtual office made up of people working from geographically dispersed locations takes hold, ISDN becomes even more attractive to companies.

According to LINK Resources, a market research organization, telecommuters number 7.6 million, and their numbers are growing at an annual rate of 15 percent. In addition, according to the Gartner Group, a corporate consulting firm, more than 80 percent of all organizations will have at least half of their staff engaged in telecommuting by 1999.

ISDN offers telecommuters an affordable, high-speed method for connecting to their office networks. ISDN's bandwidth allows people to work off site and yet interact with other people as if they were on site. A study conducted at West Virginia University found that transmission speeds of 80 Kbps made users feel as if they were actually connected to a local area network (LAN). ISDN can deliver data at up to 128 Kbps without any compression. Another tool available to ISDN telecommuters is a new generation of affordable, desktop video-conferencing systems. These easy-to-use systems let you participate in video conferences. Figure 1-6 shows a typical telecommuter ISDN configuration.

Cruising the Net with the top down

ISDN is an express lane for working and playing on the Net. Cruising the Web with ISDN instead of a modem is like driving on a wide-open freeway with the top down and the wind blowing through your hair.

ISDN offers reliable, high-speed access to the Internet, online services, and databases. In addition, a large and growing number of Internet service

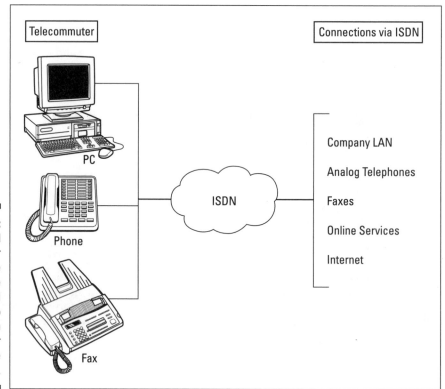

Figure 1-6:
The typical telecommuter can use multiple ISDN services to interact with people at or outside the office.

providers offer ISDN connections at affordable prices. An ISDN connection moves information at speeds that let the popular World Wide Web come alive at your desktop.

The impact of widespread ISDN deployment promises to make the Web a more exciting, cyberdelic realm of intensified sensory perception. The greatly increased data transfer speeds of ISDN will let Web site developers incorporate a wider range of data-intensive applications to their sites, such as audio, videos, and 3-D virtual reality worlds.

The benefits of ISDN for users of such online services as CompuServe, America Online, and Prodigy are the same as those for Internet users.

Face to face with desktop video conferencing

ISDN is a communications glue that allows geographically dispersed people to work together in real time. ISDN delivers the bandwidth to support desktop video conferencing and computer screen sharing. As a business tool, video conferencing delivers a low-cost alternative to travel as well as an effective strategic tool for getting things accomplished faster. ISDN is an efficient transmission medium for video conferencing because its digital basis provides virtually error-free transmission for high-quality images. You can do video conferencing over the ISDN telephone network or the Internet.

A new generation of personal video conferencing makes virtual team collaboration practical. Using a video-conferencing system, users can view each other and talk while jointly working on a file or sharing ideas using a whiteboard. Figure 1-7 shows how a video conference appears on a PC screen.

Moving multimedia files at lightning speed

The size of files grows almost exponentially as computer applications become more sophisticated. ISDN lets you move all kinds of files quickly and reliably between your computer and the Internet, another network, or a stand-alone PC. ISDN speed can easily translate to big savings on Internet access or long-distance telephone charges for people who need to move files on a regular basis. Desktop publishers, multimedia developers, software companies, and a host of others can deliver their software products economically and efficiently through ISDN.

Figure 1-7:
A desktop
video
conference
as it
appears on
your PC
screen.

ISDN Reality Check (The Good, the Bad, the Ugly)

As you enter the era of digital communications, understand that ISDN is a new technology and is therefore experiencing growing pains. ISDN is a complex system that integrates telecommunications and computers. It's composed of disparate yet interdependent players, including telephone companies, computer hardware and software vendors, and government agencies.

The good news is that many of ISDN's early problems are being corrected. Those problems included interoperability between telephone companies, lack of universal service, complex pricing, and difficult installation procedures. Telephone companies and ISDN hardware and software companies have made great strides in addressing these problems.

The bad news is that ISDN is still not a yellow brick road. Stretches of the ISDN network are under construction, incompatibilities remain, pricing is erratic, and ordering is complex. But ISDN is getting a lot better. (See the sidebar titled "What a Difference a Year Makes.")

NOTE

What a difference a year makes

I wrote the first edition of *ISDN For Dummies* in the spring of 1995. My own experience in getting ISDN service and connecting to an Internet service provider was a nightmare. It took two months and a few dozen telephone calls to get service from NYNEX, who didn't even have a telephone number for ordering ISDN service. On the Internet access front, no local Internet service providers offered ISDN access in Massachusetts. The lone ISDN provider was PSI's InterRamp service. In addition, there were only a handful of equipment options for connecting my computer to ISDN, and most were expensive and difficult to install.

Fast-forward to the summer of 1996. NYNEX has a Web site that publishes its tariffs as well as a toll-free number to order service. Most Internet service providers offer affordable ISDN service. Added to this improvement in ISDN service is a cornucopia of new ISDN equipment that is both affordable and easy to install. What a difference a year makes!

To help you become an intelligent consumer of ISDN services, the following sections present an overview of the main trouble spots in ISDN service today. Think of reading about ISDN's problem areas as part of your digital enlightenment program.

Inconsistent ISDN service

The local telephone companies deliver ISDN to homes and businesses. Currently, you can get ISDN service only from your local telephone company. (Over time, however, the long-distance carriers may enter local markets.) The U.S. has several regional telephone companies, such as Pacific Telesis, NYNEX, and Bell South. Each of these companies operates independently, which results in uneven ISDN availability, pricing, and service. Some telephone companies are aggressively trying to make ISDN easy to use; others have been slower in implementing ISDN service. Your ISDN experience can be good or bad depending on your telephone company.

Another problem with ISDN service is that it is not universally available. ISDN service is dependent on digital switches, so many places outside metropolitan areas don't offer ISDN service. In addition, there are inherent technological and economic barriers to ISDN deployment based on the proximity of your premises to a telephone company facility.

The good news is that most telephone companies now have Web sites or toll-free ISDN customer service centers to provide availability, pricing, and ordering information about ISDN in your area. As the Telecommunications Act heats up, expect to see further improvements.

Complex ISDN pricing

ISDN pricing, called *tariffs* in telephone company lingo, is based on the application of complex cost allocation and recovery rules established by both federal and state regulators. Thus, ISDN pricing varies from one telephone company to another and from one state to another. When you subscribe to ISDN service, your final price depends on a complex variety of configuration options offered by your telephone company. In some areas, ISDN pricing is still prohibitively expensive.

Adding to the confusion, telephone companies also charge different rates for different types of traffic going over your ISDN connection. Although progress is being made in standardizing prices and service packages, ordering the right package of services still remains the most difficult part of establishing an ISDN connection.

Competition resulting from the 1996 Telecommunications Act as well as the threat of competing technology from the cable industry and others should keep the pressure on the telephone companies to deliver more ISDN service for less money.

Unfriendly ISDN setup

Setting up an ISDN connection so that the equipment at the telephone company is configured to work with the equipment you use is another complex task. Efforts are being made to simplify and streamline this process. For example, all telephone companies have agreed to a universal system of preconfiguration codes for ISDN equipment. Eventually, all telephone company equipment will be configured automatically, based on the equipment at your location.

The gray area between the telephone company ISDN connection and your ISDN equipment can be a great and frustrating divide. To make an ISDN connection work, you must deal with two different players, the telephone company for the ISDN line and ISDN equipment vendors for the devices at your location. In the past, these two groups have not cooperated.

Fortunately, this state of affairs is changing as telephone companies and ISDN equipment vendors work together to make setting up an ISDN connection easier. One way is through ISDN ordering codes that act as configuration templates. The ISDN customer simply tells the telephone company representative a code supplied by the equipment vendor, and the telephone company automatically configures the ISDN line.

ISDN interoperability improves

ISDN equipment vendors have lacked standards in certain ISDN applications for ensuring the interoperability of equipment. Now, however, standards are taking hold in key ISDN applications, most notably Internet access.

The recent introduction and widespread adoption of the Point-to-Point Protocol/Multilink Protocol (PPP/MP) standard is stabilizing Internet access via ISDN. (PPP/MP is also commonly referred to as Multilink PPP.) This protocol supports full 128-Kbps access to the Internet by combining PPP connections.

PPP is the protocol used for dial-up connections to the Internet. PPP supports only one B channel for ISDN connections. The PPP Multilink Protocol, which is supported by many ISPs, delivers an Internet connection at the full-throttle 128 Kbps rate.

A new protocol called Compression Control Protocol (CCP) promises to standardize compression over ISDN. The CCP protocol supports the negotiation of different compression schemes over PPP. Currently, the de facto standard for compression over ISDN is Stac LZS.

Standards have stabilized also in desktop video conferencing. The H.320 and H.120 standards have created a solid foundation for desktop video conferencing and whiteboard applications via ISDN. Additional standards for video conferencing, including H.323 and H.324, promise to open up video conferencing over the Internet.

ISDN equipment is now cool stuff

In the past, many ISDN equipment vendors were not end-user oriented in terms of marketing and supporting ISDN products. The ISDN equipment market had more than its share of poorly designed devices, incompatible systems, and poor documentation. Now there is an explosion of easier to use ISDN remote-access devices from communications and networking companies.

At the lower end of the market, connecting the SOHO or individual PC user to the Internet or corporate LAN has become dramatically cheaper and a lot easier. A year ago, single-user ISDN remote-access products were breaking just below the $1,000 mark. Now the average ISDN single-user remote-access product is falling to the $300 range. ISDN devices are easier to set up and use than their predecessors, helping users add sophisticated networking and communication capabilities in their SOHO environments.

ISDN is loaded with jargon and acronyms

As you learn more about ISDN, you'll quickly realize that it's filled with a large vocabulary of terminology. ISDN was born from the telecommunications industry, which is notorious for buzzwords and acronyms. Here are a few: ANSI, BRI, CO, CPE, DN, EKTS, FCC, NI-1, POTS, PPP/MP, SPID, and TA. Working with ISDN is like learning a foreign language, and you need to understand the basics to function in the ISDN world. This book explains the jargon and acronyms you need to know.

Check out the glossary for a complete reference of ISDN buzzwords and acronyms.

Chapter 2

The Zen of ISDN

*B*efore you jump into the mechanics of ISDN, you need to understand the guiding principles that define its operation. These fundamentals include the systems and rules that make up ISDN and encompass the telephone network side as well as your side of the connection. Think of these fundamentals as the Zen of ISDN. Understanding them will give you valuable insights into the workings of ISDN that you can later use to your advantage. Continue on, Grasshopper.

The Transcendental Telco Side of ISDN

The integration of all local and long distance telephone companies forms one global ISDN network. You enter this digital network via your local telephone company, which brings ISDN to your doorstep through standard POTS telephone wiring. From this demarcation point, you're in charge of the ISDN connection. When you establish an ISDN connection, your premises become a node on this global network. The telephone company is one side of the connection, and the ISDN equipment at your end is the other side of the connection.

We start our discussion at the telephone company side because it defines what you can and can't do on an ISDN line.

A *cloud* is the common symbol for any large network, such as the Internet or ISDN, that delivers information transparently to the user.

In the United States, regional telephone companies provide the telephone service. Each company, called a *Regional Bell Operating Company (RBOC)* serves a specific area, as shown in Figure 2-1. These companies are Ameritech, Bell Atlantic, Bell South, NYNEX, Pacific Telesis, SBC (Southwestern Bell), and U.S. West. Another term for RBOCs is *local exchange carrier (LEC)*. Recently, Pacific Telesis merged with SBC (pending approval), and NYNEX and Bell Atlantic announced a merger.

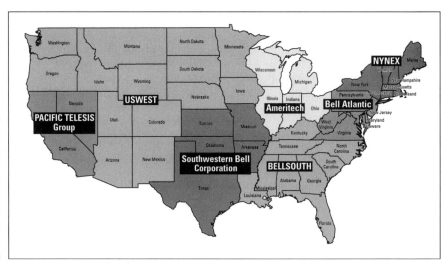

Figure 2-1: Service areas for the Regional Bell Operating Companies in the U.S.

In addition to the RBOCs, there are *independent telephone companies (ITCs)*. These companies provide local service and send that phone bill you complain about every month. Long distance telephone companies such as AT&T, MCI, and Sprint are *interexchange carriers (IC or IXC)*. They provide service between local telephone companies.

RBOCs control local switching equipment, and their service areas are divided into *local access and transport areas (LATAs)*. A LATA usually has many different area codes. For example, LATA 1 in California goes from the northern point of the state at the Oregon border south to Monterey. Within LATA 1 are several area codes, including 408, 415, and 510. California has ten LATAs and hundreds of area codes.

Computers as telco switches

A *switch* is a general term referring to facilities that route telephone traffic from one destination to another. Electronic switching software operating on computers provides the basis for the operation of ISDN. These *digital switches* provide electronic routing for telephone calls, with telephone numbers acting as a routing address system.

The telephone companies operate a hierarchy of switching depending on the call. At the local level, calls can often be completed within a single switch. Beyond this, there are switches for long distance and regional calls. During a long distance telephone connection, the call goes through your local telephone company, which switches the call to the long distance carrier, which routes the call to the local telephone company at the other end of the connection, as shown in Figure 2-2. Digital circuit switches that control the routing also manage other parts of the telephone system, such as determining toll charges and providing call-management features such as call waiting and call forwarding.

Figure 2-2:
The path of your long distance call is from your local telephone company's central office through the long distance company's network to another local telephone company.

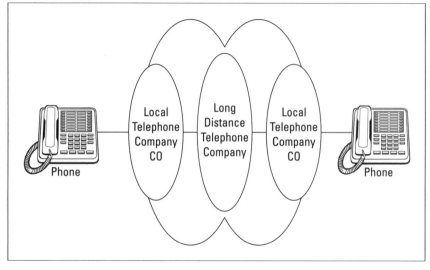

ISDN service is a circuit-switching system. The term *circuit switching* means that the communications pathway remains fixed for the duration of the call and is not available to other users. A circuit-switched connection between two users becomes a fixed pathway through the network. When the calling party initiates the call, a setup procedure tells the network the address of the calling party and sets up the route for the call. The call can be placed for the transmission of data or voice.

The leading digital circuit switches used by the telephone companies are AT&T's *5ESS* (Electronic Switching System), Nortel's *DMS-100* switch, and Siemmens EWSD. The AT&T and NT switches dominate the telecommunications industry. These computer-based switching platforms use operating system software. For the ISDN application, the AT&T 5ESS switch and the Nortel DMS-100 switch use either their own custom ISDN software or National ISDN (NI) software. The Siemens switch runs National ISDN software, which is a set of standards for ISDN service across different telephone company switching platforms.

Know your switch

You see references to telephone switching systems in all ISDN equipment documentation. Different switches support different services and capabilities. Your ISDN equipment will include specific configuration settings for each type of switch. When you order your ISDN service, you may need to relay the information from your ISDN device's documentation to your telephone company. In most cases, however, the telephone company uses a product ordering code as a template for all the necessary switch settings. For example, Intel Blue means all the configuration settings are for the ProShare Intel desktop video-conferencing system. To configure the ISDN devices on your end of the connection, you also need to know what type of switch the telephone company is using.

The central office (sounds Orwellian)

A *central office* (CO) is a local telephone company facility that houses telephone company switches. It's a mystical place that is the wiring center, or *hub,* for all telephone company subscribers. The massive cable plant at the CO provides the path from the switching device to the customer's premises. All kinds of call-management and call-routing activities go on at the CO, including local and long distance switching. It's the front line of telephone service from the telephone network to your premises and vice versa. There are approximately 19,000 central offices in the United States.

Large metropolitan areas usually have a bunch of COs, each serving a specific geographical area. These central offices connect to other COs for local calling, or to other switching facilities for long distance calls. COs are the last part of the telephone network to be upgraded to support universal ISDN service.

Local loops (no, it's not a cereal)

The term *local loop* refers to the telephone line comprising the pair of copper wires between your premises and the telephone company's CO. The local loop connects your premises to the CO, which in turn connects you to the ISDN cloud, as shown in Figure 2-3.

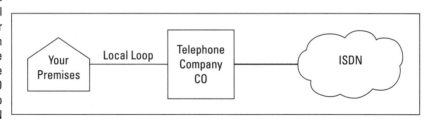

Figure 2-3:
The local
loop is your
connection
to the
telephone
company CO
and on to
the ISDN
cloud.

More than 200 million local loops (lines) are in the United States. The wiring for ISDN from the telephone company to your premises consists of the same copper wires used for POTS but requires different equipment at both ends of the connection.

The maximum length of a local loop for ISDN is approximately 18,000 feet using standard POTS wiring without any repeaters. (A *repeater* is a device that amplifies or regenerates the data signal to extend the distance of its transmission.) This limitation is one of the main reasons why ISDN service may not be available in your area. For example, if you're in a rural area, you may be more than 18,000 feet from the CO. If your telephone company employs repeaters on the line, the limit can be extended well beyond 18,000 feet.

The telephone system is in the process of moving from the use of copper wiring to fiber optics technology. *Fiber optics* sends light beams through thin strands of glass or other transparent material to transfer data. These optical fibers are immune to the electrical interference common in POTS lines. When fiber optic lines are widely deployed, the 18,000-foot distance restriction will disappear.

More power, Scotty

As you may have noticed, your telephone service remains active when the power goes off. This is because the telephone company provides the electrical power for the analog line from the CO. Unlike a POTS line, an ISDN line is not powered by the telephone company. End users of ISDN are responsible for providing the power to send digital signals through the ISDN lines between their premises and the CO.

Don't panic. The power requirements for an ISDN line are minimal. The power is supplied either by your PC or by an AC adapter that plugs into a standard electrical outlet. The power is maintained on your line only while you're using it.

In Your ISDN Interface

In the lingo of networking, an *access interface* is the physical connection between you and the network that allows you to use the network. There are two forms of ISDN access: *basic rate interface (BRI)* and *primary rate interface (PRI)*. These access interfaces deliver digital transmission services through channels. A *channel* is a conduit through which information flows in both directions. The BRI and PRI access interfaces define the channel configuration for the two types of ISDN service.

Basic rate interface (BRI)

The basic rate interface (BRI) is the affordable access service that most of us will use. Think of the BRI as the retail version of ISDN service. For BRI service, the telephone company divides the POTS wiring between your premises and the CO into three separate logical channels. The term *logical* refers to the fact that these three channels are not physical in terms of three separate wires but are defined by the logic of how the ISDN system operates. The three channels of a BRI connection include two 64-Kbps B (*bearer*) channels and one 16-Kbps D (*data*) channel, as shown in Figure 2-4. This standard BRI configuration is referred to as *2B+D*.

Figure 2-4:
The basic rate interface consists of two 64-Kbps B channels and one 16-Kbps D channel.

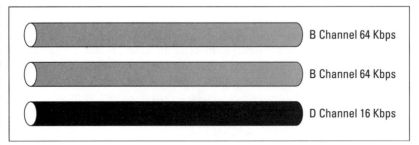

B Channel 64 Kbps

B Channel 64 Kbps

D Channel 16 Kbps

B channels are the bearers of data

The two B channels are the workhorse of an ISDN connection because they deliver the bulk of the digital information transmitted. This digital information can include voice, files, video, and sounds. You can use each B channel separately or your ISDN equipment can combine the two B channels to allow data transmission speeds of up to 128 Kbps. You can also combine multiple BRI lines to add more bandwidth power. For example, using two BRI lines and the right equipment, you can get transmission rates of 256 Kbps (64 Kbps times 4).

What's on the D channel?

The D channel delivers signaling information that tells the telephone company switches what to do with the stuff that's being delivered on the B channels. This signaling information opens and closes circuit switches to route calls. All ISDN signaling takes place within the D channel. Because it's a separate channel from the ones used to transmit data, the D channel's capacity allows ISDN to support more capabilities than analog communications.

This expanded channel allows for more powerful voice communications than analog systems. In analog systems, all the tricks of telephone services — call waiting, call forwarding, and other services for which you pay extra — are contained in the telephone company switch. With ISDN, that functionality is downsized to the telephone set sitting on your desk, thanks to the D channel. Voice communications using ISDN telephones, however, is not a well-developed ISDN application, compared to remote access or desktop video conferencing.

The D channel has a capacity of 16 Kbps, which is more than enough for ISDN signaling needs, so some telephone companies offer packet-switched data service (X.25 data). The biggest use of the D channel for X.25 communications is for connecting credit-card readers for credit or debit card transactions. Most ISDN users will not be using this feature.

Keeping your signals straight

In-band signaling is the process of sending through one communications channel not only the data being transmitted but also the information to operate the channel. When you pick up the handset on your phone, you send an off-hook signal to the central office switch. This switch detects the condition and connects you to a dial tone, which indicates that the system is ready for your call. On touch-tone phones, you enter various tones using the buttons on your telephone keypad. These buttons generate unique in-band signals called dual tone multiple frequency (DTMF).

With *out-of-band signaling,* information used to control the network is sent on a separate channel than the one used to deliver the user's information. ISDN uses out-of-band signaling on the D channel, so the two B channels are free to carry user data.

Because few local telephone companies have not implemented out-of-band signaling connections to and from the long distance telcos, some long distance calls combine the signaling that goes through the D channel with the two B channels. Because the D channel can use up to 16 Kbps for in-band signaling, 8 Kbps is merged into each B channel. As a result, your data in the B channel is delivered at 56 Kbps or 112 Kbps instead of 64 Kbps or 128 Kbps for the two B channels.

Because a B channel can potentially be transmitting data at either 56 Kbps or 64 Kbps, most ISDN equipment supports both. You'll typically see reference to this support as 56/64 Kbps in hardware data sheets and documentation.

Signaling System Number 7 (SS#7) is a collection of signaling switching protocols that allow out-of-band signaling to work across the different switches of the telephone network. The telephone industry Q.931 standard defines the user-network messaging signals that make up the user side of SS#7 — the local loop portion of the ISDN system.

Primary rate interface (PRI)

Primary rate interface (PRI) is the wholesale version of ISDN service. PRI delivers 23 64-Kbps B channels and 1 64-Kbps D channel. PRI service is referred to as *23B+D*. As you might guess, this digital communications power comes with a price tag that is out of reach for most. This bandwidth power is comparable to a T1 line. Companies installing multiple ISDN lines use PRI as a kind of wholesale delivery of B channels, which are then divided at the premises. Internet service providers and large organizations use PRI service for handling incoming BRI connections.

The primary rate interface costs hundreds of dollars per month. As such, it's clearly beyond the reach of individuals and the SOHO market. This book focuses on working with the BRI (basic rate interface) form of ISDN.

Playing by the Rules

ISDN is a network that works because of protocols and standards. A *protocol* is a set of rules for data communications. A *standard* is a set of detailed technical guidelines used to establish uniformity. Protocols and standards create an environment of universal capability. (Protocols from the analog modem world include V.34 for 28.8 Kbps modems and V.32bis for 14.4 Kbps modems.)

As a consumer of ISDN products, you may frequently see references to protocols and standards in product data sheets and documentation. Table 2-1 describes the main standards organizations that help bring order to ISDN service and equipment.

Table 2-1　ISDN Protocol and Standards Organizations

Organization	Description
International Telephone Union (ITU)	An agency of the United Nations that is the primary source of ISDN standards. This organization was once the Telephone Consultative Committee or Comité Consultatif International Télégraphique et Téléphonique (CCITT)
International Multimedia Teleconferencing Consortium	An organization that provides standards for using video and audio over ISDN.
American National Standards Institute (ANSI)	The primary standards-setting body in the U.S., ANSI plays a significant role in the development of ISDN standards. In the U.S., ANSI defines the operations of the local loop.
North American ISDN Users' Forum (NIUF)	Formerly the National Institute for Standards and Technology (a federal agency that is part of the Department of Commerce) in conjunction with ISDN industry players to identify ISDN applications and encourage ISDN equipment vendors to develop the products of interest to ISDN users. NIUF is involved in the development and packaging of ISDN service ordering codes.
Corporation for Open Systems (COS)	An organization that specifies and performs the testing and certification for ISDN within the U.S.
Federal Communications Commission (FCC)	A federal agency that develops and publishes rules and regulations governing communications and communications equipment in the U.S.
Bell Communications Research (Bellcore)	Formed as the research and development arm of the seven RBOCs in the U.S. As such, Bellcore played a leading role in defining ISDN standards for the RBOCs and has developed National ISDN, which is a collection of specifications for uniform implementation of ISDN. Bellcore also worked on ordering codes in conjunction with NIUF. The RBOCs recently divested themselves of Bellcore.
Internet Engineering Task Force (IETF)	An organization that sets the technical standards for the Internet and protocols, such as PPP/MP.
National ISDN Council (NIC)	Standards body for features incorporated into the National ISDN standards. This group consists of telephone switch manufacturers and telephone companies.

National ISDN standards

In 1988 the North American ISDN Users' Group, the National Institute of Standards and Technology, and Bellcore teamed up to develop the National ISDN series of specifications starting with National ISDN 1 (NI1), which was finalized in 1991. This was followed by NI2, which was released in 1994, and NI3, released in 1995.

These series of specifications are designed to make ISDN equipment and service interoperable. Nearly all major switch manufacturers, telephone companies, and CPE (customer premises equipment) vendors in the U.S. support National ISDN specifications. Each new addition to National ISDN adds more standardization of ISDN services and products. The NIC (National ISDN Council) now directs the ongoing development of National ISDN standards. It standardizes the features and functions of the telephone company switch vendors. These standards then carry over to the ISDN equipment at the consumer side of the ISDN connection.

Implementing ISDN standards is a slow process. It can take 3 to 4 years before they are set up across the entire telephone network.

Defining ISDN functions and reference points

Several key ISDN protocols define the unique functional and communication tasks required for an ISDN connection. The protocols that define the types of devices used in an ISDN connection are called *functional devices*. The protocols that define the communication between functional devices are called *reference points,* commonly referred to as interfaces.

The important thing to remember about functional devices and reference points is that they're protocol definitions. These protocols become embodied in ISDN equipment in a variety of configurations depending on what the ISDN equipment does. As a buyer of ISDN equipment, you need to understand functional devices and reference points to make sure that you choose the right equipment for your end of the ISDN connection.

Figure 2-5 shows the complete layout of an ISDN connection's functional devices and reference points. Each is explained in the following sections.

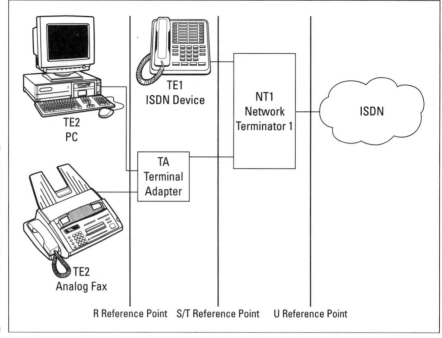

Figure 2-5:
ISDN
functional
devices and
reference
points are a
collection of
protocols
that define
the ISDN
connection.

ISDN Functional Devices

Functional devices are definitions for specific functions that need to be performed as part of an ISDN connection from the user side up to the telephone company's CO (central office). ISDN equipment typically embodies multiple functional devices. The following sections explain the functional devices in an ISDN connection.

ISDN hardware equals CPE

The encompassing term for any equipment on the customer side of the ISDN connection is *customer premises equipment (CPE)*. The more formal reference point is *terminal equipment (TE)*, which refers to any end-user device connected to an ISDN line. This is the general class of equipment that covers both ISDN-ready equipment and non-ISDN equipment such as analog telephones, faxes, and modems. CPE is the hip term, not TE, but you see both used.

All digital roads lead to network termination 1 (NT1)

Network termination 1 (NT1) represents the boundary between the ISDN system and the end user's equipment. NT1 includes the physical and electrical termination functions of ISDN service coming into your premises from the telephone company's CO. Specifically, NT1 is the device that provides an interface between the twisted-pair wires used by telephone company in the BRI and the four-wire cables used by ISDN equipment. Because the ISDN line, unlike the analog line, doesn't have any power, NT1 also includes the power function for operating the ISDN line.

Each BRI access has only one NT1 device. The NT1 function is typically embodied in the ISDN device used for remote access. The NT1 function can be handled also by a stand-alone device that supports multiple ISDN applications.

A *network termination 2 (NT2)* device handles switching functions and is embodied in PBXs (private branch exchanges). The NT2 device performs intelligent operations such as switching and concentrating traffic across multiple B channels in a PRI line. Working with PBXs and the primary rate interface is beyond the scope of this book.

ISDN-ready out of the box

Terminal equipment 1 (TE1) refers to ISDN devices that support the ISDN interface directly, including digital phones, digital faxes, and integrated voice/data terminal devices. These TE1 devices provide direct access to an ISDN connection without any adapters. Most ISDN-ready equipment is too expensive to be practical at this time. As ISDN service becomes universal, new computers and other devices will be ISDN-ready right out of the box.

Not ready for ISDN

Most of the computer and telephone equipment you use today is not ISDN-ready. This means you must use an ISDN adapter to make it work with ISDN. For example, you use an ISDN adapter card to connect your PC to ISDN so that you can access the Net.

Terminal equipment 2 (TE2) includes any device that isn't ISDN-ready. This category includes the equipment you now use for analog communications. Any device in this class, such as a modem, a PC, or an analog telephone or fax, requires an adapter to work with ISDN. The terminal adapter function, explained in the next section, provides this conversion of analog to ISDN. A number of ISDN equipment vendors offer remote-access products that consolidate the terminal adapter, NT1, and remote-access functions in a single unit.

Terminal adapters to the rescue

The functional device called a *terminal adapter (TA)* allows a non-ISDN ready device to work over an ISDN connection. The TA device is a protocol converter that adapts equipment not designed for ISDN. Beyond TAs for telephones and fax machines, other types of terminal adapters convert Ethernet to ISDN, RS-232 to ISDN and PC bus to ISDN. As PCs, telephones, faxes, and modems become ISDN-ready out of the box, TAs will disappear. For now, however, terminal adapters are the cornerstone to your ISDN connection. TAs are embodied in a variety of ISDN devices to connect both computers and analog equipment to ISDN. The most common use of terminal adapter functions in ISDN are adapters for allowing your PC to communicate with ISDN, and adapters for connecting analog telephones, faxes, and modems to an ISDN line.

Points of Reference

ISDN reference points define the communications between the different devices as well as define the operating parameters for the functional devices. The common term for reference points is *interfaces*. Four interfaces are commonly defined for ISDN: R, S, T, and U interfaces.

Understanding ISDN reference points is important because most CPE vendors refer to their equipment capabilities in terms of the interface it embodies. For example, you may see a reference to a CPE as U interface, meaning it has the network terminator 1 (NT1) function device built in.

The R interface

The R reference point defines the relationship between the terminal equipment 2 (TE2) functional device — a non-ISDN-ready device. There are no specific standards for the R interface, so the TA manufacturer determines and specifies how a TE2 and TA communicate with each other. In other words, it is a proprietary specification.

The S/T interface

The S interface is between ISDN user equipment (TE1 or TE2 with a TA) and the NT1 (network termination 1) device. The T interface is the interface between the local switching device (NT2) and the local loop termination (NT1). As mentioned, the NT2 device handles switching functions and is embodied in PBXs (private branch exchanges). In the absence of the NT2 — which is the case for BRI users — the reference point is commonly called an S/T interface. An S/T interface CPE cannot be plugged directly into the ISDN line without the addition of an NT1 device.

The U interface

The U reference point is where the local telephone company network arrives at your doorstep up to the NT1 device. The U interface is also called the *U-loop* because it represents the loop between your premises and the telephone company's CO. ISDN devices that terminate the U interface with network termination can be plugged directly into an ISDN line. A U-interface device can also have ports to plug in S/T-interface and analog devices.

Know your interfaces

Most ISDN CPE vendors sell equipment that supports either the S/T interface or the U interface. You'll see references to the type of interface the product supports on the packaging. Just remember that an S/T device requires an NT1 device to work with your ISDN connection. A U interface device includes the NT1 device, so it can plug directly into your ISDN line.

As you read in Chapter 4, a variety of CPE configurations enable you to integrate different ISDN equipment to the same line based on matching U- and S/T interfaces.

Where to Now?

Learning about ISDN is like peeling away the layers of an onion. At times, it can make you cry. Wipe your eyes and go to the next layer. Chapter 3 explains the nuts and bolts of starting down the road to establishing an ISDN connection.

Chapter 3

ISDN Connection Essentials

● ●

In This Chapter

▶ Developing an ISDN connection game plan

▶ Checking on ISDN availability and telephone company switch types

▶ Determining your ISDN service needs

▶ Figuring out the cost for your ISDN service

▶ Ordering the right configuration for your ISDN service

● ●

*I*n the olden days of POTS communications, getting started was simple. You ordered a POTS line with a telephone number from the telephone company, plugged in your telephone, fax, or modem, and started communicating.

Establishing an ISDN connection is a more complex undertaking. It involves making several line configuration and CPE decisions *before* you order the service from the telephone company. This chapter focuses on the key elements involved in configuring your ISDN connection as a foundation for CPE decision making, as explained in Chapter 4.

Your ISDN Connection Game Plan

The process of establishing an ISDN connection involves several elements that converge to define the configuration of your ISDN service from the telephone company to your premises. We can break down an ISDN connection game plan into the following four subprocesses:

✔ Finding out whether ISDN service is available at your location and what type of switch the telephone company uses at the local central office

✔ Defining your ISDN service needs

✔ Figuring out what ISDN service will cost

✔ Ordering your ISDN service from the telephone company

The entire process centers on ISDN provisioning, which is the configuration of your ISDN service by the telephone company. Your telephone company programs its switch to work with your specific CPE at your premises. The requirements for provisioning your ISDN line are defined by the specific equipment you will be using on your ISDN line. Provisioning information is always provided with your ISDN CPE, and many include unique ordering codes that act as ISDN service configuration templates.

Getting ISDN Service?

There are several routes you can follow to establish your ISDN service. A growing number of CPE vendors offer ISDN customer service groups that coordinate the entire process of getting your ISDN service. Many Internet service providers offer similar services. You can also take the do-it-yourself route by dealing directly with the telephone company, using your CPE documentation as your guide. Whatever option you choose, you should understand the configuration essentials for establishing ISDN service because they're relevant to the kinds of CPE choices you make.

No matter who handles your ISDN ordering, only your local telephone company can actually establish an ISDN line to your premises.

Using a CPE vendor's ISDN ordering services

Many ISDN equipment vendors offer customer service groups to help you get up and running with ISDN service. These services will typically provide details on setting up ISDN service for your locality, including contact numbers, installation charges, and ISDN provisioning information for their (and other vendor) products. These groups work with the local telephone and long-distance companies.

An example of an ISDN CPE group is U.S. Robotics I-Team. Call their toll-free number (888-USR-ISDN), and the I-Team will order ISDN service for you through the local telephone company and arrange the scheduling and installation of ISDN service. U.S. Robotics doesn't charge for these services, as is the case with most other vendors. Motorola, Farallon, Microsoft, Intel, and others provide similar services.

Respective CPE chapters later in this book provide detailed information on the vender's ISDN customer service groups, if available. Additionally, Appendix B has a comprehensive listing of ISDN CPE vendors providing ISDN ordering and provisioning services.

Using Internet service providers

A number of ISDN Internet service providers (ISPs) will also provide help in setting up your ISDN service. Many also sell ISDN CPE, sometimes at discounted prices. One of the advantages of going the ISP route is that they get your ISDN line established and also set up your Internet account.

 Keep in mind that different ISPs offer different ISDN service plans and configurations, so you need to become an educated Internet access consumer. Refer to Chapter 8 for more information on how to choose an ISP for your ISDN service. Appendix B lists ISDN Internet service providers.

Going the do-it-yourself route

Contacting the telephone company to handle the ordering of ISDN service yourself can be a good or bad experience, depending on your telephone company. Most telephone companies now have separate ISDN ordering centers staffed with ISDN-literate representatives. One of the best places to start your quest for ISDN service is to check out your telephone company's Web site. (There's more on contacting telephone companies for ISDN service later.)

Checking ISDN Availability and Switches

As explained previously, ISDN isn't universally available. Before you go any further, you must find out whether ISDN service is available in your areas, and more specifically to your premises. If there isn't a switch at the local CO that supports ISDN to your premises, or if your premises are outside the radius of ISDN service from the CO, the remaining steps are superfluous unless you plan to relocate.

The cost of ISDN service in your area is another critical factor in determining whether you can or want to get ISDN service. Pricing for ISDN service is a complex maze that varies from telephone company to telephone company. Before you can determine what ISDN service will cost, however, you need to know the configuration of the ISDN service. For this reason, figuring out the cost of ISDN is covered later in this chapter.

If ISDN service is available in your area, you need to find out the type of switch used by the telephone company for the ISDN line. Different switches run different software and vary in the number and type of ISDN devices they allow you to use on your line.

Checking ISDN availability

The absolute first step in getting an ISDN connection is determining whether it's available in your area by contacting the telephone company. Telephone companies differ considerably in their implementation of ISDN service.

Figure 3-1 shows the current ISDN deployment based on the percentage of POTS lines that support ISDN. You can use this chart as a rough gauge of the responsiveness of a telephone company to ISDN service.

Some RBOCs offer a service called *virtual ISDN*. This lets a telephone company offer ISDN service from a CO that doesn't have the switches to handle ISDN service. The telephone company routes the local loop termination at your local CO to another CO via an internal high-speed data link. Unfortunately, telephone companies may charge you extra for this service. For example, NYNEX charges approximately $35 more a month for virtual ISDN service. In addition, your telephone number reflects the actual CO where the switch is located, which will affect your usage charges.

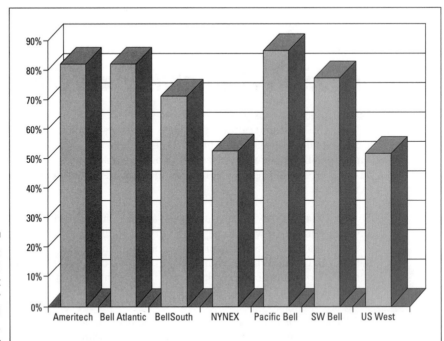

Figure 3-1:
ISDN
deployment
by RBOC for
1995 and
1996.

Euro-ISDN

If your telephone company says ISDN service isn't available, consider moving to Europe — just kidding! Euro-ISDN is a pan-European implementation of ISDN. As you can see in Figure 3-2, Europe leads the world in the number of ISDN B channels in service; 70 percent compared to 15 percent for the U.S. and 15 percent for Japan. Germany is the leader in ISDN deployment in Europe.

The United States lags in ISDN availability in large part due to the fragmentation of telecommunications companies. European telephone companies typically control the telecommunications market for an entire country.

Determining the switch type

The switch at the telephone company's CO defines the capabilities of your ISDN service. The switch type determines the number of ISDN devices and other features you can use on the line. It's important to determine in advance the type of switch the telephone company will use for your ISDN service.

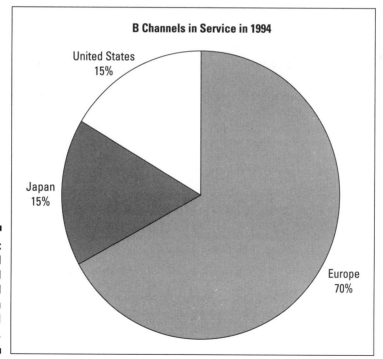

Figure 3-2:
The United States and Japan trail Europe in ISDN deployment.

Most telephone companies have three main types of ISDN switch software options: AT&T 5ESS Custom, AT&T 5ESS NI-1 (National ISDN-1), and NT DMS-100. Before you determine the applications you plan to use on your ISDN line, you need to know what type of switch the telephone company will provide. Different switches have different capabilities for handling multiple ISDN devices and other configuration options. The importance of the type of switch that your ISDN line is connected to has an impact if you're planning on adding multiple devices to your line. Most ISDN devices support all the leading telco switches and software.

The following lists the number of devices supported by each type of switch:

AT&T 5ESS NI-1	8 devices
AT&T Custom	8 devices
NT DMS-100	2 devices

You also need to know the switch type to configure your CPE to work with your ISDN line. CPE documentation includes specific configuration information for each of these switches.

All switches are not created equal. If you have a choice, ask for the AT&T 5ESS Custom. This switch offers the most flexibility in configuration options.

Getting answers from the telephone company

Getting information about ISDN service from telephone companies has improved but can still be a hit-or-miss proposition. Most telephone companies now offer ISDN service centers, automated voice systems for checking ISDN availability, or Web sites for checking availability and other information, such as tariffs and provisioning options. Table 3-1 lists telephone numbers and Web site URLs for obtaining ISDN information from telephone companies.

Table 3-1	Telephone Company Sources of ISDN Information
Telephone company	*Information source*
Ameritech	24-hour voice and fax-back system: 800-832-6328 Home ISDN service: 800-419-5400 Business ISDN service: 800-417-9888 World Wide Web: `http://www.ameritech.com/products/data/isdn/index.html`

Telephone company	Information source
Bell Atlantic	ISDN InfoSpeed Solutions Center: 800-204-7332 Small businesses: 800-843-2255 TeleProducts: 800-221-0845 World Wide Web: `http://www.bell-atl.com/`
BellSouth	ISDN individual line service: 800-858-9413 World Wide Web: `http://www.bell.bellsouth.com/`
Cincinnati Bell	513-566-3282
GTE	24-hour, menu-driven voice and fax-back system: 800-888-8799 Voice: 214-718-5608 World Wide Web: `http://wcn.gte.com/`
Nevada Bell	Small businesses: 702-334-4811 Large businesses: 702-688-7100
NYNEX New York	24-hour, menu-driven voice and fax-back system: 800-438-4736 Voice: 914-644-5152 World Wide Web: `http://www.nynex.com/`
NYNEX New England	24-hour, menu-driven voice and fax-back system: 800-438-4736 ISDN Service Center: 800-650-4736 World Wide Web: `http://www.nynex.com/`
Pacific Bell	24-hour voice and fax-back system: 800-995-0345 ISDN Service Center: 800-472-4736 World Wide Web: `http://www.pacbell.com/`
Rochester Telephone	716-777-1234
Southwestern Bell	Austin: 800-792-4736 Dallas: 214-268-1403 South Houston: 713-567-4300 North Houston: 713-537-3930 ISDN DigiLine Service: 800-792-4736 x500 World Wide Web: `http://www.sbc.com/`
U.S. West	24-hour voice and fax-back system: 800-728-4929 Voice: 800-246-5226 World Wide Web: `http://www.uswest.com/`

With the automated system, you can check availability by using your touch-tone telephone to enter your area code and exchange number (the three numbers after the area code). Most of the Web sites provide tariff information, ordering instructions, and an availability database.

One way or another, you must check with your local telephone company to get a confirmation that ISDN service is available to your premises. Some telephone companies have this information available in databases and can tell you right away. Others must perform a *loop qualification*, in which the telephone company checks your local loop to see whether it supports ISDN; this process can take days to complete.

Don't trust automated systems as your final answer for ISDN availability. Even if the system says ISDN is available in your area, it may not be available at your premises because of the distance from a CO.

For detailed ISDN tariff and contact information, see Appendix A.

Determining Your ISDN Service Needs

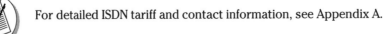

You need to know what specific CPE you plan to connect to ISDN before you can order your ISDN line from the telephone company. The telephone company needs to know what equipment you plan to connect to your ISDN line so that they can configure their switch at the central office, a process called *provisioning*. If you decide to change equipment, most telephone companies will charge you a change-order fee.

You can use multiple ISDN devices on your ISDN connection, so you need to coordinate your CPE activities into a unified ISDN system. Keep in mind that the more CPE devices and applications you plan to use with your ISDN connection, the more configuration specifications you need for the ISDN line. Chapter 4 details the specific planning issues for developing a CPE strategy that will make the best use of your ISDN line.

Connecting multiple devices to a B channel is a little more complicated. ISDN can support up to eight devices on the same B channel, but no two devices can use a single B channel at the same time. To allow multiple devices to share a B channel, your telephone company may use SPIDs (*service profile identifiers*). Later in this chapter, you'll learn more about SPIDs and why you need to know whether your telephone company assigns them.

Although ordering ISDN service remains one of the most difficult aspects of getting up and running with ISDN service, the situation is improving. Most vendors provide detailed configuration information in their documentation. Additionally, most telephone companies use ordering codes to streamline the configuration of ISDN service. The following sections explain the essential configuration options for ISDN service.

In the future, telephone companies may automate the provisioning of ISDN lines — users will simply hook up their equipment and the switch will automatically configure the line.

Making it easier to order ISDN service

ISDN ordering codes simplify the process of ordering and configuring your ISDN connection. An ISDN ordering code represents an established set of commonly used ISDN services. Unfortunately, the current order code environment hasn't matured, and different telephone companies use different order code systems. If your telephone company supports ordering codes, however, the process of provisioning your ISDN service will be streamlined.

CPE documentation includes ordering information for a number of ordering code systems. Your CPE vendor also provides specific provisioning information for each switch type in case your telephone company doesn't use ordering codes.

Compatibility packages

Bellcore Compatibility Packages are a widely used series of ISDN ordering codes. These packages, labeled A through Q, represent solution sets as defined for broad applications. They are complicated but very useful. The most common of these is Bellcore Compatibility Package M, which is similar to the Intel Blue code (see the next section).

Product codes

Another collection of ordering codes defines the provisioning of an ISDN line around a unique CPE product code. This set of product codes is more widely used and easier to work with. For example, the CPE code for the Intel ProShare Personal Video Conferencing System 200 is "Intel Blue." The ISDN provisioning requirements for Intel Blue work for a wide variety of ISDN remote-access devices. When you order your ISDN service, you simply tell the telephone company the code name supplied by your vendor. The other popular product vendor code is the Motorola BitSURFR Pro.

EZ-ISDN codes

NIUF (National ISDN User's Forum) introduced EZ-ISDN codes, which are designed to make ordering ISDN service easier. These four configuration templates provide preconfigured packages of ISDN services that are most useful for end-users or the mass market. The four codes are named EZ-ISDN 1, EZ-ISDN 1A, EZ-ISDN 2, and EZ-ISDN 2A. CPE vendors can register their equipment as compliant or compatible with these codes. At this stage in the evolution of ISDN service, these codes are just beginning to be used.

Choosing your B channel configurations

The basic rate interface standard typically includes two B channels and one D channel. However, many telephone companies offer a menu of BRI (basic rate interface) channel configurations, which do more to confuse people than to add real benefits. Table 3-2 shows the variety of available BRI configuration options that NYNEX offers.

Table 3-2	BRI Configuration Options from NYNEX for Massachusetts
Interface type	*Interface configuration*
0B+D	D channel only
1B	1B voice
1B	1B data
1B	1B alternate voice/data
1B	1B packet data
1B+D	1B voice D packet data
1B+D	1B data D packet data
1B+D	1B alternate voice/data D packet data
2B	1B voice 1B data
2B	1B voice 1B packet
2B	2B data
2B	1B data 1B voice/data
2B	1B data 1B packet data
2B	1B voice/data 1B packet data
2B+D	1B voice 1B packet data

Interface type	Interface configuration
2B+D	2B data
	D packet data
2B+D	1B data
	1B voice/data
	D packet data

Before you order the 2B+D configuration, make sure your Internet service provider or other network can support two B channels. You may be able to connect through only a single B channel.

Your BRI channel configuration determines the type of information that is transmitted through each B channel. You determine the channel configurations when you order your ISDN service. If you make any changes, your telephone company will probably charge you.

The following are the available channel configuration options:

✓ **Circuit-switched voice (CSV) only.** This option allows only voice traffic for the B channel. This is a restrictive option that doesn't allow the full bandwidth of the BRI connection because it ties up a B channel for just voice.

✓ **Circuit-switched data (CSD) only.** This option allows circuit data only for data transmission speeds of up to 64 Kbps uncompressed for each B channel.

✓ **Alternate circuit-switched voice/circuit-switched data (CSV/CSD).** This option allows either circuit data or voice communications to be carried over the channel. This channel configuration allows for the most versatile use of an ISDN line.

✓ **Packet data only.** This option allows for only X.25 packet data. In most cases, you won't use this provisioning option for your B channels.

Typically, you'll order the basic 2B+D channel configuration, with one B channel as alternate voice/data and the other as data only or alternate voice/data. As with other aspects of ISDN service, however, your CPE will determine the configuration of your B channels.

Every BRI connection has a D channel for out-of-band signaling. Beyond the requirement of signaling, the D channel offers 16 Kbps of X.25 packet data capacity. Some telephone companies let you specify whether you want the extra X.25 capacity on the D channel. If you specify not to have the X.25 capacity, your BRI line still uses a D channel for out-of-band signaling, but you don't have the 16 Kbps of X.25 packet data available.

Data over voice to save money

Some telephone companies, such as NYNEX, don't tariff local voice calls made over an ISDN line. If your ISDN remote-access device can initiate voice calls for data (most do), you can connect to an Internet service provider at 56 Kbps (one B channel) or 112 Kbps (two B channels) and not be charged for the call. The same call initiated as a data call over ISDN will be charged the ISDN tariff rate. NYNEX tries to thwart this low-cost approach, however, by not allowing the provisioning of the second B channel for voice unless you pay an additional charge. In PacBell territory, charges for data and voice calls are the same. Check your telephone company tariffs.

Getting to the point-to-point or multipoint?

An ISDN line can be either point-to-point or multipoint. Point-to-point configuration refers to the operation of one device on an ISDN line. Point-to-point on the AT&T Custom switch is the easiest to provision for the telephone company as well as to configure for your own ISDN remote-access device. In many cases, the point-to-point configuration is less expensive.

Multipoint configuration refers to the operation of multiple devices on the ISDN line. For a multipoint configuration, you need to use the SPID so that the device knows its ID in the switch. For example, if you have a telephone and a fax on a multipoint line, the switch delivers the called number as part of the call setup. The correct device — either the telephone or the fax machine — answers the number because the switch knows the device to which the number is associated. Within a multipoint configuration, each switch allows a certain number of devices to be connected to the line. At most, eight devices can be supported.

X.25 defined

X.25 is the widely used protocol for packet transmission over the worldwide telephone system. For example, CompuServe is based on the X.25 protocol. The X.25 packet-switching protocol breaks data into small chunks; each chunk is sent across the telephone network in a packet that contains source and destination information. Because each packet has its addressing information built-in, it can travel independently. Although the packets may arrive out of order, each packet also contains sequence information, so the receiving computer can reconstruct the original data.

If you're working with multiple ISDN devices that will share your ISDN line, you'll need the multipoint configuration. For example, your PC may have an ISDN adapter card that includes one or two analog ports, or you might want to add another device at a later time. An important criterion for ISDN equipment is to make sure it supports the multipoint protocol, which most do.

Supplementary services

The collection of voice communications features supported by ISDN are referred to as *supplementary services*. These services are an extensive set of defined call-management features you can implement as part of your BRI service. You're already familiar with many of these features from the analog world — call waiting, call forwarding, and conference calling are examples of supplementary services. The total set of supplementary services available at your premises depends on your telephone company and the services available from the central office serving your premises.

Supplementary services is a big collection of extras for your ISDN service. Don't get overwhelmed by all these options. Most ISDN devices you'll be using include information in their documentation about which supplementary services the device supports.

If you're using Intel Blue, Motorola BitSURFR Pro, Bellcore Compatibility Package M, or another vendor-supplied ordering code, the supplementary services are already specified. For example, an ISDN remote-access product may specify No CACH EKTS, call appearances, Caller ID, or other calling services as part of its configuration. Your CPE documentation will be your guide as to which supplementary services you must have and which services are supported but not required.

Because ISDN moves the power of a PBX to the desktop either by the user adding an ISDN-ready telephone or connecting an analog telephone to a terminal adapter for handling voice connection, the available options can be as extensive as those in many PBX systems. Supplementary services can be broken down into number identification, call offering, call completion, multiparty services, community of interest, charging services, and other services.

Although voice communications as well as fax and modem communications are available through ISDN, the tariffs imposed by different telephone companies can make using ISDN more expensive than using a standard POTS line. With ISDN, you may be charged for origination fax and voice calls, depending on tariffs. In the POTS world, the origination of calls is dependent only on local and long distance toll tariffs. See the section, "Data over voice to save money," for information on taking advantage of lower POTS charges for an ISDN data call. Check Appendix A for more information on tariffs.

Directory numbers and call appearances

The major advantage of ISDN for voice communications is its capability to handle multiple calls. Depending on the type of switch at the CO, you can have multiple directory numbers for each BRI line. Each directory number can have up to 64 different *call appearances* available from a single BRI connection. Multiple call appearances of the same directory number enable you to operate call waiting with incoming telephone calls coming into the same directory number. You can handle an increased number of calls because, unlike analog call waiting with its two-call limit, an ISDN telephone can receive several incoming calls.

Getting keyed-up ISDN

On your side of the connection, you configure your remote-access or other ISDN device that supports voice communications to work with the call-management features. This involves specifying *key systems* that define the functions of different buttons on the telephone for executing a particular task. As is the case for all supplementary services, these settings are specified in your CPE documentation or are part of a specific ISDN ordering code. The key system for ISDN voice communications follows.

Electronic Key Telephone Set (EKTS) is a National ISDN standard. It supports call appearances based on the directory number for the voice terminal. You can have multiple directory numbers, but only one call appearance per directory number. With EKTS, however, you have access to a multitude of common ISDN call-management features, such as caller ID, automatic callback, conference calling, and call forwarding.

- CACH EKTS stands for Call Appearance Call Handling Electronic Key Telephone Set, a supplementary service offered for National ISDN-1. With CACH EKTS, you can have multiple directory numbers and multiple appearances of each directory if you're using an AT&T 5ESS switch. There is a limitation of only one call appearance per directory number on the DMS-100 if the directory number is shared on another ISDN device.

- Feature Key Signaling enables you to assign specific call-management tasks to a given key on your ISDN telephone. Feature keys are identified by a unique number. For example, you might assign a key to call forwarding; when you press that key, the switch at the CO knows you're specifying call waiting and responds accordingly. You can reassign keys as new services become available or if you no longer use certain services.

- Keypad signaling is similar to the actions you perform on an analog telephone for services such as call waiting, call forwarding, and conference calling. This type of call handling is typically incorporated into NT1 Plus devices that connect analog telephones to an ISDN line.

Common supplementary services

You can order your supplementary services when you establish your BRI service or at a later time. Different telephone companies sell ISDN supplementary services differently. For example, a telephone company might sell call appearances and supplementary services in units of ten, which you can then define as you want. If you ordered ten units, for example, you might use four units to create four call appearances, and then use the remaining six units to add three-way conferencing, call forwarding, caller identification, repetitive dialing, and return last incoming call.

You must define your supplementary services so that the telephone company can program their switch at the CO. Depending on your telephone company and the type of switch used at your local CO, you can have up to 64 call appearances and supplementary services. Other telephone companies offer a package of the most common supplementary services for a flat charge.

An extensive collection of supplementary services is available for ISDN. For most small businesses and individuals, however, a core of services address most voice communications needs. The following list breaks down supplementary services into their key groupings. Table 3-3 lists the specific calling features within the main categories of supplementary services.

- ✔ Number identification supplementary services control the presentation of one party's ISDN number to the other party.
- ✔ Call offering supplementary services affect the connection and routing of calls.
- ✔ Call completion supplementary services affect the completion of incoming calls centering around a variety of call waiting features.
- ✔ Multiparty supplementary services pertain to conference calling.

Table 3-3   Common ISDN Supplementary Services

Service	Description
Number Identification	
Multiple Subscriber Number	Allows multiple telephone numbers to be assigned to a single BRI connection.
Calling Line Identification Presentation	Displays the caller's telephone number on an LCD display at the called party.
Calling Line Identification Restriction	Allows the calling party to prevent the delivery of the calling ISDN number to the called party.

(continued)

Table 3-3 *(continued)*

Service	Description
Connected Line Identification Restriction	Allows the connected party to restrict the display of its ISDN number to the calling party.
Calling Offering	
Call Transfer	Allows you to transfer an established call to a third party.
Call Forwarding Busy	Allows you to have the network automatically forward incoming calls to another number when your line is busy.
Call Forwarding No Reply	Allows you to have the network automatically forward incoming calls to another number if there is no answer on your line within a specified amount of time.
Call Deflection or Call Forwarding Unconditional	Allows you to have the network automatically forward all incoming calls to another number even if your line is available.
Call Completion	
Call Waiting	Allows you to be notified of an incoming call even when no information channel is available. You can then either accept, reject, or ignore the incoming call.
Call Hold	Allows you to interrupt communications on an existing call and then reestablish the connection.
Completion of Calls to Busy Subscribers	Allows you to camp on a busy telephone line until it's available. When it's available, you're notified and the call is established.
Multiparty	
Conference Calling (CONF)	Allows multiple users to communicate with each other simultaneously.
Three-Party Service (3PTY)	Allows you to place an active call on hold and place a new call to a third party. You can then switch back and forth between the two calls, join the calls together to form a three-way conversation, and split a three-way conversation back to two separate calls.

Figuring Out Your ISDN Service Costs

Now it's time to get down to the bottom line: What will all this digital enlightenment cost? The total cost of your BRI line depends on a variety of fixed and variable costs. Many of these costs are similar in structure to those of a POTS connection. ISDN service costs include a one-time installation charge, recurring monthly charges, and usage charges. This section explains each of the factors that make up the cost of your total ISDN service package.

See Appendix A for a summary of specific ISDN tariffs for each telephone company.

One thing is certain about ISDN service: It costs roughly twice as much as POTS. Because ISDN service lets you perform both analog and digital communications on the same line, you may be able to leverage the cost of ISDN service by adding a fax machine to the ISDN line and canceling the POTS line you used for your fax machine. Unless your telephone company offers standard POTS calling plans for your ISDN line, however, be careful about moving outgoing voice and modem communications to your ISDN line. Otherwise, you may find you're paying more for the "privilege" of using your ISDN line for analog communications.

ISDN is about speed and saving connection times. The expanded bandwidth of ISDN enables you to transfer more data in less time. For example, if you transfer lots of large files, the cost performance of ISDN over POTS and a modem are substantial. For working on the Internet, ISDN can substantially cut connection time, saving both telephone call charges and charges levied by online and Internet service providers.

Business versus residential rate

As is the case for analog telephone service, ISDN service can be based on a business or a residential tariff. Generally, the cost of business telephone service is higher than residential service. Many telephone companies, such as Pacific Telesis, offer residential ISDN telephone rates; others, such as NYNEX, don't. Without a residential tariff rate, the telephone company charges you the more expensive business rate. The residential rate is cheaper not only for installing an ISDN line but also for recurring charges and usage charges.

Installation charges

It costs about $150.00 to install an ISDN line. Your exact installation charge depends on your channel configurations, whether you're installing a new line or converting an existing POTS line for ISDN, and any wiring work performed at your premises. Table 3-4 shows the range of BRI installation charges for the major telephone companies. Keep in mind that specific costs break down on a state-by-state basis. Note that if you cancel your ISDN service, some telephone companies charge a termination fee that can run over $100.

Table 3-4	The Range of BRI Installation Costs
Telephone company	*ISDN BRI installation cost*
Ameritech	$100-$147
Bell Atlantic	$120-$173
BellSouth	$24-$288
NYNEX	$67-$325
PacBell	$159-$195
SWBell	$452
USWest	$67-$210

If the telephone company wires your home or business — that's twisted-pair wiring — the charge is around $55 to $75 per hour. You can also use independent contractors or do the wiring yourself within your own premises for ISDN, as explained in Chapter 4.

The U interface, or the line the telephone company terminates at your premises, is a two-wire interface, so it uses an RJ-11 jack and cord. This is the standard cabling used by analog telephones. The S/T interface, on the user's side of the NT1, uses the RJ-45 (8-pin) jack. Most CPE vendors provide a short RJ-45 cord to go from the NT-1 to the equipment. You can plug in an RJ-11 connector into an RJ-45 jack.

Don't let the telephone company installer sell you an RJ-45 jack for ISDN service — you don't need it. All you need is the standard RJ-11 jack, which you can probably install yourself. (You can also buy an RJ-45 jack for a lot less than what the telephone company would charge you. For example, NYNEX charges $12.50 for the RJ-45 jack.) See Chapter 4 for more information on ISDN wiring.

Monthly costs

ISDN service has a recurring monthly charge. The amount of this fee depends on your BRI configuration. Table 3-5 shows the range of monthly recurring costs charged by telephone companies for a BRI connection. These charges don't reflect a variety of charges that can be added to your monthly costs for adding specific features. Also note that these charges don't include usage.

Table 3-5	The Range of Monthly Costs for a BRI Connection
RBOC	*Average monthly BRI cost*
Ameritech	$28-$94
Bell Atlantic	$26-$50
BellSouth	$33-$126
NYNEX	$24-$90
PacBell	$24-$28
SWBell	$57-$104
USWest	$35-$104

Usage charges

Beyond the installation and monthly costs of ISDN service, there are usage charges. Like their POTS counterparts, these charges can easily dwarf your recurring monthly costs, depending where you're calling. The local telephone company charges you for local calls and the long distance telephone company bills you for long distance calls. These charges can be higher than for POTS service.

Unlike your POTS service, your local and long distance ISDN usage may not arrive in a consolidated bill. You'll receive a separate long distance bill from the long distance carrier that you specified at the time you ordered ISDN service.

ISDN toll charges generally follow the formula used for POTS service, which breaks down the charges according to the time the call is made and the distance of the call. The three standard calling time categories are day, evening, and night. The day rate is the most expensive, and the night rate is the least expensive. The toll rates for ISDN are just as complex to figure out as POTS charges, plus ISDN has additional charges. For example, if you're using both B channels during a connection, you'll be charged twice the published tariff because the two B channels are treated as two separate lines. If you're using the D channel (or B channel) to send X.25 data, the telephone company charges various rates based on the amount of data you move through the channel.

Charges for switched data are usually handled differently from those for voice. For voice, standard POTS voice rates for residential or business service usually prevail. For circuit-switched data usage, most telephone companies charge a higher tariff. Table 3-6 shows the NYNEX charges for circuit-switched data. Keep in mind that if you're using both B channels in an ISDN call, the rate is doubled.

Table 3-6   The Usage Charges of NYNEX New England

Calling area	Charge per call	Per minute charges (or fraction)
Within the calling area		
Zone 1 exchanges	$.0603	$.016
Zone 2 exchanges	$.0603	$.016
Outside the calling area		
Day rate	$.01	$.105
Evening rate	$.01	$.055
Night rate	$.01	$.036

In addition to the local usage charges, there are long distance charges. Table 3-7 lists the toll charges for AT&T long distance ISDN service, which is based on a mileage formula. These rates reflect the charge per minute for each B channel; if you're using both B channels, the charge is doubled.

Table 3-7   AT&T's Day Rate for Each B Channel

Mileage	First minute	Each additional minute
0-55	$.2790	$.1990
56-124	$.3090	$.2290
125-292	$.3310	$.2510
293-430	*$.3530*	*$.2730*
431-925	$.3790	$.2990
926-1910	$.3880	$.3080
1911-3000	$.4000	$.3200
3001+	$1.1470	$1.0670

Don't forget the Internet service provider's charges

Getting connected to the Internet requires an ISDN account with an Internet service provider. The cost of the ISP connection is in addition to all the charges for your ISDN line from the telephone company. ISDN Internet access accounts typically cost more than POTS-based accounts. A typical ISDN, single-user access account costs $26 to $40 a month for a block of free hours (often around 30 or so hours). Many ISPs also charge a one-time setup fee. As is the case with POTS accounts, a variety of plans are offered by ISPs. You need to shop around.

For more information on shopping for an ISDN ISP, see Chapter 6.

On-demand versus dedicated ISDN service

The typical ISDN service used by individuals and small businesses is the on-demand version. This type of service is a usage-based service, where charges are based on the amount of time you are connected.

Another form of ISDN service that isn't widely available yet is dedicated ISDN service. Dedicated service is an ISDN BRI line that is billed at a fixed monthly rate regardless of the amount of time you are connected. In other words, there are no usage charges. A dedicated ISDN line operates strictly as a point-to-point link. For example, you could have a dedicated ISDN connection to an Internet service provider, but that is the only connection you can make.

These dedicated ISDN lines are commonly referred to as Centrex service, because both ends of the connection must go through the same switch at the telephone company. Dedicated ISDN lines are rare, but they are beginning to become available in some areas. Centrex connections to the Internet typically cost from $200 to $600 a month. The Centrex option may be less expensive than dial-up ISDN if you're connecting a LAN to the Internet and plan to be connected for longer than several hours a day. Another reason you may want a dedicated ISDN line is for running a Web server to the Internet. A server on the Internet must be connected 24 hours a day, seven days a week.

Ordering Your ISDN Service

The final part of establishing ISDN service is contacting the local telephone company to order your service. You should order your ISDN service only after you've assembled the information on the devices you plan to use, the BRI channel configurations you want, and any other specifications. With this information in hand, you're ready to order your ISDN line from the telephone company.

Before you order your ISDN service, read Chapter 4 to develop your CPE blueprint. Also remember that you may want to use a CPE vendor to handle your ISDN connection arrangements. For a listing of vendors offering these services, see Appendix B.

As you'll recall, ordering an ISDN connection involves exchanging information with the telephone company. This information includes line and switch configuration information for each CPE you plan to use on the line. From the telephone company, you receive information for configuring your CPE to work with the ISDN connection. The following sections explain what information you'll receive from the telephone company after you give them your configuration information. Be aware that it may take some time for the telephone company to establish your line and give you the information you need to configure your devices.

Switch type

As explained earlier, the three types of ISDN switches are AT&T 5ESS Custom, AT&T 5ESS NI-1 (National ISDN), and NT DMS-100. You need to know what type of switch the telephone company is using at their end of the ISDN line so that you can configure your ISDN devices. Most ISDN devices support all the ISDN switches, but you must specify which one when setting up the device.

SPID on your ISDN connection

Your telephone company assigns a number called a *SPID (service profile identifier)* to each device connected to the ISDN line. SPIDs let the telephone company switch know which ISDN services a given device can access. A unique SPID is required for every device on a multipoint ISDN line or for each B channel. The SPIDs for two B channels, for example, may be 50862890210000 and 50862809620000. Typically, a SPID is a telephone number with several digits after it.

You usually need to configure the software for an ISDN device to tell it the SPID assigned to that device. Multipoint ISDN lines can handle multiple SPIDs. The AT&T 5ESS Custom switch and the AT&T 5ESS National ISDN switch support up to eight SPIDs. The NT DMS-100 National ISDN 1 supports only two SPIDs.

All the telephone companies have adopted standards established by the National ISDN Council (NIC) that will totally automate SPID capabilities in network switches by 1998.

Directory numbers

A *directory number (DN)* is the telephone number for the ISDN line assigned by the telephone company. Each ISDN line receives at least one directory number. You can have several directory numbers for each B channel, depending on the switch being used by your telephone company. If the CO switch is an AT&T 5ESS Custom, you can have one DN for each device. For example, a fax machine, a telephone, and a PC could all use one B channel, but each with a different number. Of course, you must have TE1 devices that can communicate with the D channel. If the CO switch is an NT DMS-100 NI-1, you must have two DNs — one for each B channel.

Chapter 4

Wired for ISDN and CPE Basics

In This Chapter

▶ Wiring your premises for ISDN

▶ Creating your CPE game plan

▶ Common CPE configuration recipes

*O*n your side of the ISDN connection is a cornucopia of *consumer premises equipment (CPE)* options that you need to understand before finalizing your ISDN service configuration and ordering. Different uses of ISDN service require different CPE pieces, and using an ISDN line for multiple applications requires still other CPE configurations. This chapter explains how to get wired for ISDN, the main CPE categories, and key factors for developing your CPE game plan.

Getting Wired for ISDN

ISDN and POTS use the same wiring, but ISDN wiring configurations operate differently. You need to understand several important wiring issues before dealing with your ISDN CPE.

ISDN line installation

The physical wiring is the same for an ISDN line and a POTS line. You may, however, have restrictions on adding a new telephone line, depending on your location and whether it's a business or residence. In most cases, business sites have no restrictions for bringing in additional lines.

For residences outside metropolitan areas, the number of telephone lines may be restricted to two. Standard telephone wiring consists of single, 4-wire cable and therefore allows for two lines. Most homes in metropolitan areas can add a number of lines beyond two lines.

Before you decide about converting an existing analog line, check with your telephone company to see whether you can bring in an additional line. If you can't bring in another line at your home, you'll need to convert an existing POTS line to ISDN. Remember, you can use an ISDN line for analog communications. For example, if you use a second analog line for a fax, you can still use the fax with an ISDN line and a *TA (terminal adapter)* device.

Typically, the conversion involves the telephone company canceling your POTS line (and number) and replacing it with an ISDN line. In most cases, you shouldn't convert your primary analog voice line to ISDN service because ISDN tariffs can be more expensive than POTS. Also, you may want to use your ISDN line exclusively for data transmission and not to tie it up with incoming voice calls.

Wiring from the telco to your premises

The U interface covers the wiring from the telephone company's central office (CO) to your premises as well as your site's internal wiring up to the NT1. The division of telephone wiring responsibility between the telephone company and the end user is different in the United States than in the rest of the world. The telephone company is responsible for any wiring to your doorstep; from that point, it's your responsibility. In most other areas of the world, the telephone company is also responsible for the NT1 function.

The *demarcation point* is the division between the telephone company's wiring and the premises' wiring. As shown in Figure 4-1, the demarcation point is usually a box. The physical device that provides the means to connect the telephone company's wire to the premises' wire is the *network interface* (NI).

The demarcation point and network interface box are the same for POTS and ISDN service. If your premises consist of an older structure, however, you may not have a network interface box. As a result, the incoming telephone line connects directly to a device called a *protector block*.

The FCC places a restriction, commonly referred to as the *12-inch rule*, on both the customer and the telephone company. This rule states that if you have a protector block, the network interface box must be located within 12 inches of it. The FCC prohibits customers from working at the protector block. Therefore, if your house doesn't have a network interface box, you need to have one installed by the telephone company. Only the telephone company can install the network interface device or any device directly wired to the telephone line.

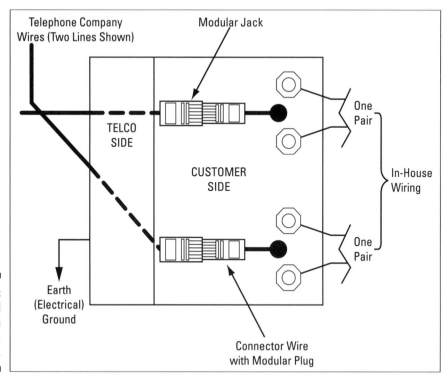

Figure 4-1:
A typical demarcation box for a residence.

Wiring your place

From the demarcation point, the telephone wiring is your responsibility. You can choose to have the telephone company or an independent contractor do the inside wiring for a new line, or you can do it yourself. If you have a choice, bring in your ISDN line as a separate line and use only one of the wire pairs. This will make it easier to install and set up your ISDN equipment. If you're using one of two pairs of wires in a line, you need to know which pair of wires is used for which line. Typically, the red and green wires are used for one line, and the yellow and black for the other line.

If your existing wiring works properly for analog service, it should continue to work for ISDN service. You may run into problems if the existing wiring is complex, such as office wiring originally installed for older key-based telephone systems. If this is the case, consult your telephone company or wiring contractor.

The EIA/TIA (Electronic Industries Associations and the Telecommunications Industry Association) standard for new residential wiring of analog and ISDN service specifies 24-gauge *unshielded twisted-pair* (UTP) cable of category 3 or above. The designation *unshielded* refers to the fact that the sheath does not include an electrical shield. You can buy this wiring at any hardware or electronics store.

The connectors

At the end of your wiring are the connectors. Standard analog wiring uses RJ-11 modular connectors, which snap into a surface-mounted or flush-mounted jack. RJ-11 connectors are 4-wire connectors used for analog equipment. ISDN devices use 8-wire RJ-45 connectors and cabling to connect to the NT1 device. From the U interface to the NT1, you can use RJ-11 connectors and cabling. Figure 4-2 shows the wiring of RJ-11 and RJ-45 connectors. S/T-interface devices (CPE without built-in NT1) use the RJ-45 connector.

Figure 4-2:
The 4-wire
RJ-11 and 8-
wire RJ-45
modular
connectors.

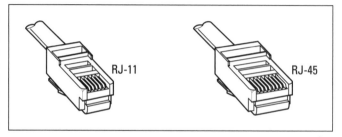

Daisy chains, stars, and passive buses

For POTS service, you normally add a new telephone or other analog device by simply splitting the RJ-11 jack or tapping into the existing line and adding a jack. This type of wiring arrangement is called a *daisy chain* configuration and is shown in Figure 4-3.

The daisy chain wiring arrangement, however, doesn't work for an ISDN line. Your ISDN service comes in as a single line and terminates at the network termination 1 (NT1) device. You can't add any ISDN devices to the line before it gets to the NT1. After the ISDN line terminates at the NT1, you can add multiple ISDN devices using multiple RJ-45 connectors.

The wiring arrangement for ISDN is the *star configuration,* as shown in Figure 4-4. In this arrangement, each piece of terminal equipment is wired separately to a central point, which is the NT1 or NT1 Plus device.

The star wiring scheme for connecting ISDN devices to the NT1 device using RJ-45 wiring is referred to as a *passive bus* configuration. Typically, most small businesses and individuals can use this ISDN device configuration. The

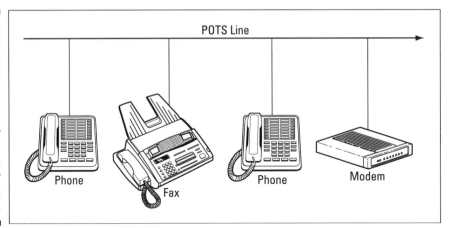

Figure 4-3:
The typical POTS wiring scheme enables you to tap into an existing line at any point to add a telephone or another analog device.

passive bus arrangement allows the connection of multiple devices on a single ISDN line without the need for repeaters to boost the digital signal. Chapter 5 explains the specifics of wiring ISDN devices to NT1 devices.

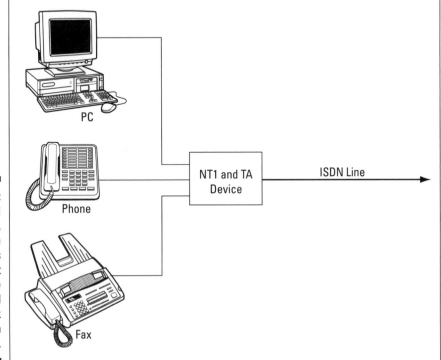

Figure 4-4:
For ISDN wiring, separate lines connect each device to a central network termination device.

CPE Game Plan Essentials

To get the most out of your ISDN service, an ISDN CPE game plan is essential. Different combinations of applications require different CPE configurations. And the CPE configuration determines how you provision your ISDN line.

To start, you need an overview of the main types of ISDN devices and applications you'll use on your ISDN line. From this overview, you can create your CPE blueprint. From the blueprint, you can order your ISDN line and provide the necessary information to the telephone company.

It is important that you know how to choose and integrate your ISDN equipment into a complete system. Buying the wrong matchup of ISDN CPE can be an expensive mistake.

Equipping yourself for ISDN

ISDN devices range from those required for basic ISDN service, such as network termination 1 (NT1) devices, to those for specific ISDN applications, such as Internet access and video conferencing. Although ISDN applications and equipment are evolving, the following CPE categories remain fairly stable:

- Stand-alone NT1 device that provides the network termination and ISDN line powering functions. The NT1 device allows you to plug in two S/T-interface devices. The NT1 function is also built into many ISDN remote-access products.

- Stand-alone NT1 Plus device that includes built-in terminal adapters for connecting analog devices to the line, the NT1 function, and ISDN line powering. Most ISDN remote-access products now include analog ports, so you typically don't need to use an NT1 Plus device.

- PC adapter cards for ISDN remote access (Internet access or telecommuting). These devices are available with or without built-in NT1 and typically include an analog port.

- Serial-based ISDN remote-access devices that connect to your PC via the COM port and RS-232 serial cable. These devices are available with or without the built-in NT1 and analog ports, although most include the NT1.

- Stand-alone Ethernet-based remote-access equipment that connects your LAN to ISDN through Ethernet. These devices, which can be bridges or routers, are available with or without the built-in NT1 and analog ports.

- Desktop video-conferencing (DVC) systems that include a video capture card, an ISDN adapter, and a video camera. Most ISDN DVC systems require a stand-alone NT1 device or an ISDN remote-access device to work.

Later chapters cover each of these ISDN CPE categories in order.

To do a U or S/T interface

ISDN equipment comes in two flavors, U interface and S/T interface. CPE vendors typically sell their products in both flavors. ISDN equipment made for the U interface has the NT1 functional device built in. ISDN equipment made for the S/T interface requires the NT1 function to connect to ISDN.

The significance of these two interfaces is pivotal to your CPE game plan. You can have only one NT1 per ISDN line. Therefore, a single ISDN line can't have more than one U-interface device because it includes the network termination function. A single ISDN line can have multiple S/T-interface devices. (S/T-interface devices require an NT1 device to connect to the ISDN line.)

The Zen of NT1 placement

The network termination 1 (NT1) device represents the boundary to the ISDN network from the end-user side. The placement of the NT1 function within your ISDN CPE configuration is the key factor in determining the number of applications you can use on an ISDN line. The NT1 functional device can be embodied in a stand-alone device or included in a specific device, such as a PC adapter card used to connect to the Internet.

Determining which route to go for your NT1 device depends on your entire ISDN applications package. If you want to use your ISDN line for connecting to the Internet or telecommuting and add an analog device, you can purchase an ISDN remote-access device that includes built-in NT1 and RJ-11 analog ports for adding a telephone, a fax, or a modem. This is a common configuration for ISDN remote-access devices.

If you want to use your ISDN line for connecting to the Internet or telecommuting as well as for using a desktop video conferencing system, the NT1 device must have at least one additional S/T-interface port. Remember, the S/T-interface is an RJ-45 port that connects an ISDN-ready device to the NT1 device.

An S/T-interface device requires you to use a stand-alone NT1 device, or you can use an ISDN remote-access device with built-in NT1 that includes an S/T-interface port (RJ-45). Most desktop video-conferencing systems as well as ISDN telephones are S/T-interface devices. If you use an Internet- or TCP/IP-based video-conferencing system, the data goes through your remote-access device.

A stand-alone NT1 device provides the network termination and line-powering functions for your ISDN connection. It typically enables you to connect two S/T-interface devices to your ISDN line. Remember that one of those S/T-interface devices — such as a remote-access adapter card — can include analog (RJ-11) ports for connecting a fax, a telephone, or a modem. The remote-access device that you plug into the NT1 device cannot have built-in NT1.

You can use a stand-alone NT1 Plus device to support two analog devices and two S/T-interface devices. This configuration enables you to plug in the maximum number of ISDN and analog devices to your line.

For more detailed and hands-on information on working with stand-alone NT1 and NT1 Plus devices, see Chapter 5.

Better living through ISDN CPE standards

Standards create a level playing field for users so that they can choose equipment from different vendors and be assured that it will work with equipment at the other end of the ISDN connection.

Interoperability means related devices from different vendors can work together. In the analog communications world, a modem from one vendor can connect to a modem from another because all modem manufacturers follow standards. Likewise, in the ISDN realm, several protocols establish interoperability across CPE from different vendors.

This section explains the key standards in place for ISDN.

PPP/MP for two B-channel Internet access

In the Internet access area, the Point-to-Point Protocol Multilink Protocol (PPP/MP) supports PPP over two B channels and allows different CPE vendors' remote-access products to work with each other. The PPP/MP standard has been universally adopted by CPE vendors as well as the Internet Engineering Task Force (IETF), a world-wide group with responsibility for developing the technical protocols for the Internet.

Desktop video conferencing with H.320 and T.120

Desktop video-conferencing products are also based on two key standards: H.320 and T.120. The H.320 standard provides the basis for interoperation of different video-conferencing systems. This standard was established by *International Telecphone Union* (ITU), a global standards organization.

The ITU-T T.120 general multimedia-conferencing standard is designed for interoperability of real-time animation, file transfers, share applications, and faxes within the context of video-conferencing systems. The ITU H.323 and

H.324 standards will most likely be implemented in ISDN video-conferencing systems in the future for video conferencing over TCP/IP (the Internet) and LANs.

Rate adaptation for serial communications over ISDN

V.120 is a standard of the ITU-T that governs what a system should do when the data rates offered by ISDN can't be matched by the device. To make rate adaptation happen, bits must be added to the transmission to make a lower stream of, say, 19.2 Kbps from your PC serial port fit into a 64 Kbps B channel. It's widely used in North America as the method of adapting the rate of an asynchronous serial port on a computer to ISDN.

Bonding power (no, it's not James Bond)

Bonding, which stands for bandwidth on demand interoperability group, is a method for combining multiple channels to form a single channel. For ISDN, bonding allows the two B channels to be combined into a 128-Kbps transmission for the same application. Combining multiple B channels allows more data to flow over an ISDN connection. Applications such as file transfers and video conferencing depend on bonding. Bonding is embodied at the CPE level; equipment vendors may or may not include it as a feature of their product.

De compression

Compression is an important technology for getting more through your ISDN line. Using compression over ISDN can give you a data transmission rate between two and four times the uncompressed 128 Kbps for two B channels. The final standard for ISDN compression, *Compression Control Protocol* (CCP), is in limbo because Motorola owns the patent to this technology and isn't letting it become an Internet standard. Therefore, most ISDN vendors continue to use proprietary data compression schemes. In the meantime, the leading compression schemes for ISDN are Stacker LZS Compression Protocol and Ascend Stack compression.

NT1 plus CPE equals NT1 Plus CPE

An NT1 Plus device is often the best starting point for working with ISDN if you plan to use analog devices, such as a telephone, a fax, or a modem. These are hybrid devices that include the NT1 and terminal adapter functions. As you recall, the terminal adapter (TA) functional device allows non-ISDN devices to communicate via ISDN. The configuration of the available ports depends on the product. Because NT1 Plus devices let you work with ISDN's voice services, they require more effort to set up.

Chapter 5 explains working with NT1 Plus devices.

Remote-access CPE (where the action is)

Remote-access CPE encompasses connecting your PC or LAN to the Internet or connecting your PC to an office LAN for telecommuting. Remote access can also be connecting a LAN to another LAN, or a single PC to another PC.

Internet access is provided by an Internet service provider through TCP/IP. Telecommuting is made possible by connecting to a Windows NT TCP/IP, Novell, or other network environment at a company site. Consider the following:

- ✔ Stand-alone serial-based ISDN remote-access device. This unit looks like a standard PC modem and connects your PC to ISDN through a serial port.

- ✔ ISDN bus adapter card. A bus card uses the PC's bus configuration to communicate to the PC. This card fits into an expansion slot in a PC and is available as a U- or S/T-interface device. Most of these cards include analog ports for voice and modem communications.

- ✔ Stand-alone Ethernet-based remote-access CPE. These devices connect to your PC through a LAN adapter in your PC to ISDN. The two types of Ethernet CPE products are bridges and routers. A *bridge* connects two physical networks into a single logical network that acts like a single physical network. A *router* can be configured to route data to different networking protocols based on information in the network packets. Therein lies the difference — bridges can't route data based on different network packets. Both bridges and routers can be used by single PC users or to connect LANs to the Net or other networks.

Part II explains ISDN-based remote-access options for connecting your PC to the Internet and other networks.

Smile for desktop video conferencing

Desktop video-conferencing systems are one of the most exciting uses of ISDN. The bandwidth ISDN delivers makes real-time video communications come close to being alive. Video-conferencing systems typically include a video compression card, a sound card, a video camera, and software. The cards plug into a PC and provide both video and audio services. Because most PC video-conferencing systems comply with standards, you can communicate with people who use different systems. These PC-based systems can communicate also with room-size systems.

The two basic desktop video-conferencing systems are those that work over the Internet and ISDN and those that work over ISDN only. The Internet systems use TCP/IP to operate across the Internet with the data routed through your remote-access device.

Part III explains working with desktop video-conferencing systems.

ISDN CPE Recipes

Understanding the pieces is one thing; understanding how to assemble them into an integrated package is another. Different recipes are required to build systems for different application mixes. To guide you through the assembly process, the following sections present typical ISDN CPE configuration recipes.

Starting with your PC

ISDN is a powerful communications connection that requires matching PC power. Using a slow processor, an older graphics adapter, or too little memory causes bottlenecks that will affect the overall performance of your system. For example, downloading graphics to your systems at ISDN speeds is dramatically diminished if your graphics card redraws your screen too slowly.

Here is the optimal PC configuration for working with ISDN access. In most cases, you can get by with less, but you'll pay in terms of performance. Your PC should include the following:

✓ A Pentium PC

✓ An accelerated VESA bus or PCI bus graphics card that supports at least SVGA with 800 x 600 x 256 colors recommended

✓ 16MB to 32MB of RAM

✓ One to three empty 16-bit ISA bus slots or PCI slots depending on your ISDN applications

✓ Microsoft Windows 95 or Windows NT Workstation (or Server) 4.0

Numero uno: Internet access

Surfing the Internet is the number one reason for getting ISDN service. You can establish an ISDN connection to the Internet using a variety of affordable products. If you only want to connect to the Internet through ISDN, you can simply add to your PC an ISDN serial remote-access device or an adapter card that includes the built-in NT1. Many of these serial devices and adapter cards also include analog ports that you can use to attach a telephone, a fax, or a modem to your ISDN line. To connect one or more PCs through an Ethernet network, you can use an ISDN router. Figure 4-5 shows the schematic for a basic ISDN connection to the Internet.

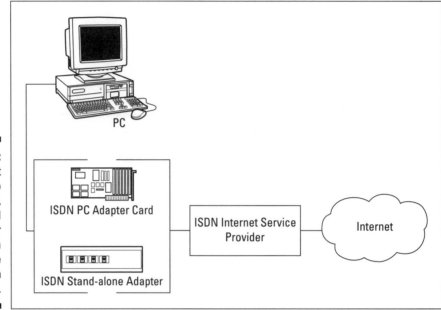

Figure 4-5:
To connect
your PC to
the Internet,
use an ISDN
adapter
card or a
stand-alone
unit with
built-in NT1.

The only software you need to access the Internet is Windows 95, a Web
browser, and any TCP/IP application software you want to use for e-mail, FTP,
telnet, and so on. To connect to your Internet provider, use the Windows 95
dial-up networking feature, Windows NT's Remote Access Service, or your ISDN
remote-access device. You can also connect to the Internet by using a third-
party TCP/IP package, such as NetManage's Chameleon. In most cases, the ISDN
remote-access CPE that you use for Internet access can be used also for
telecommuting connections to your office LAN.

Chapter 7 explains how to use ISDN with Windows 95. Chapter 8 explains how
to use ISDN with Windows NT 4.0.

Combining remote access with analog devices

You can easily add analog devices to remote-access applications. For example,
many remote-access devices include one or two ports for plugging in a telephone, a fax, or a modem. You probably won't want to make an ISDN line your
primary incoming voice line because doing so would tie up high-speed data
communications capabilities with voice communications and because ISDN
service typically has higher tariffs than POTS.

Adding a fax machine to your ISDN line may make better sense than adding a telephone. Doing so is like maintaining a separate line for your fax, complete with its own telephone number. While you're using your ISDN line for remote access, your fax line will send a busy signal to anyone trying to fax you.

The most common and least expensive way to add voice communications is to attach an analog telephone to an ISDN remote-access adapter card that has one or two built-in RJ-11 telephone jacks. You can also use a POTS port on an NT1 Plus device to plug in a fax machine or modem instead of a telephone. If the NT1 Plus supports two POTS ports, you can plug in both a telephone and a fax or a modem. Figure 4-6 shows a schematic for connecting remote access and analog equipment. Remote LAN access, telephone calls, and fax calls are accomplished through the telephone network.

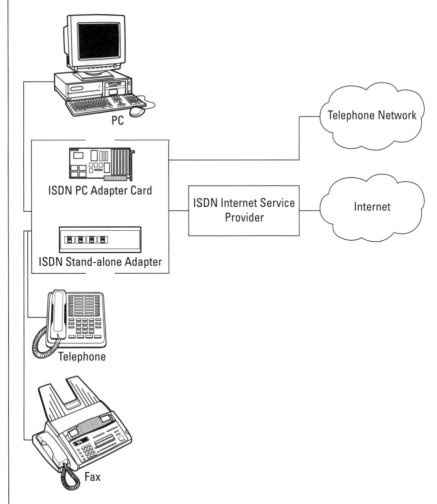

Figure 4-6:
To connect analog equipment and for remote access, use a remote-access device with built-in NT1 and an analog port.

The deluxe package: remote access, video conferencing, and analog devices

If you want the maximum possible use from your ISDN line, you can combine voice, remote access, and video conferencing. You can handle the added element of video conferencing in two ways. The first option is to use a video-conferencing system that works only across ISDN. You dial up another video-conferencing system through the telephone company network. This system includes a separate adapter card with an S/T interface that connects to a stand-alone NT1, NT1 Plus, or remote-access device that includes an S/T-interface port. Figure 4-7 shows a schematic for remote access, video conferencing, and analog devices on an ISDN line.

The other option for video conferencing is through your ISDN Internet connection. This approach uses your remote-access device to carry the video conference across the Internet to another person. This system typically includes a software package, such as CU-SeeMe, a video capture card, and a video camera.

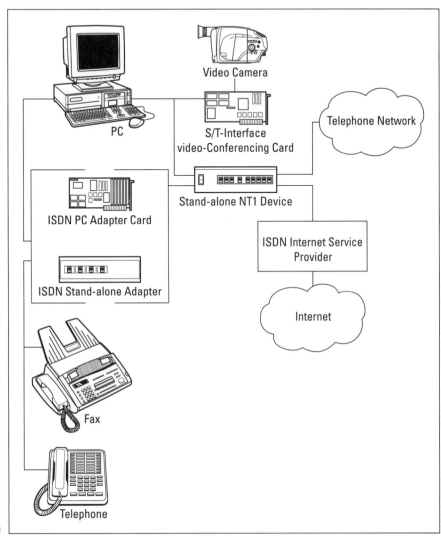

Video Camera

Telephone Network

PC

S/T-Interface
video-Conferencing Card

Stand-alone NT1 Device

ISDN PC Adapter Card

ISDN Internet Service
Provider

ISDN Stand-alone Adapter

Internet

Figure 4-7:
The
schematic
for
connecting
remote
access,
video
conferencing,
and analog
devices on
an ISDN
line.

Fax

Telephone

Chapter 5

Close Encounters of the NT1 and NT1 Plus Kind

*T*o use remote access and a desktop video-conferencing system on your ISDN line, you may need a stand-alone NT1 or NT1 Plus CPE. This chapter explains the workings of NT1 and NT1 Plus devices and takes you on a tour of the leading products. You can skip this chapter if you don't plan to go beyond remote access and analog devices using ISDN.

The Workings of NT1 Devices

A typical NT1 device looks like a small modem. It usually has a series of LEDs on the front, with one U-interface port and two S/T-interface ports at the back of the unit. All the ports are RJ-45 jacks. You can connect an RJ-11 cable into the U-interface port. You connect RJ-45 cables from your ISDN devices into the S/T-interface ports.

The passive bus configuration for a BRI (*basic rate interface*) connection can support up to eight devices, but in most cases you'll want to connect only two S/T-interface devices to an NT1. Adding more than two ISDN devices by using a Y connector is complicated because you need to work with external resisters. NT1 devices include a switch to set the termination for your bus configuration, which is explained in the section "Passive Bus Options."

NT1 devices have different power options depending on whether you need to power your customer premises equipment from the NT1 or you need to power only the NT1. Most NT1 devices support both point-to-point and multipoint ISDN CPE configurations. They're also compatible with all CO switch types.

With a stand-alone NT1 device, you can add another S/T-interface device to your ISDN connection in addition to the remote-access device. The most common additional device you might add to your ISDN connection is a desktop video-conferencing system. All leading ISDN video-conferencing systems use an S/T interface, which means the NT1 function is not built in. In addition, most remote-access devices don't include an S/T-interface port. The only other S/T-interface device you might use is an ISDN telephone. A typical stand-alone NT1 device costs under $200.

A number of vendors offer NT1 devices. This chapter covers working with ATI's UT620 NT1, Tone Commander's NT1U-220TC, ADTRAN's NT1 Ace, and Motorola's NT1D.

Appendix B provides a listing of NT1 vendors.

Powering options

Your NT1 requires power for your ISDN line. Beyond the powering requirements of your ISDN line, which are minimal, the NT1 may need to supply additional power. The CCITT defines the power for ISDN devices as Powering Source 2 (PS2). PS2 provides dedicated power to S/T-interface devices that don't have their own power supply.

An ISDN device that doesn't include power, such as an ISDN telephone without its own power supply, must have the PS2 power supply with your NT1. (ISDN devices that are powered themselves, such as ISDN adapter cards in a PC, don't need the PS2 power supply.) Some NT1 devices have only the PS2 powering option, which you can use even if your ISDN devices don't need power from the NT1.

If the operation of the NT1 is disrupted due to something in an ISDN connection, often you need to reboot the NT1. Unfortunately, most NT1 devices don't include a reset button, so you must unplug these devices to reboot them. Some NT1 devices have a reserve power option to give you enough time to shut down a connection in the event of a power loss.

Passive bus options

The term *passive bus* refers to the capability to connect multiple devices to a single BRI connection. The configuration of the passive bus combines the terminating resistors for all the devices connected to your NT1, which must add up to 100 ohms. Termination options for NT1s are 50 ohms, 100 ohms, or none (unterminated).

How you set these options depends on the devices you're using with your ISDN line. For example, if you're using a video-conferencing system that includes a built-in 50-ohm terminator resistor, set the NT1 termination option to 50 ohms, for a total of 100 ohms. The distances between the devices and the NT1 on a passive bus arrangement vary depending on the device and the type of NT1 or NT1 Plus that you use.

ATI's UT620 NT1

The ATI UT620 is a compact NT1 device that lists for around $200. You can choose two different power supply options depending on whether you need to power ISDN devices or only the NT1. The power source is connected to a 4-pin mini DIN power connector on the side of the UT620.

If you use the UT620 with an SP62020 switching power supply, the UT620 can provide CCITT-standard Power Source 2 (PS2) power through the S/T interface to the ISDN CPE. If the UT620 is used with the AD62010 power adapter, the UT620 does not provide PS2 power to the ISDN CPE.

LEDs

The three LEDs (light-emitting diodes) on the front panel of the UT620 indicate the status of the power supply, the S/T and U interfaces, and the ISDN line. The Power LED indicates that the power supply is functioning normally. When you first install the UT620, the S/T&U LED flashes for a few seconds, and then goes off. The UT620 communicates to you through its LEDs as follows:

✔ If the U interface isn't connected, the S/T&U LED flashes eight times per second.

✔ If the U interface isn't activated, the S/T&U LED stays lit continuously.

✔ If the S/T interface isn't activated, the S/T&U LED flashes once per second.

✔ If both the S/T and U interfaces are linked, the S/T&U LED goes off.

✔ The U loopback LED lights during a CO loopback test with the UT620.

DIP switch settings

On the bottom of the UT620 is a block of four DIP switches. Use the DIP switches to configure the UT620 according to the settings in Table 5-1. In most cases, you'll choose the Short passive bus option for DIP switch number 3.

Table 5-1	UT620 DIP Switch Configuration Options		
DIP Switch	*Function*	*On*	*Off*
1	S/T termination	Yes	No
2	S/T termination	Yes	No
3	Bus timing mode	Short passive bus	Point-to-point, or extended passive bus
4	PS2 selection	SP62020 switching power supply	AD62010 AC/DC power adapter

Installation

Installing the UT620 is an easy process that involves setting DIP switches, plugging in the power supply, and connecting the U-interface and S/T-interface cables. Here are the steps for installing ATI's UT620:

1. **Set the DIP switches for your setup.**

2. **Connect the power supply to the UT620 and plug it into the AC power outlet.**

   The Power LED lights up.

3. **Connect an RJ-11 or RJ-45 cable between the UT620 U-interface connector and the U-interface outlet at your premises.**

4. **Switch on the power to the ISDN terminal equipment.**

5. **Connect one end of an RJ-45 cable to an S/T port on the UT620, and the other end to the ISDN terminal equipment, such as an adapter card in your PC.**

6. **If you're connecting two ISDN terminals, repeat Steps 4 and 5 for the second device.**

   The S/T&U LED may begin to flash for a few seconds. The LED will go off when the communication paths have linked up. When the LED goes off, the ISDN CPE is ready for communication.

Tone Commander's NT1U-220TC

Tone Commander's NT1U-220TC lists for around $200. It includes the standard NT1 U-interface and S/T-interface ports, and also has PS2 powering for ISDN devices not powered locally. The NT1U-220TC includes a handy feature not found in other NT1 devices — a power reset button that enables you to reboot the device.

LEDs

The NT1U-220TC has four LEDs on the front panel: TERMINAL ERROR, ACTIVE, LINE ERROR, and POWER. Here's how to interpret them:

✔ During the power up of the NT1U-220TC, all four LEDs light for about a second.

✔ If the input power to the NT1U-220TC is too low, the POWER button flashes.

✔ If the TERMINAL ERROR LEDs lights up, no active TE is connected or there is a problem with the TE.

✔ If there is a problem with the U interface, the LINE ERROR LED lights up or flashes and the TERMINAL ERROR LED flashes.

Setup

Setting up the NT1U-220TC is similar to setting up other NT1 devices:

1. **Set the TERMINATION switch for your configuration.**

   Check the documentation of your ISDN devices to determine how to set the NT1U-220TC.

2. **Connect the power supply to the NT1U-220TC and plug it into the AC power outlet.**

   All the LEDs on the front panel light for about a second.

3. **Connect one end of an RJ-11 or RJ-45 cable to the NT1U-220TC, and connect the other end to the U-interface (ISDN line) outlet at your premises.**

4. **Switch on the power to the ISDN terminal equipment.**

    5. **Connect one end of an RJ-45 cable to an S/T port on the NT1U-220TC, and connect the other end to the ISDN terminal equipment, such as an adapter card in your PC.**

    6. **If you're connecting two ISDN terminals, repeat Steps 4 and 5 for the second device.**

ADTRAN's NT1 Ace

ADTRAN's NT1 Ace, which is shown in Figure 5-1, has the standard ports: one U-interface port and two S/T-interface ports. The NT1 unit also has line power-ing and 9.5 seconds of reserve power for bridging AC power interruptions. The NT1 Ace lists for $325.

LEDs

Three LED status indicators display the status of various parts of your ISDN connection. The POWER LED lights when the NT1 Ace has power. When the ERROR LED lights, the U interface is not ready or an S/T-interface device is not ready. The READY LED lights when the network is ready to place a call.

Figure 5-1:
The
ADTRAN
NT1 Ace.

(Photo courtesy of ADTRAN.)

Local bus configuration

The two option switches on the side of the unit are used to configure the local bus of the NT1 ACE. You use the TERMINATION switch to select the local bus termination; the options are NONE, 50, or 100. The CONFIGURATION switch has two settings. When you set the switch in the LONG position, the local bus is configured for extended passive bus. When you set the switch in the SHORT position, the local bus is configured for short passive bus. In most cases, use the SHORT option.

Setup

Setting up the NT1 Ace is easy. You set the termination settings, plug in the power supply, and connect your U-interface and S/T-interface cables. Here are the details:

1. **Set the CONFIGURATION and TERMINATION switches for your configuration.**

   Check the documentation of your ISDN devices to determine these settings.

2. **Connect an RJ-11 or an RJ-45 cable from your ISDN line to the NT1 Ace Network U port.**

3. **Connect the power cord to the Power port on the NT1 Ace, and plug the AC cord into a standard electrical wall outlet.**

4. **Connect one end of an RJ-45 cable to an S/T port on the NT1 Ace, and connect the other end to the ISDN CPE.**

5. **Repeat Step 4 for a second S/T-interface CPE.**

The Motorola NT1D

The Motorola NT1D sells for around $200 and includes the standard two S/T-interface ports. You choose between no termination and a 100-ohms termination; unlike the other NT1 devices, the Motorola NT1D doesn't include the 50-ohms termination option.

The Motorola NT1D has a power supply to power any ISDN devices not locally powered, such as an ISDN telephone.

Table 5-2 explains the functions of the six LEDs on the front of the unit.

Table 5-2	The LEDs on the Motorola NT1D
LED	*Description*
SC (Sealing Current)	When on, this LED indicates that the ISDN switch has bounced back a termination test voltage from the NT1D.
ACT (Activity)	When on, this LED indicates that a link between the terminal equipment and the ISDN switch at the CO via the NT1D has been established.
	The LED flickers if a disruption occurs between the U interface and the ISDN switch.
	The LED blinks once per second if a disruption occurs between the S/T interface and the terminal equipment.
	The LED goes off if a disconnection occurs on both the U and S/T interfaces.
LB (Loop Back)	When on, this LED indicates that the ISDN switch has sent a 2B+D loopback command to the NT1D.
LP (Local Power)	When on, this LED indicates that the local AC power is active.
RP (Remote Power)	When on, this LED indicates that the power at the remote site is functional.
RPR (Remote Power Reversed)	When on, this LED indicates that the power at the remote site is not functioning properly.

NT1 Plus Devices

NT1 Plus devices, like the NT1, include the network termination function with two S/T-interface ports. In addition, though, NT1 Plus devices include analog ports for analog devices to your ISDN line. NT1 Plus devices sell for around $350.

Figure 5-2 shows a typical NT1 Plus configuration for an ISDN line.

Because many remote-access devices now include one or two analog ports, the role of NT1 Plus devices has diminished. However, if you want the flexibility of a remote-access device that doesn't include the built-in NT1 device, and you still want to use a telephone, a fax, or a modem, an NT1 Plus CPE will do the job. An NT1 Plus device requires extra configuration steps to support analog communications.

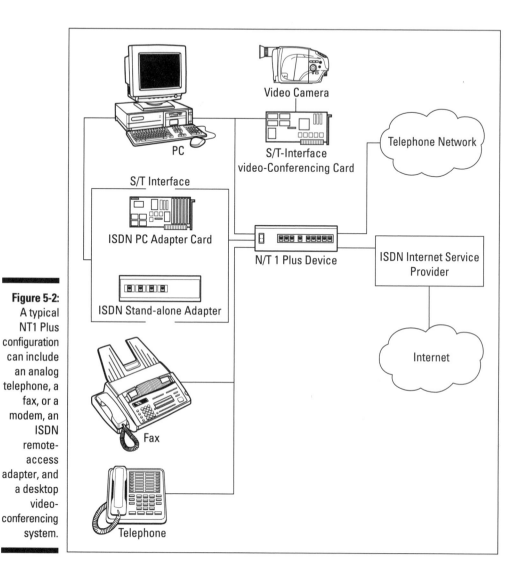

Figure 5-2:
A typical NT1 Plus configuration can include an analog telephone, a fax, or a modem, an ISDN remote-access adapter, and a desktop video-conferencing system.

The typical NT1 Plus device requires a multipoint configuration with two directory numbers. You configure one B channel for voice using the alternate voice/data configuration. The second B channel can be data only or alternate voice and data. If you're using a Nortel DMS-100, don't specify a voice-only B channel; otherwise, you won't be able to use the channel for high-speed circuit data tasks, such as remote access or video conferencing. On the AT&T 5ESS, however, you specify just a voice channel for the directory number that has the modem, the fax, or whatever. Then for the directory number that has the remote-access or video-conferencing device, you specify two channels for data or voice/data.

The core ports that define an NT1 Plus device are at least one RJ-45 S/T-interface port and at least one RJ-11 POTS port. (Every NT1 Plus device has the U-interface port.)

✔ The S/T-interface port is an RJ-45 jack. This type of port allows you to connect ISDN devices, such as an ISDN adapter card for remote access or video conferencing.

✔ The RJ-11 port is used to connect standard analog devices, such as a telephone, a fax, or a modem. You can add multiple analog devices to an RJ-11 port.

Any NT1 Plus device you get should support National ISDN National-1, AT&T 5ESS Custom, and DMS-100 CO switches. It should also provide support for automatic switching between 56-Kbps and 64-Kbps service. As you recall, long distance ISDN service may drop to 56 Kbps because the signaling and bearer services are combined.

Leading NT1 Plus Devices

Only a few NT1 Plus devices are on the market. The top two are the IBM NT Extended and Alpha Telecom's Super NT1.

The IBM Network Terminator Extended

The IBM ISDN Network Terminator Extended was the first NT1 Plus device on the market. It's a stand-alone unit that includes one U-interface port, one S/T-interface port, and one analog port. It includes power for the NT Extended and PS/2 power for nonpowered ISDN devices. The NT Extended also provides a standby battery for backup power to maintain analog telephone service during power outages. The NT Extended lists for $350. The IBM NT Extended has been superseded by the ATI Super NT1, which supports two S/T interfaces and two POTS ports.

In NT Extended lingo, the use of a B channel for analog devices is referred to as *extended analog*. You plug your analog telephone into an RJ-11 port to take advantage of ISDN's supplementary services for voice communications. The NT Extended acts as a terminal adapter to make your telephone act like an ISDN telephone. You can also connect a fax or a modem to the NT Extended.

IBM sold its WaveRunner ISDN product line, which includes the IBM 7845, to Network Express. Network Express was sold to Cabletron. Cabletron decided not to keep the WaveRunner product line and sold it to a startup company called WaveRunner, Inc. See Appendix B for more information.

The Super NT1

Alpha Telecom's Super NT1 device has two analog ports and two S/T-interface ports, which is one more of each port than the IBM NT1 Plus has. The Super NT1 also has a small LCD screen for setting up analog devices to work with your ISDN line. In addition, the Super NT1 includes an internal power supply and a battery backup option for power loss protection for your analog communications. Attaching an analog telephone to the Super NT1 allows you to work with ISDN's supplementary services for call management.

ATI's Super NT1 is the only serious NT1 Plus device on the market. If you plan to add both remote access and desktop video conferencing, the Super NT1 is a reasonable solution. Keep in mind that the Super NT1 does not route analog and ISDN calls. Each port is assigned its own directory number. The following sections take you on a step-by-step tour of setting up the Super NT1 to use on your ISDN line.

Provisioning ISDN Service for Super NT1

Before ordering your ISDN service based on using the Super NT1, make sure that you know what S/T-interface devices you plan to plug in to it. The provisioning of any analog devices that you connect to ISDN is handled through the Super NT1. The provisioning of the S/T devices that you plug in to the Super NT1, however, is determined by the S/T-interface devices.

Keep in mind a few basic facts when dealing with the phone company. It will have to tell you what type of switch is supporting your BRI. The phone company must also give you the SPID or SPIDs to be used on this line. The SPID number, which is composed of your telephone number and a one- to four-digit TID (terminal identifier), must be entered into ISDN equipment before it can communicate with the switch at the telephone company.

Switches and software supported

The Alpha Telecom Super NTI supports the following switch types and software protocols:

Switch type	Software
AT&T 5ESS	Custom and National ISDN-1
Northern Telecom	Custom and National ISDN-1
Siemens	National ISDN-1

For the AT&T 5ESS switch running CUSTOM, request at least the following from the telephone company:

✔ Data line class = multipoint

✔ One SPID for each TEL port you will use, and one or two SPIDs for each TA

✔ Supplementary service type for each TEL port SPIDs = Term Type A

For the AT&T 5ESS running National ISDN-1, request at least the following:

✔ One SPID for each TEL port you will use

✔ Electronic key telephone set (EKTS) = No

✔ Call appearance handling (CACH) = No

✔ Supplementary service type for each number = Term Type A

For a Northern Telecom or Siemens National ISDN-1, request the following:

✔ PVC issue set to 1 for Custom and 2 for National ISDN-1. For Nortel DMS-100 only.

✔ One SPID for each TEL port you will use

✔ Electronic key telephone set (EKTS) = No

✔ Call appearance call handling (CACH) = No

✔ MAXKEYS set to 3 for most devices. ISDN phones may require more if features are added to keys.

✔ RING set to YES

Information you need from the telephone company

You must get some information from the telephone company after you order your service so that you can configure the Super NT1 device. Also remember, you'll need additional information for each S/T-interface CPE that you connect to ISDN via the Super NT1. The following is the required information for setting up the Super NT1:

✔ ISDN switch type

✔ ISDN protocol version (Custom or NI-1)

✔ ISDN phone number(s) or directory number(s)

✔ *Service profile identification* (SPID) number(s) with prefixes and suffixes

Connecting Your Devices to the Super NT1

To connect your ISDN line to the Super NT1, connect one end of the RJ-11 or RJ-45 cable to the U-interface port on the rear of the Super NT1. Plug the other end of cable to the telephone outlet. Only the inside pair of wires are used, so the Super NT1 U-interface can use either RJ-11 or RJ-45 jacks depending on what you're using at the ISDN outlet.

You use 8-pin RJ-45 cable to connect your CPE to the S/T ports. You can use either S/T port because they are electrically the same point. Both S/T ports will provide PS2 power for your ISDN devices, if necessary. No configuration of the Super NT1 itself is required for S/T-interface devices, but you need to configure your S/T-interface devices separately using their CPE vendor's documentation.

The S/T bus on the Super NTI is terminated internally with 100 ohms. This will cover most S/T bus configurations. The terminating resistor included with the Super NTI is only needed if an S/T device with 50 ohms is used in the S/T port. In this case, plug the S/T terminating resistor into the other S/T port.

You can connect multiple analog devices to a single analog port in the Super NT1, but you can use only one device at a time. To use more than one analog device per TEL port, you need a Y splitter cable.

Never plug an analog line in to the Super NTI U interface. Doing so could damage the Super NTI!

Powering on the Super NT1

After all cables are properly connected, you can plug the AC power cord into the wall outlet. When the Super NTI is powered on, it will perform a self test by checking its internal hardware. The LCD screen will display Alpha Telecom and the firmware release number.

Reading the LEDs

On the front panel of the Super NT1 are several LEDs that provide a variety of power and connection status information, as follows:

LED	Function
Power	When this green LED is lit, the power is on.
BAT Low	When this red LED is lit, the backup battery is in a low voltage status.

Line Error	This red LED indicates a synchronization problem for either the U or S/T interface. If the LED is flashing quickly (4 times per second), the U interface can be synchronized. This means the problem lies between the Super NT1 and the telephone company CO. If the LED is flashing slowly (1 time per second), the S/T interface cannot be synchronized. This means the problem lies between the ISDN S/T-interface device and the Super NT1.
Line LPBK	This yellow LED indicates that the telephone company is running a 2B+D loopback test on the ISDN line. When this light is on, you must wait for the telephone company to finish testing before using the ISDN line.
TEL1	When this green LED is lit, TEL1 is in use.
TEL2	When this green LED is lit, TEL2 is in use.

Configuring the Super NTI

The Super NTI provides two independent analog ports labeled TELl and TEL2. To utilize analog devices on TEL1 or TEL2 ports, the Super NT1 must first be configured. This involves setting up the switch type and SPID as well as choosing whether the TEL port(s) will be used for voice or fax/modem.

SPIDs are provided by the local telephone company when an ISDN line is provisioned. As mentioned, the SPID is composed of your phone number and a one- to four-digit TID.

Configuring the TEL ports

Before you can use an analog phone, internal or external fax/modem, or answering machine on the TEL ports, you must configure them. You can set up only one TEL port at a time.

To configure the analog port TEL1, use an RJ-11 cable to connect a push-button analog phone to TEL1. (Likewise, to program the analog port TEL2, connect the analog phone to TEL2.) You can also configure the TEL port by using a fax or modem to enter the digits. The LCD screen on the Super NT1 shows the status of your configuration.

When you pick up the hand-set of the analog phone attached to TEL1, the status LCD for TEL1 flashes green (which means TEL1 is in use). You also hear a fast busy signal in the hand-set to warn you that the port is not ready for use yet. Other status and warning messages are displayed on the LCD screen to help you, as explained later.

During the configuration mode, both the top and bottom of the LCD screen are used for displaying messages for the TEL port that you're configuring. The corresponding LEDs for TEL1 or TEL2 will blink during the configuration process. Afterwards, when you're using the Super NT1, the top line of the LCD shows the status of TEL1 and the bottom line shows the status of TEL2.

Step-by-step configuration

This section details how to set up the Super NT1.

1. **Pick up the receiver on your analog telephone and press #**# on the analog phone keypad.**

   You hear a prompt tone in the receiver, and the LCD screen displays

   ```
   CONFIGURATION
   0: # EXIT: ON_HK
   ```

   When either one of the analog ports is in the configuration mode or engaged in an active call, the other TEL port is not allowed to enter into configuration mode. This restriction does not apply to the S/T-interface ports.

2. **Press #.**

   The LCD displays the beginning screen of the switch options. After any key is entered, the tone in the receiver is turned off. Following are the Super NT1-supported ISDN switch protocols:

Switch type	Description
AT&T Custom	5ESS switch using AT&T customized point-to-multipoint management protocol
AT&T NI-1	AT&T 5ESS switch using National ISDN-1 standards
Nortel Custom	DMS-100 running NORTEL custom software
Nortel NI-1	DMS-100 using National ISDN-1 standards
Siemens NI-1	National ISDN-1 standards

3. **Press * on the telephone keypad to toggle sequentially through all the switch options. Then press # to install the desired switch option.**

   The LCD screen displays the following message:

   ```
   SPID (1 or2):
   DEL: *
   ```

4. **Enter your assigned SPID (up to 20 digits) by pressing the corresponding numbers on the telephone keypad.**

   (If a previously entered SPID is displayed, you can remove it by pressing *.) As you enter the SPID, it will appear on the bottom line.

5. **Press # when you're finished.**

   The LCD screen displays the following:

   ```
   ANALOG: SPEECH
   0: # CHG: *
   ```

6. **Press * on the telephone keypad to toggle between the SPEECH and FAX/MODEM options.**

   (These options tell the Super NTI how to set up your outgoing calls.)

   In most cases, either option will work. Some telephone company switches, however, require you to use one or the other. The telephone company may also bill you differently depending on the type of calls you place.

7. **Press # to select the option you want.**

   The LCD screen displays the following:

   ```
   SAVED? NO
   0: # CHG:
   ```

8. **Press * to confirm the configuration setup.**

   The LCD screen displays the following:

   ```
   SAVED? YES
   ON-HK TO CONFIRM
   ```

9. **Hang up the telephone handset.**

   On successful loading of the new configuration, the LCD screen displays

   ```
   CONFIGURATION OK
   ```

10. **To configure the other TEL port, repeat Steps 1 through 9.**

Warning messages

The Super NT 1 includes built-in diagnostic capability to watch the TEL ports. When a TEL port fails to operate properly, the LCD screen displays diagnostic information that can help you identify the source of the problem. Table 5-3 lists the Super NT1 warning and other status messages, their probable cause, and solution options. The display is used only for the TEL ports.

Table 5-3   Super NT1 Error and Status Messages

Warning or Status Message	*Cause*	*Solution*
U NOT READY	The TEL port device has gone off-hook before Super NT1 is in sync with ISDN line.	Give the SuperNT1 more time to get in sync before going off-hook with TEL ports. Wait for the error light to stop flashing.
	ISDN line is not activated.	If the error light doesn't stop flashing, there is a problem with your ISDN line. Contact your telephone company.
NO SPID ENTERED	You are attempting to use a TEL port without first configuring a SPID into that port.	Enter the SPID number for the port by using the Super NT1's configuration mode.
INVALID SPID	An incorrect SPID has been entered for the port.	Check your SPID entry. If the SPID is correct, call your telephone company to confirm the SPID.
	The analog device was taken off-hook before the TEL port was ready.	After powering on the Super NT1, wait at least 30-60 seconds before using the TEL ports.
DUPLICATE SPID	The same SPID has been used for both TEL ports.	Remove the SPID from one of the TEL ports and turn the power off and on to reset the configuration. Each port must have a unique SPID.
TEL (1 OR 2) NOT READY	The ISDN line isn't in sync with the Super NT1.	Wait for a minute. Make sure that the SPID was not used in any other devices.
CALL IDLE	Normal condition.	Line is ready to use.
CALL IDLE 21	TEI device has been removed.	Try powering the Super NT1 off and on and then waiting 90 seconds before using TEL port.

(continued)

Table 5-3 *(continued)*

Warning or status message	*Cause*	*Solution*
CALL IDLE 31	Switch management protocol is incorrect.	Verify that the switch type is correct. Try powering the Super NT1 off and on and then waiting 90 seconds before using the TEL port.
CALL IDLE 32	The same SPID is entered in two devices.	Verify that S/T device does not have the same SPID. Try powering the Super NT1 off and on and then waiting 90 seconds before using the TEL port.

Part II

Internet Surfing and Telecommuting the ISDN Way

The 5th Wave   By Rich Tennant

"IT HAPPENED AROUND THE TIME WE SUBSCRIBED TO AN ON-LINE SERVICE."

In this part . . .

You've completed ISDN boot camp (if you read Part I). Now you're ready to roll up your sleeves and start using ISDN for Internet access and telecommuting. The following chapters explain your ISDN remote-access CPE options; sort through them to help you choose the right solution. You discover how to connect your PC or LAN via ISDN to ramp on to the Internet or any network. You read how to use Windows 95 and Windows NT 4.0 communications features for your ISDN connections. You also experience — hands-on — the entire process of installing, configuring, and using leading ISDN remote-access products — from ISDN modems and adapter cards for a single PC to sophisticated routers for connecting an entire LAN to ISDN.

Chapter 6

Remote Access in the ISDN Fast Lane

● ●

In This Chapter

▶ Understanding ISDN remote access

▶ Learning the nuts and bolts of ISDN-based remote access

▶ Knowing the three ways to connect your PC to ISDN

▶ Choosing the right ISDN remote-access CPE features

▶ Finding the right ISDN Internet service provider

● ●

*C*onnecting via ISDN to the Internet, to a corporate LAN, or to any computer acting as a host is where the digital communications light shines brightest. A variety of CPE solutions for connecting your PC to ISDN are available. This chapter builds the foundation for understanding your ISDN connectivity options by explaining the key underlying technology elements.

Do All Kinds of Data-Moving with ISDN

Whether you're connecting to the Internet or to the office for telecommuting, the expanded bandwidth of ISDN translates into moving larger amounts of data in shorter periods of time. You can use ISDN for all kinds of remote-access activities:

✔ ISDN delivers a high-speed connection for working and playing on the Internet. An ISDN connection moves data at speeds that make the popular World Wide Web come alive at your desktop. Not only does ISDN speed up your Web travel adventures, it also dramatically improves the reliability of your Internet connection.

- ✔ ISDN delivers an affordable, high-speed connection from your home PC to the company LAN. Using a seamless ISDN connection, you can connect to your office LAN to work with applications and files. The speed at which ISDN delivers data makes you feel like you're working right at the office.

- ✔ ISDN dramatically reduces software downloading times. More and more companies distribute their software via the Internet, so using ISDN can save you a lot of connection time. Most ISDN CPE vendors routinely put upgraded software drivers and installation programs on the Net for downloading.

- ✔ ISDN provides a great conduit for connecting a small office LAN to the Internet or another network using a router. Multiple users can share the ISDN line and make connections to different networks at the same time.

- ✔ ISDN enhances remote-control applications, which enable you to operate another computer remotely or perform remote system administration.

- ✔ ISDN offers an attractive route for faster connections to online services (such as CompuServe, America Online, and Prodigy).

Remote access via ISDN is based on the core concepts of inter-networking (communicating across different networks) and client/server computing. To make any PC connection, the client and server (host) must be able to communicate with the same protocols. For example, to connect to the Internet, both your PC and the Internet service provider's host computer must be using the TCP/IP protocol.

ISDN itself is a network operated by the telephone companies that acts as a conduit for connecting networks to networks or for connecting PCs to networks. It delivers data between networks in a way that is transparent to users of computers attached via ISDN. To the network users, the operation of the ISDN system looks and feels like a point-to-point connection even though the information can travel over different links.

Windows 95 includes TCP/IP and a variety of other networking protocols, so you can use your PC to connect to the Internet and other networks. Chapter 7 explains working with Windows 95 and ISDN.

The ISDN Conduit for Client/Server Computing

The foundation for networking is *client/server* computing, in which one computer acts as a client and the other acts as the *host,* or *server.* In the case of remote access, your PC acts as the client computer that connects to a server. The server can be a corporate LAN server, an online service, a computer connected to the Internet, or any computer that accepts your incoming connection.

At the heart of the client/server model is the splitting of application functions between the client and the server. The World Wide Web is an example of a client/server computing system. You use a Web client program such as Netscape Navigator to connect to Web servers via the Internet. Information is downloaded to the client computer, which then recreates the Web documents using the Web browser and the computing resources of the client. The result is that computer processing is distributed.

ISDN's role in client/server computing is that of a background conduit for connecting client and server computers. Figure 6-1 shows client/server computing in action using ISDN to connect to the Internet. Notice that you connect to your Internet service provider via the ISDN system, which is a separate network from the Internet.

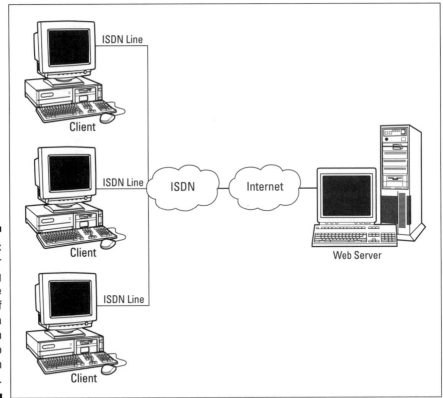

Figure 6-1:
Client/server computing forms the basis of making a connection via ISDN to a server on the Internet.

Matching Network Protocols

The term *protocol* is used extensively when talking about networking standards. A protocol is a set of rules that specifies how network communications occur. In any remote-access connection, both the client and the server must support the same protocol.

The leading networking protocols are listed in Table 6-1. When you choose an ISDN remote-access option, make sure that it supports the protocols of the networks you plan to access. Currently, Windows 95 supports all the protocols in Table 6-1 except PPP/MP. Most ISDN CPE vendors, however, include software to add PPP/MP capabilities to Windows 95.

Because of the explosive rise of the Internet, which is based on the TCP/IP networking protocol, you'll probably use TCP/IP for most of your remote-access connections.

Table 6-1 Leading Network Protocols for Windows-based Inter-networking

Network Protocol	Description
TCP/IP (Transmission Control Protocol/ Internet Protocol)	The networking protocol that forms the basis of the Internet. TCP/IP was developed by the Department of Defense. It's also part of the UNIX operating system and Windows NT.
IPX (Internet Packet Exchange), SPX (Sequential Packet Exchange)	Novell's NetWare inter-networking protocols; also supported by Windows NT servers.
IEEE 803.2	The protocol that defines an Ethernet network at the physical layer of network signaling and cabling.
PPP (Point-to-Point)	One of the protocols that can be used for connections to the Internet via TCP/IP for one B channel.
PPP/MP (Point-to-Point/ Multilink Protocol)	A new protocol for connecting to the Internet via ISDN using both B channels.
NetBIOS (Basic Input/Output System)	Developed by IBM and used in DOS-based and Windows NT networks.
NetBEUI (NetBIOS Extended User Interface)	Used in Windows for Workgroups, Windows 95, NT, and OS/2.

Inter-networking

Networks are prolific in the modern computing environment, and communicating across different networks — referred to as *inter-networking* — is essential. The role of inter-networking is to connect networks based on different protocols.

The two classes of inter-networking functions are bridges and routers. A *bridge* is a simple device that passes data from one network to another. A *router* is a more sophisticated device that allows data to be routed to different networks based on the packet address information associated with the data. A router is typically used on a network to handle a variety of inter-networking functions. A bridge is used for connecting a single PC or LAN to another network only one network protocol at a time. However, a bridge can support multiple network protocols.

WAN It with ISDN

A *wide area network* (WAN) is created by connecting two or more physically isolated networks. The connection between these networks is where ISDN comes into play. To communicate between these dispersed networks, you need a conduit that lets the networking protocols work with each other over long distances. Figure 6-2 shows the role of ISDN in connecting two networks via bridges or routers.

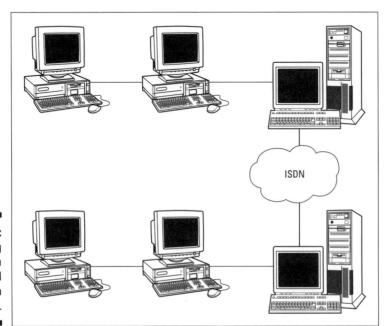

Figure 6-2: Connecting LANs via ISDN creates a WAN.

Networking Basics

The network BIOS (Basic Input/Output System) expects to see the data sent by a network adapter in a specific format. Similarly, the network BIOS sends data to the network driver in a specific format. The network adapter driver receives the information and converts it to a format that the network interface card (NIC) understands. This function is handled by a software driver that acts as an interface between the network adapter card and the network operating system, called NOS for short.

The *network driver interface specification* (NDIS), developed by Microsoft, provides a common set of rules for network adapter manufacturers to use for communication between the network adapter and the NOS. Most network adapters ship with an NDIS driver or are included with Windows 95. Figure 6-3 shows the relationship of the NDIS and ODI (*Open Datalink Interface*) interfaces to the Ethernet adapter hardware and network operating system.

The standard that serves the same purpose as the Microsoft NDIS is the ODI specification developed by Novell. ODI supports multiprotocol stacks and is the standard supported in Novell's NetWare.

Although NDIS provides compatibility between any network adapter and NOS that supports it, NDIS was developed primarily to support multiprotocol stacks. These stacks enable you to run different protocols concurrently with the same network adapter.

By running multiprotocol stacks, you can use the network adapter in your computer for your LAN while also using it to access another network, such as the Internet, using the TCP/IP protocol. Without the support for multiprotocol stacks provided by NDIS, you would have to unload one stack, and then load another stack to access a system that uses a different protocol. This crude approach requires rebooting your computer.

Figure 6-3:
The NDIS or ODI specification is the layer between the network adapter card and the network operating system.

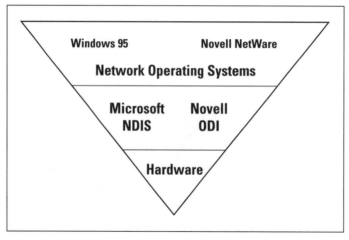

TCP/IP Primer

Internet access uses TCP/IP (*Transmission Control Protocol and Internet Protocol*).
TCP/IP is the collection of networking protocols that keeps the Internet as a
whole connected. TCP/IP is not a single entity, but a set of software protocols
that provides network services, such as FTP (*File Transfer Protocol*), and telnet.
TCP/IP is a packet-based network, which means data is transferred in chunks,
or packets. Each packet includes the data as well as error control and routing
information. These packets can travel on multiple routes across the Internet;
when they reach their intended target, they are reassembled.

IP addresses (Code of the Net)

Think of *Internet Protocol* (IP) addresses as the unique telephone numbers for
specific computers over a TCP/IP network, which is what the Internet is based
on. Each computer that uses TCP/IP protocols is distinguished from other
computers on the Internet by a unique IP address. An IP address is organized
into four groups of numbers separated by periods (referred to as dots), for
example, 199.3.135.8.

For a single dial-up ISDN connection, you need only one IP address, which can
be assigned each time your connect, or your ISP assigns you a unique IP
address, which you use each time you connect.

For LAN access to the Internet, your ISP typically will provide IP addresses for all
the computers connected to your LAN, plus a single IP address for the router. These
multiple IP address accounts cost more than single-user accounts. Your IP
addresses are an important part of configuring Internet access using Windows 95.

Note: A new generation of low-cost IP routers allows you to connect a LAN
using a single-user dial-up account instead of a LAN account. This means that
you don't need to get any assigned IP addresses for the PCs connected to the
LAN. Chapter 11 explains working with routers that support this new feature.

Your service provider typically provides you with the following IP numbers for
dial-up accounts:

- An IP address for your machine.
- An IP address for the gateway device (router) used to make your connection
  to the Internet. This is the host machine at your service provider's location.
- One or more IP addresses for *Domain Name System* (DNS) servers. DNS
  servers are used for matching IP addresses with domain names, as the
  next section explains.
- If you connect a LAN to an Internet service provider, you may need to get
  multiple IP addresses, one for each PC on your local area network and one
  for your gateway device.

From numbers to names (DNS)

Instead of using the full 32-bit IP address, most systems on the Internet adopt more meaningful names for their devices and networks. These text-based names act as pointers to IP addresses, hence the name Domain Name System, or DNS.

Domain names are organized in a hierarchical fashion with the most specific (computer name) at the left and the general top-level domain to the right. For example, `author.angell.com` translates to the specific machine `author` connected to the `angell` host machine; `.com` is the top-level domain name. At the highest level are `.com` for commercial organizations; `.edu` for educational institutions; `.gov` for government organizations; `.net` for networking organizations; and `.org` for anything that doesn't fit elsewhere, such as non-profit organizations and professional groups. There are also geographical names, such as `.ca` for Canada and `.ru` for Russia.

ISDN Remote-Access CPE Options

Basically, three categories of ISDN CPE devices connect to the Internet or another network. All these devices act as terminal adapters for your PC to allow it to handle communications over ISDN.

- **Stand-alone serial-based devices** connect to your PC via the serial port using a standard RS-232 cable.

- **Internal adapter cards** use your PC's bus to connect to ISDN.

- **Ethernet-based devices** use Ethernet networking to facilitate communications between a LAN and ISDN.

ISDN via the PC serial port

The first category of ISDN remote-access hardware is the serial-based external terminal adapters. These are stand-alone units that look like modems. Serial remote-access devices are commonly referred to as *digital modems* or *ISDN modems*. These are marketing terms that make the idea of connecting your PC to ISDN appear like connecting your PC to a modem.

A serial ISDN device typically includes its own power supply and connects to your PC's serial port using a standard RS-232 cable. Because these ISDN devices work through your serial port, they use the same Hayes Standard AT command set used by standard analog modems. This means that a serial ISDN device works with Windows 95 in a similar manner as an analog modem, except at ISDN speeds. The devices use an asynchronous to PPP driver to make the conversion from the asynchronous serial port to the data stream in the ISDN lane.

The major advantage of using serial ISDN modems is that they are typically easier to set up and operate than other ISDN remote-access devices. It's a lot easier to work with ISDN serial devices in Windows 95 than in Windows 3.1 and Windows for Workgroups 3.11, which supported serial data rates up to only 19,200 bps. Windows 95 supports up to 921,600 bps. Another advantage of stand-alone ISDN serial devices is that you can connect them to a PC or Macintosh serial port.

The major disadvantage of serial ISDN modems is the reduced data communications speed because of their reliance on the asynchronous form of serial communications. PCs can use two forms of serial communication: asynchronous and synchronous. ISDN can support both. Asynchronous communications use a start bit and a stop bit to define each chunk of 8-bit data being sent, which reduces the amount of data actually transferred by 20 percent. Although asynchronous communications can transfer data at speeds of up to 115.2 Kbps via ISDN, or 57.6 Kbps for each B channel, the extra start and stop bits result in a true data transfer rate of about 92 Kbps for both B channels.

Synchronous communication is faster because it doesn't require the start and stop bits used in asynchronous communication. You can transfer data at the full 128 Kbps using synchronous communications with the PPP/MP protocol. Synchronous data transmission sends information in larger blocks as a continuous stream using a synchronized timing method. Synchronous data transmission is the standard for digital communications; asynchronous is the standard for analog communications.

The leading serial ISDN products are Motorola BitSURFR Pro, 3Com Impact IQ, Farallon Netopia, and U.S. Robotics Courier I-modem. Most of these devices come in U-interface (built-in NT1) form with one or two RJ-11 ports for connecting analog devices (faxes, modems, or telephones) to your ISDN line. You can find more on serial-based ISDN remote-access devices in Chapter 9.

It's in the cards

ISDN adapter cards fit into an ISA slot in your PC. Because these adapter cards use your PC bus to communicate to ISDN, they deliver data faster than serial devices. Typically, these cards come in both U-interface and S/T-interface models, and include an RJ-11 port for connecting a telephone, a modem, or a fax. Most of these products come with easy-to-install programs.

ISDN is fast, except when compared to PC buses — so you don't need to worry about which bus card to get. ISA (*Industry Standard Architecture*) is the current standard supported by most ISDN adapter cards. PCI (Peripheral Component Interconnect) offers the most potential for future ISDN adapter cards. As of this writing, ISDN PCMIA cards (for laptops) are not available, although a number of vendors including Xircom are planning to come out with them.

Windows 95 has improved the process of installing and working with adapter cards. The Windows 95 plug-and-play feature simplifies installation by automatically avoiding conflicts with other devices connected to your PC. (More on this feature in Chapter 7.) Windows 95 handles an ISDN adapter card as a network adapter card because most ISDN adapter cards use an NDIS driver.

The leading ISDN PC adapter cards are U.S. Robotics Sportster ISDN 128 Kbps and the Diamond Multimedia NetCommander ISDN. You can read more on these cards in Chapter 10.

LAN-based access

To connect a local area network to ISDN, you must use a bridge or a router. These devices connect via your Ethernet network. Ethernet forms the basis of most popular local area networks, including Windows 95 and Windows NT, and provides a fast way for PCs to interface with ISDN. Using an Ethernet-based ISDN device is the only way for multiple PCs to share an ISDN line.

A bridge lets multiple users connect to a single different type of network via ISDN. The more sophisticated routers allow data to be routed to different networks depending on the packet addresses of the data. Using a router, people on a network can send data simultaneously to different networks depending on the type of data being transmitted.

Routers use routing tables to forward data based on the address information associated with each data packet. The router acts as an independent node on the Ethernet network, routing traffic between the local network and the remote networks through ISDN. Figure 6-4 shows the layout of a router on a local area network. Most ISDN devices for connecting LANs to other networks via ISDN are routers.

In the early days, ISDN routers were expensive and difficult — if not impossible — for the nontechnical person to set up and run. The latest generation of ISDN routers are both affordable and a lot easier to use.

The ISDN router market is competitive. ISDN router prices are falling rapidly, making them an affordable option for even the smallest of networks. The leading vendors of ISDN routers are Ascend Communications, Farallon Computing, 3Com, Cisco Systems, and a host of other companies. You can see more on working with routers in Chapter 11.

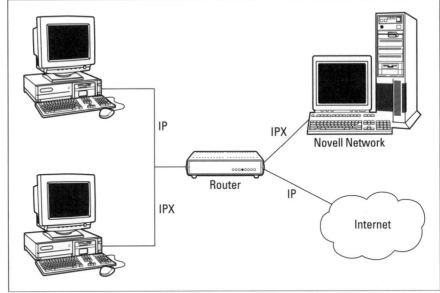

Figure 6-4:
The multiuser router routes different protocol network traffic from PCs on the local network to multiple remote networks.

Key Elements of ISDN Remote Access

In addition to ISDN remote-access CPE categories, you need to understand a few other elements. These include the placement of the NT1, support for PPP/MP, and compression.

Where's the NT1?

As you may recall, only one NT1 device can be on your side of a BRI connection. The location of the NT1 device is important if you plan to connect multiple devices to your ISDN line. Most vendors offer remote-access devices in both U-interface and S/T-interface models. If you want to use your ISDN service only to connect to the Internet and other networks, get an ISDN device with built-in NT1.

Many ISDN remote-access devices with built-in NT1 also include analog RJ-11 ports for connecting a telephone, a fax, or a modem. None of the leading ISDN serial or adapter card vendors include S/T-interface ports for connecting another ISDN device, such as a desktop video-conferencing system. If you want to add a desktop video-conferencing system, you need to get an S/T-interface remote-access device and a stand-alone NT1 device, as I explain in Chapter 5. Some ISDN routers, however, include an S/T-interface port.

PPP/MP is standard

Until recently, connecting to the Internet via ISDN usually required proprietary implementations of the Point-to-Point Protocol (PPP). As a result, PC adapters from different vendors frequently didn't work with each other. In addition, PPP supports only 64 Kbps data communication via one B channel. The introduction and acceptance of the Point-to-Point Multilink Protocol (PPP/MP) is changing this situation. PPP/MP allows remote-access devices to connect to the Internet using both B channels and allows interoperability between different vendors' products. Most CPE vendors are adopting PPP/MP, and it is incorporated in a number of ISDN remote-access devices.

Although PPP/MP is now widely implemented in ISDN remote-access devices, some Internet service providers don't support it because they haven't upgraded their equipment.

Make sure that the ISDN remote-access device you want to use supports the PPP/MP protocol.

Dynamic bandwidth allocation

A key feature of ISDN remote-access devices is support for dynamic bandwidth allocation, which is the automatic adjustment of the number of B channels in use depending on the volume of data being sent or received. The feature saves you money. Remember, each B channel is usually billed as a separate charge. Automatically adjusting bandwidth up or down depending on your data volume means that you use only what you need.

Get into a compressing situation

ISDN supports up to 128 Kbps of data transmission without compression and up to 512 Kbps with compression, a fourfold increase. (This compression is referred to as a 4:1 compression ratio.) A growing number of ISDN remote-access devices include support for compression. A compression scheme is worthwhile, however, only if it is supported on both ends of the connection.

Unfortunately, most Internet service providers do not offer compression. The main reasons are the cost to upgrade their equipment to support compression, and the fact that compression reduces their online charges because file transfers occur more quickly.

The Stac Hardware and Lempel Ziv Algorithm are already de facto compression standards. Another standard that may be implemented soon is *Compression Control Protocol* (CCP). It allows two devices to figure out which type of compression algorithm they both support and carry on from there.

Getting ISDN Internet Service

Internet service providers (ISPs) nationwide are jumping on the ISDN band-width bandwagon. Availability and cost, however, depend on the telephone companies that supply ISDN. Where ISDN service is widely available, ISDN dial-up access to the Internet, including 30 to 100 hours of connection time, costs between $25 to $40 a month. Expect to see the number of ISDN providers go up and the cost go down. Some telephone companies are also getting into the ISDN Internet access market.

Internet access via ISDN is available from national, regional, and local Internet service providers. In many cases, you may prefer regional or local ISPs to the larger national providers. Local ISPs are more likely to offer better services and rates equal to or slightly lower than those of the nationals. Regional or local ISPs are also often more willing to tailor their service to specialized requirements, and are usually in a better position to adapt more quickly to new ISDN solutions.

In the United States, there are relatively few choices at the national level for ISDN service. A national provider uses local access points distributed across the country, commonly referred to as *points of presence,* or POPs.

A number of sources on the Web point to ISPs offering ISDN service. The best starting point is Dan Kegel's ISDN Page at `http://alumni .caltech.edu/~dank/isdn/`.

What to look for when choosing an ISDN ISP

When comparing Internet service providers, typical selection criteria are performance, price, and responsive technical support. Here are general guide-lines to keep in mind as you shop for an ISDN ISP:

- ✔ Make sure that you don't have to pay any telephone usage charges beyond a local call. Most ISDN service is metered even for local calls, but you don't want to pay additional charges due to an ISP service that is outside your local calling area.

- ✔ Figure out how much time you spend online and compare charges based on that. ISDN users are typically moderate to heavy Internet users.

- ✔ Determine whether your ISP is overloaded by asking about the customer-to-CPE ratio, which should be between 8 to 1 and 12 to 1. You may not get an accurate answer, but it's worth trying. Ask others about what service providers are the best in your area.

- ✔ Make sure that the ISP offers telephone support with a staff who knows about ISDN and different ISDN devices. Check the ISP's Web site to see whether it provides an online reference.

✔ Shop around for the best total ISDN package pricing plan for your needs. A common plan is a monthly flat rate for 30 to 40 hours per month and a one-time setup fee. Some Internet service providers have a higher setup fee but a lower monthly charge; others have a lower setup fee but a higher monthly charge. Keep in mind, though, that pricing isn't the only consideration.

✔ Ask what ISDN remote-access devices the ISP supports or has experience working with. An ISDN ISP may support only one or two ISDN remote-access devices or may support several.

✔ Analyze your ISDN Internet access options. Talk to your friends, associates, and several ISPs.

✔ Check to see whether the ISP offers compression. Most do not. Signing up with one who does may be the best deal because of the faster data transfer rates that the ISP can offer. Remember, a 4-to-1 compression rate can mean a data communications rate of up to 512 Kbps.

Dial-up or dedicated ISDN Internet service?

Two kinds of ISDN-based Internet access service are available: dial-up and dedicated. *Dial-up service* is the most common and least expensive. It is similar to the way a dial-up modem account works. As the name implies, you must *dial up* the Internet service provider to begin an active session. At the completion of the session, the telephone connection is terminated.

Dedicated service is a connection that stays open 24 hours a day, 7 days a week. Large office LANs and the operation of Web servers usually use this type of service. Dedicated ISDN is sold in most regions as a configured service called Centrex. As you might guess, this service can be expensive, typically costing several hundred dollars per month.

What type of call?

Telephone company tariffs are usually cheaper for analog calls than for digital data calls. In some telephone company service areas, you may be charged a flat rate for analog local calls, but billed by usage at a higher metered rate for digital calls.

Some ISDN remote-access devices let you initiate a call as a voice signal instead of a data signal so that the telephone company switch thinks the data call is a voice call. As a result, you're charged the lower analog flat rate instead of the higher digital rates. This can save money because in most cases your Internet service provider is a local call. As such, the cost of connecting to your ISP falls within the flat monthly rate. If you connect to your Internet provider for more than a few hours, the savings can add up.

This works only when there are two separate tariffs for analog and ISDN. Pacific Telesis, for example, charges one metered rate for all calls over ISDN, regardless of the type of call. NYNEX, on the other hand, charges a lower analog rate so that initiating a call as voice will get you the lower rate. However, NYNEX reduces the value of initiating a data call as a voice call by allowing only one B channel to be configured for both voice/data.

Check out how IP addresses are handled

Depending on your Internet service provider, you may be assigned a dynamic IP address or static IP address(es). With a dynamic IP address, your PC isn't assigned a specific IP address, but instead is automatically assigned an IP address for each connection session. This allows the ISP to ration IP addresses on an as-needed bases. A number of ISPs use dynamic IP addresses for dial-up accounts.

For connecting a LAN to the Internet, your ISP may assign you IP addresses for every machine on your local area network. These business accounts are more expensive than single-user accounts. However, new router technology is coming online that supports the use of multiple PCs using a single-user dial-up ISDN connection.

Matching hardware

Regardless of which type of ISDN remote-access device you use for an Internet connection, the devices at both ends of the connection must be able to communicate with each other. In spite of PPP/MP, you can still have problems with connections between CPE devices from one vendor and another. As such, you must know what devices an ISP has worked with successfully.

Many ISPs offer hardware and access packages that let you buy your ISDN remote-access device below list or at retail.

B channel options

Most ISDN remote-access devices support two B channel connections. Many ISPs, however, offer ISDN service in units of one B channel. Recall that the telephone company typically charges you for the use of each B channel. Where ISDN service is more expensive, ISPs provide the option of getting a single B channel to save money. If you can afford it, go with the full two B channel ISDN Internet access account. To download files quickly and to keep up with growing demands of the Web as multimedia and Java applets become commonplace, more bandwidth is always better.

The speed of an ISDN connection does not always match the speed at which the Internet responds. Factors affecting speed are the current amount of traffic on the Internet plus the size of the communications link and the type of equipment at the location where the data is being accessed.

Compression support

As you recall, compression can speed up file transfers by a 4-to-1 ratio. Unfortunately, most ISP don't offer compression support. If an ISP supports a compression scheme that your ISDN remote-access device supports, however, you can improve your download times dramatically. The leading compression schemes for ISDN are Stacker LZS Compression Protocol and Ascend Stack compression. At some point, Compression Control Protocol (CCP) will become a standard for negotiating which compression algorithm you will agree to use.

CHAP

Ask your ISP whether it uses CHAP (*Challenge Handshake Authentication Protocol*) to verify your name and password when you dial in. Some ISDN devices, particularly serial devices, don't support this feature. CHAP arranges an exchange of random numbers between machines. The receiving machine performs arithmetic on those numbers using a previously agreed secret. (A *secret* is a string of up to 16 characters used as an encryption key.) CHAP can become a hassle for an ISDN dial-up account because it requires reauthentication if you drop a channel for voice and then reconnect.

Chapter 7

ISDN Meets Windows 95

● ●

In This Chapter

▶ Discovering what's under the Windows 95 networking hood

▶ Setting up TCP/IP in Windows 95 for dialing your Internet service provider

▶ Installing other network protocols for telecommuting

▶ Setting up and using Windows 95 Dial-Up Networking

▶ Using the Internet Setup Wizard

● ●

*M*icrosoft Windows 95 provides new networking and remote access enhancements that make connecting to the Internet and other networks easier. This chapter explains the Windows 95 features and facilities that support your ISDN connection. You learn, hands-on how to work with ISDN remote access within the Windows 95 context.

Under the Windows 95 Hood

Windows 95 delivers a collection of new features that makes it a good platform for ISDN connections. These new elements include support for faster serial communications, Plug and Play for easier installation of adapter cards, built-in TCP/IP, and Dial-Up Networking.

Faster serial communications support

Windows 95 eliminated the 19,200 bps limitation for serial communications ports inherent in Windows 3.1 and Windows for Workgroups. Windows 95 can support up to 921,600 bps. For ISDN users, this means that you can use serial ISDN remote-access products that connect directly to your PC's serial port, such as BitSURFR Pro.

Windows 95 support for the higher data transmission rates is based on your PC using the 16550A UART (universal asynchronous receiver/transmitter) chip. UART chips are the part of the PC's COM port that handle communications between the CPU and any device connected to the COM port.

Most newer PCs use the 16550A UART chip. If you're not sure whether you're using a 16550A UART, you can find out by using the *Microsoft Diagnostics program* (MSD). (You execute the MSD program from the DOS prompt, which is available from the Windows 95 Start menu. At the DOS prompt, type **msd**.)

Plug and Play

Windows 95 Plug-and-Play system automatically detects any Plug-and-Play compatible devices attached to your system. Windows 95 Plug and Play automatically allocates resources such as IRQs (interrupt requests) and I/O (input/output) addresses, without any manual configuration. This means that any resource conflicts are automatically handled by communications between peripheral devices, the BIOS, and the operating system.

With Plug and Play, you no longer need to supply configuration information as you did for earlier versions of Windows. Plug and Play also makes system configuration changes automatically. The BIOS part of Plug and Play is a function of your PC BIOS. Plug and Play also allows Windows 95 to load and unload dynamically any device drivers that your system needs.

A growing number of ISDN CPE vendors are making their device Plug-and-Play compatible to simplify the installation process. The Windows 95 Plug-and-Play feature is particularly helpful for installing ISDN adapter cards.

Plug and Play isn't perfect because it relies on participation of peripheral devices, the BIOS, and the operating system. As more PC hardware vendors comply with Plug and Play, it should eliminate the earlier hassles of manually configuring different components to work together.

Built-in TCP/IP

Transmission Control Protocol and Internet Protocol (TCP/IP) is the collection of networking protocols that form the basis of the Internet. TCP/IP is a packet-based network, which means data is transferred in chunks (packets). In earlier versions of Windows, you had to purchase a third-party program, such as NetManage's Chameleon, to get TCP/IP capability. Windows 95 now includes a TCP/IP stack that provides the networking protocol for connecting your PC to the Internet.

TAPI

Windows *telephony application program interface* (TAPI) was developed by Microsoft and Intel specifically for Windows 95 and Windows NT. TAPI basically lets the telephone system interact with your PC to enable voice-handling services on your PC. To make TAPI work, the user simply installs the TAPI.DLL on the computer. TAPI supports both POTS and ISDN services. TAPI provides a standardized way of controlling any kind of telephone access and also arbitrates conflicts between applications requesting the use of communications ports, modems, and so on.

Setting Up Windows 95 for Remote Access

Similar procedures are involved in setting up Windows 95 for Internet access and telecommuting. The differences are in which network protocols you set up. For Internet access, you use the TCP/IP protocol. For connecting to a Windows for Workgroups network, you use the NetBEUI protocol.

Setting up Windows 95 to communicate via ISDN for Internet access or telecommuting involves working with the following facilities:

✔ For Internet access, you must first install the Microsoft TCP/IP protocol. Next, you install your ISDN remote-access device. If it's a serial device, you create a modem profile using the Modem wizard in the Control Panel. Finally, you set up a Dial-Up Networking profile to make the connection for your ISDN device to communicate to your Internet service provider.

✔ For telecommuting, you install the appropriate network protocol for the network you want to connect to. For example, if you're connecting to a Windows for Workgroups network, you use the NetBEUI protocol. Next, you configure the NetBEUI dial-up adapter. Finally, you set up a dial-up profile to make the connection for your ISDN device to communicate with the network.

Installing Windows 95 TCP/IP

Before you can use ISDN to connect to your Internet service provider, you must install the Windows 95 TCP/IP WinSock, commonly called a TCP/IP stack. Installing the Microsoft TCP/IP stack also installs the TCP/IP dial-up adapter.

Make sure that you have the original distribution disks. Windows prompts you for various disks to complete the installation:

1. Double-click the Network icon in the Control Panel.

The Network dialog box appears (Figure 7-1).

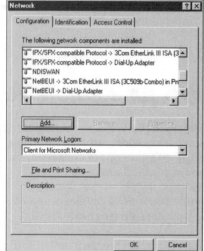

Figure 7-1:
The
Network
dialog box
contains the
settings for
Windows 95
networking.

2. Click the Add button.

This displays the Select Network Component Type dialog box.

3. Double-click Protocol.

The Select Network Protocol dialog box appears (Figure 7-2).

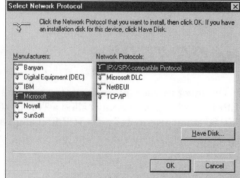

Figure 7-2:
The Select
Network
Protocol
dialog box
lists the
types of
network
components
you can
install.

4. **Select Microsoft.**

   The available protocols appear in the Network Protocols list on the right side.

5. **Double-click the TCP/IP item or select it and click OK.**

6. **Follow the Windows 95 prompts to complete the installation.**

7. **Restart Windows 95 when prompted.**

Now that you've installed the TCP/IP stack, you have to install the ISDN CPE device using its setup program. You work with the three types of ISDN remote-access devices — serial devices, adapter cards, and routers — in Chapters 9, 10, and 11, respectively. After you install your ISDN CPE, you can set up Windows 95 for remote access using Dial-Up Networking.

Installing Other Network Protocols

Windows 95 supports a number of networks from other vendors. Table 7-1 lists the networks supported by Windows 95 out of the box. Installing these network protocols involves the same procedures you use to install the TCP/IP protocol. If you have a disk from a network vendor, you can also install it from the Network icon in the Control Panel.

WinSock it to you

WinSock, short for Windows Sockets, is an application program interface (API) developed in 1991. WinSock is the *de facto* standard for Windows-based communications applications. WinSock 1.1 supports only TCP/IP. WinSock 2.0 supports TCP/IP, IPX/SPX (NetWare), AppleTalk, and OSI. It also supports wireless *asynchronous* *transfer mode* (ATM) and ISDN. This forms the basis of easier implementation of ISDN CPE in the Windows 95 environment. In addition, the WinSock API works in concert with telephony API (TAPI), which was designed by Microsoft to control telephone communications with Windows.

Table 7-1	Networking Protocols Supported by Windows 95 Out of the Box
Network Vendor	**Drivers**
Banyan	Banyan VINES Ethernet Protocol
	Banyan VINES Token Ring Protocol
Digital Equipment (DEC)	PATHWORKS V4.1 Ethernet
	PATHWORKS V4.1 Token Ring
	PATHWORKS V5.0 and above Ethernet
	PATHWORKS V5.0 and above Ethernet (ODI)
	PATHWORKS V5.0 and above Token Ring
IBM	Existing IBM DLC Protocol
Microsoft	IPX/SPX compatible Protocol
	Microsoft DLC
	NetBEUI
	TCP/IP
NetManage	NetManage TCP/IP V5.0 Dialup Only
	NetManage TCP/IP V5.0 NDIS Dialup
	NetManage TCP/IP V5.0 ODI Dialup
Novell	Novell IPX ODI Protocol
SunSoft	PC-NFS Protocol

Before you install the network drivers included in Windows 95, make sure that you have the original distribution disks. Windows prompts you for various disks to complete the installation:

1. **Double-click the Network icon in the Control Panel.**

2. **Click the Add button.**

   The Select Network Component Type dialog box appears.

3. **Double-click Protocol.**

   The Select Network Protocol dialog box appears.

4. **Select the Network vendor.**

   The available protocols appear in the Network Protocols list on the right side.

5. **Double-click the item or select it and click OK.**

6. **Follow the Windows 95 prompts to complete the installation.**

7. **Restart Windows 95 when prompted.**

Each network protocol is associated with a dial-up adapter. For example, if you selected the Microsoft NetBEUI protocol, the following entry appears in the Network Protocols list:

```
NetBEUI->Dial-Up Adapter
```

You use this entry for making a connection to the remote network from your PC. Selecting it and clicking Properties displays any configuration options for that network. Each network's properties are different.

Installing Dial-Up Networking

You use the Windows 95 Dial-Up Networking facility to manage all outside ISDN (and POTS) connections, whether you're dialing out to an Internet service provider or to another network, such as your office LAN.

The Windows 95 Dial-Up Networking facility is fine for most connections, but you can use a third-party communications program instead.

Before you start setting up your system as a remote-access client, the Dial-Up Networking software must be installed on your system. Check your My Computer folder for an icon labeled Dial-Up Networking. If you don't see it, you must install the Dial-Up Networking software from your original Windows 95 disks or CD-ROM, as follows:

1. **Double-click the Add/Remove Program Properties icon in the Control Panel.**

   The Add/Remove Programs Properties dialog box appears (Figure 7-3).

2. **Click the Windows Setup tab.**

3. **Double-click the Communications option.**

   The Communications dialog box appears (Figure 7-4), displaying the available communications and networking components of Windows 95.

4. **Click Dial-Up Networking and then click OK.**

   This returns you to the Windows Setup page.

5. **Click OK.**

   This starts the installation process.

6. **Follow the Windows 95 prompts for the disks or CD-ROM it needs to install Dial-Up Networking.**

   When the process is completed, Windows 95 reboots to enable the software drivers.

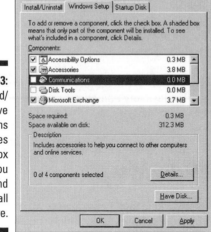

Figure 7-3:
The Add/
Remove
Programs
Properties
dialog box
allows you
to install and
uninstall
software.

Figure 7-4:
The
Communi-
cations
dialog box
displays
what
Windows 95
components
are installed
and not
installed.

Making Windows 95 Take Notice of Your ISDN CPE

Before you can use Windows 95 Dial-Up Networking, you need to install your ISDN CPE. Most CPE devices have their own setup programs that add the devices to Windows 95 and manage your ISDN line configuration. How the device installs and appears in Windows 95 varies depending on the technology:

✔ Windows handles serial-based ISDN devices as if they were a modem. After you install a serial ISDN device, you use the Modem wizard in the Control Panel to add it as a modem. Then you create a Dial-Up Networking profile. Chapter 9 explains setting up specific ISDN serial devices in Windows 95.

✔ Windows handles ISDN adapter cards as it does network adapter cards. When you install an ISDN adapter card, it appears as a network adapter in the Network control panel, and you can then create a Dial-Up Networking profile. (Unlike a serial device, an ISDN adapter card is not added like a modem.) Chapter 10 explains setting up specific ISDN adapter cards in Windows 95.

✔ Routers are accessed via the network adapter card. You configure your TCP/IP Ethernet card with your PC's IP address, which then communicates with the router. All the activity for making connections is handled by the router. Chapter 11 explains setting up a specific ISDN router for Windows 95.

After you have successfully installed your ISDN remote-access device, you are ready to create a Dial-Up Networking ISDN connection. Make sure that you have installed the cables provided with your adapter, that the line indicators are good, and that the line is active.

Before you can create a Dial-Up Networking profile for connecting to the Internet, you need a few pieces of information provided by your Internet service provider:

✔ Your machine's IP address, if your service provider assigned your a static address. Many ISDN Internet service providers use dynamic IP addressing, which means that your PC is not assigned a unique IP address.

✔ The subnet mask. The subnet mask indicates to TCP/IP which part of the IP address is used to identify your network and which part is used to identify each device on that network. A subnet mask is composed of the numbers 255 or 0. Typically, the subnet mask is 255.255.255.0.

✔ The IP address of the default gateway, which is the host machine you connect to. Again, if your ISP is using dynamic IP address, you won't have a default gateway IP address.

✔ The host and domain name.

✔ DNS server IP addresses.

✔ IP addresses for the router and all the PCs on your local area network, if you're installing a router.

Working with Dial-Up Networking

You can create Dial-Up Networking connection profiles in two ways, depending on what you're dialing up to. With the first, you use the Make New Connection program in the Dial-Up Networking folder, which is located in the My Computer folder on the desktop. The second and easier method uses the Internet Setup wizard. The Make New Connection program is used for any dial-up connection; the Internet Setup wizard is only for Internet access connections.

After you create a Dial-Up Networking connection profile, you can make your connection by simply clicking the icon in the Dial-Up Networking folder. Or for Internet access, if you use the Internet Setup wizard, you simply double-click the Microsoft Internet Explorer or Netscape navigator icon on your desktop. The Web browser opens along with the Dial-Up Networking Connect To dialog box. Clicking the Connect button automatically connects you to your Internet service provider.

Making a Dial-Up Networking connection profile

Each Dial-Up Networking profile is unique for the network and CPE you're using. You can create multiple Dial-Up Networking connection profiles. The following steps show you how to set up a Dial-Up Networking profile for connecting to any network. These steps assume that you've already installed an ISDN device and that it's working properly.

1. **Double-click the My Computer icon on the desktop, double-click the Dial Up Networking folder, and then double-click the Make New Connection icon.**

   The Make New Connection Wizard appears (Figure 7-5).

Figure 7-5:
The Make New Connection Wizard walks you through configuring Windows 95 for making a dial-up connection.

2. **Type a name to identify your connection (such as ISDN) and select your ISDN device from the list of modems.**

   This list includes any serial-based ISDN devices as well as any ISDN adapter cards that you've installed.

3. **Click Next.**

   A page appears for you to type the telephone number of the host computer you want to call, such as your Internet service provider's access number (Figure 7-6).

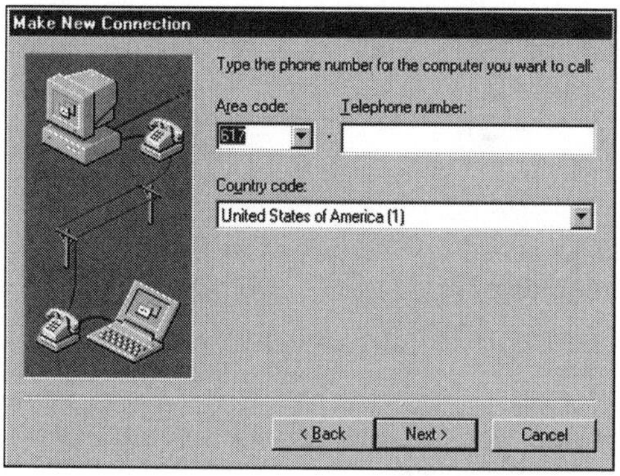

Figure 7-6:
The page for entering the access number for the remote host.

4. **Type the area code and telephone number of the host and then click Next.**

   Even if you don't use the area code, enter it. The default country code is U.S.

5. **Click Finish.**

6. **Double-click the My Computer and Dial Up Networking icons.**

   You see a new icon with the name you entered for your connection.

7. ***Right-click* the connection icon.**

   A menu appears.

8. **Select Properties.**

   A connection profile dialog box appears with the name of your connection in the title bar (Figure 7-7).

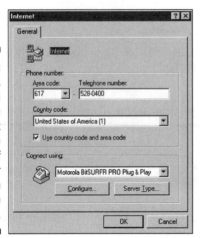

Figure 7-7:
A
connection
profile
dialog box
with the
name of
your
connection
in the
title bar.

9. **If you're using an ISDN serial device, click Configure in the General tab and then select a Maximum speed of 115,200 bps. Click OK.**

10. **If your CPE requires AT commands to place a call (check your CPE documentation):**

   • Click Configure and then click the Connection tab to display the Connection properties sheet.

   • Click the Advanced button to display the Advanced Connection Settings dialog box (Figure 7-8).

   • In the Extra settings box, type the appropriate string of AT commands for your CPE to place a call.

   • Click OK twice.

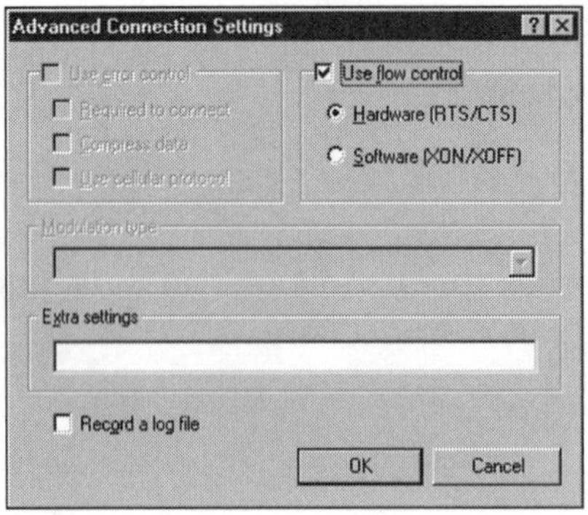

Figure 7-8:
The
Advanced
Connection
Settings
dialog box
includes
settings for
devices that
use the AT
Command
set.

11. Click the Server Type button.

The Server Types dialog box appears (Figure 7-9).

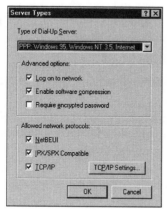

12. If you want to make the connection profile for dialing up to a Windows for Workgroups or Windows NT 3.1 network:

- Select Windows for Workgroups and Windows NT 3.1 from the Type of Dial-Up Server list.

- Make sure that only the NetBEUI item in the Allowed network protocols area is checked.

- Click OK twice and you're finished.

13. If you want to make the connection profile for dialing up to a Novell network:

- Select NRN: NetWare Connect from the Type of Dial-Up Server list.

- Make sure that only the IPX/SPX Compatible item in the Allowed network protocols area is checked.

- Click OK twice and you're finished.

14. **For connecting to the Internet, to Windows 95, or to Windows NT 3.51 network:**

   - Select PPP: Windows 95, Windows NT 3.5, Internet from the from the Type of Dial-Up Server list.

   - Check only the TCP/IP item in the Allowed network protocols area.

   - Click the TCP/IP Settings button.

   The TCP/IP Settings dialog box (Figure 7-10) appears.

   - If your ISP uses dynamic IP addressing, select Server assigned IP address.

   - If your service provider has assigned you a specific IP address, select Specify an IP address and enter the IP address in the Primary DNS and Secondary DNS boxes.

   - Click OK three times, and you're finished.

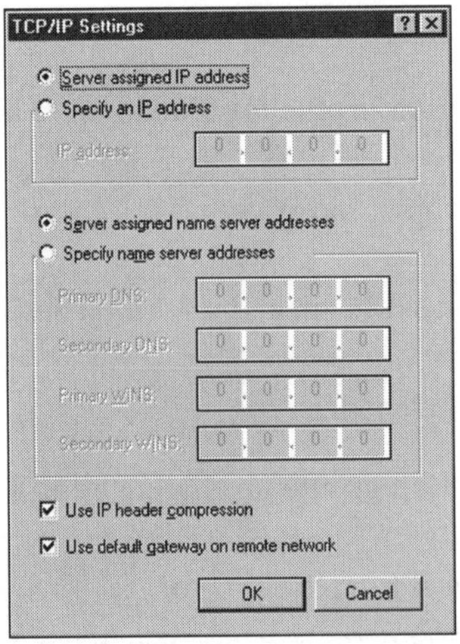

Figure 7-10:
Use the
TCP/IP
Settings
dialog box to
enter the IP
addresses
of the
network
you're
connecting
to.

Internet Setup Wizard to the rescue

The Internet Setup Wizard makes creating an Internet access connection a breeze. After the connection is set up, you simply double-click any Web browser icon on your Windows desktop, and the Connect To dialog box appears. Click the Connect button, the connection is made, and you're on the Web. This section describes how to set up an Internet connection using the Internet Setup Wizard.

If you're using the Windows 95 upgrade version, you need to get a copy of the Microsoft Plus add-on package to get the Internet wizard. The Microsoft Plus pack is sold by Microsoft for a list price of $54.95.

1. **Choose Start⇨Programs⇨Accessories⇨Internet Tools⇨Internet Setup Wizard.**

   The Internet Setup Wizard Welcome page appears (Figure 7-11).

Figure 7-11: The Internet Setup Wizard Welcome page.

2. **Click the Next button to begin.**

   A page appears asking which method you want to use to connect to the Internet.

3. **Choose Connect using my phone line setting (the default); then click Next.**

   A page appears asking how you want to connect to the Internet — through the Microsoft network or through your own account.

4. **Click I already have an account; then click Next.**

   A page appears asking whether you want to use Microsoft Exchange or another program to send and receive your e-mail.

5. **Select the program you want to use for e-mail and then click Next.**

6. **If you chose Yes (for using Exchange), follow the Windows 95 prompts for installing the software.**

   The Internet Setup Wizard displays a page prompting you for the name of your Internet service provider.

7. **Type a name to identify the dial-up networking profile and click Next.**

   A page appears (Figure 7-12) for entering the telephone number of your Internet access provider.

8. **Type the area code and the telephone number to dial for access to your Internet provider.**

Type the area code even if it's a local call.

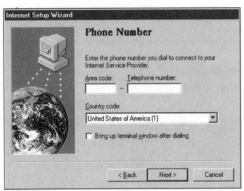

Figure 7-12:
The page for entering the access number for your ISDN Internet connection.

9. **Leave the Bring up terminal window after dialing option unchecked. Click Next.**

A page appears for entering your username and password.

10. **Enter the username and password you use to log on to your Internet provider's host computer and then click Next.**

A page appears for entering IP addresses (Figure 7-13).

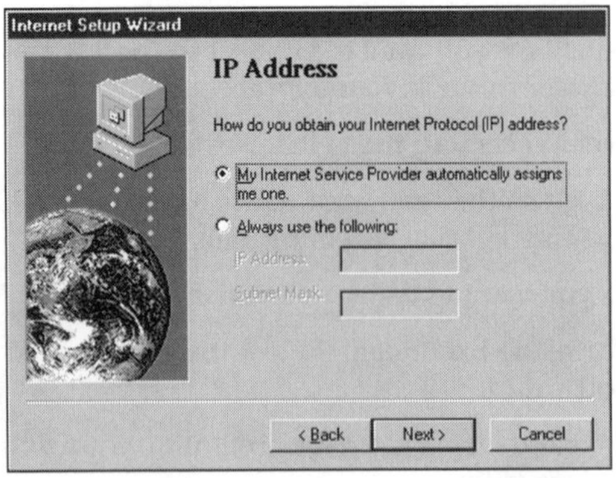

Figure 7-13:
The IP Address page is for specifying whether your ISP uses static or dynamic IP addressing.

11. **If your ISP provided you with a static IP address, click Always use the following; then enter your IP address and subnet mask IP address. If your provider automatically assigns an IP number when you log on (a dynamic IP address), click My Internet Service provider automatically assigns me one setting.**

12. **Click Next.**

    The DNS Server Address page appears, as shown in Figure 7-14.

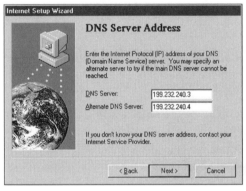

Figure 7-14:
Use the
DNS Server
Address
page to
specify your
ISP's DNS
server
addresses.

13. **Type the IP addresses for your Internet service provider's DNS (Domain Name System) server(s) and then click Next.**

    You must use numeric IP addresses, not a domain name.

    The Internet Mail page appears (Figure 7-15).

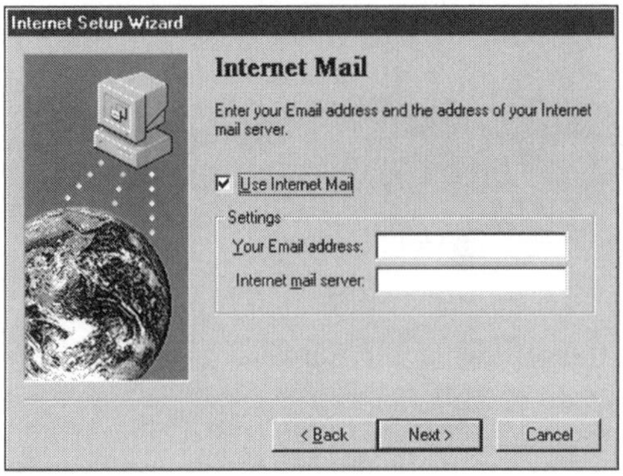

Figure 7-15:
Use the
Internet
Mail page to
configure
Microsoft
Exchange
for your
e-mail.

14. **If you're using Microsoft Exchange for your e-mail, check the Use Internet Mail setting; then type your e-mail address and Internet mail server address. If you're using another mail program, make sure that the Use Internet Mail setting is not checked.**

15. **Click Next.**

    The next page displays a notice that your Internet setup is complete.

16. **Click Finish.**

Now you're ready to connect to the Internet using Internet Explorer.

Managing Internet properties

The Internet Wizard creates a new Control Panel entry for the Internet access settings. Double-click the Internet icon in the Control Panel or *right-click* the Internet icon on the desktop. Choose Properties, and the Internet Properties dialog box appears (Figure 7-16).

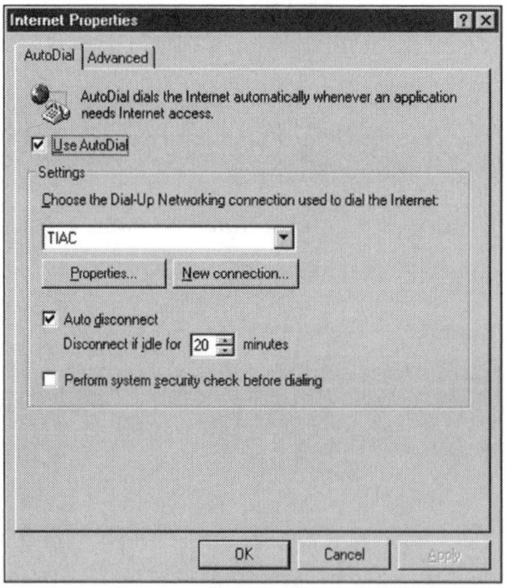

Figure 7-16:
The Internet
Properties
dialog box
lets you
control
settings
for the
Windows
AutoDial
feature.

The following describes the settings in the AutoDial properties page:

✔ Use AutoDial. This setting is checked by default. It allows Internet Explorer or Netscape Navigator to automatically dial the Internet when you open the Web browser.

✔ Choose the Dial-Up Networking connection used to dial the Internet. Use this setting to specify which Dial-Up Networking profile you want to use for AutoDial. The default is the last profile you created using the Internet Setup wizard.

✔ The Auto disconnect setting lets you specify how long Windows stays connected to the Internet when it is idle. The default is 20 minutes. For ISDN connections, this feature can save you money.

✔ Perform system security check before dialing. If this setting is checked, Windows prompts you for your Windows 95 username and password before enabling you to initiate an Internet connection.

The AutoDial feature links with only one Web browser at a time. If you use another Web browser from your desktop, Windows 95 displays a dialog box asking whether you want to assign it as the default browser. Clicking Yes does so. Clicking the Advanced tab displays settings for determining which server will be used for access via proxy. On a LAN, a *proxy server* is a computer connected to the Internet through which other computers on the LAN can access the Internet.

Making the connection

After you've created your Dial-Up Networking profile manually or with the Internet Setup wizard, you're ready to make your connection. If you used the Internet wizard and have the AutoDial setting ready, simply double-click the Web browser icon. The browser window opens along with the Connect To dialog box, as shown in Figure 17-17.

Click the Connect button. The connection is made and the home page appears in your Web browser. To disconnect, click the minimized Connect To dialog box on the taskbar and then click Disconnect.

Do the following to make a connection to your Internet provider or other network from the Dial-Up Networking folder:

1. **Double-click the Dial-Up Networking icon you created.**

   The Connect To dialog box (Figure 7-18) appears.

2. **Type your username (also known as hostname) and password for logging on to the Internet, if necessary.**

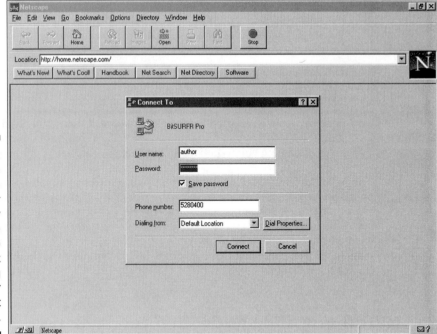

Figure 7-17:
Opening the
Netscape
browser
automatically
displays the
Connect To
dialog box
for making
your
Internet
connection.

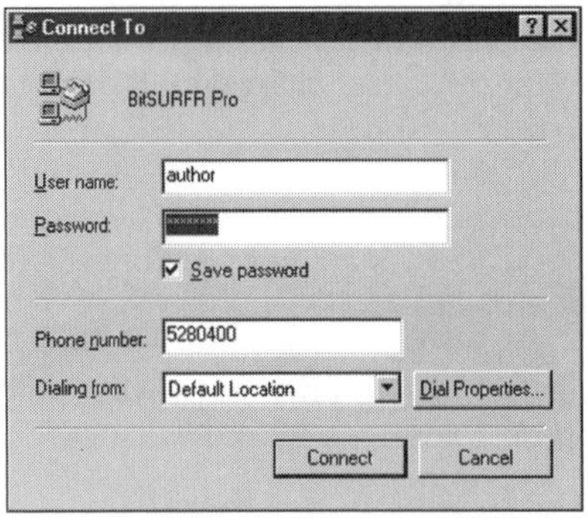

Figure 7-18:
The Connect
To dialog
box.

3. **Click the Connect button to make your connection.**

The Status dialog box appears. It indicates dialing, verifies the username
and password, and then displays Connected. After you are connected to
the Internet, you can immediately use your Web browser or other Internet
applications.

While connected to the network, the Connect To dialog box appears minimized on the taskbar. You can open this at any time (Figure 7-19) to see the bps rate and the duration of your connection.

Figure 7-19:
The
Connected
to dialog
box lets you
know that
you're
connected
and the
speed of the
connection.

4. To end your connection, click Disconnect.

If your Internet service provider does not support PAP or CHAP, a terminal window opens to display text received from the ISP's server after you're connected. Enter your username and password when prompted. When the terminal window reports your IP address, press F7. The terminal window closes, and your Internet connection is active.

Changing locations for the nomadic laptop

The Windows 95 Dial-Up Networking adapts to the needs of the mobile user. It enables you to create new locations for the same dial-up connection as you move around.

To create a different location, open the Dial-Up Networking connection you want to change from the Dial-Up Networking folder. This displays the Connect To dialog box. Click the Dial Properties button to display the Dialing Properties dialog box (Figure 7-20).

In the Where I am area, click the New button to create a new location entry in the I am dialing from option. Enter the area code you are currently calling from if it's different from the one you usually call from.

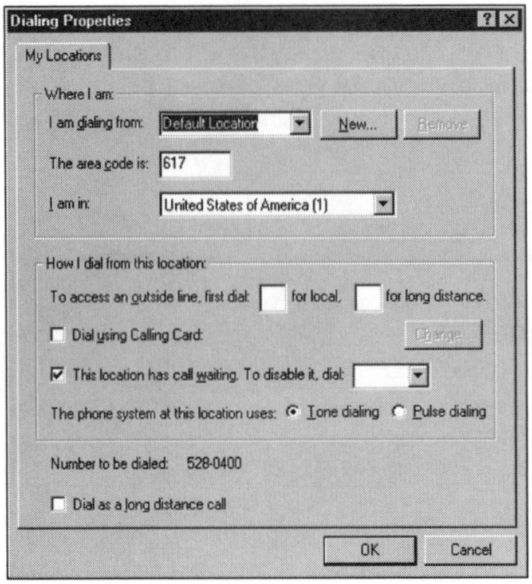

Figure 7-20:
The Dialing
Properties
dialog box.

After you create your new location, specify how Dial-Up Networking makes the call in the area titled How I dial from this location. You can add prefixes to get an outside line and for making a long-distance call.

Select the Dial using Calling Card option if you want to charge your call to a telephone company credit card. You can specify multiple calling cards for a single location entry. Clicking the Change button displays a Change Calling Card dialog box (Figure 7-21). The Calling card to use drop-down list displays telephone calling cards and telephone access numbers to select from. The Calling Card number field is where you enter your PIN number.

Figure 7-21:
The Change
Calling Card
dialog box.

If the location has call waiting, which disrupts modem communications, you can shut it off using the This location has call waiting setting in the Dialing Properties dialog box. The drop-down list includes common codes for shutting off call waiting before making the outbound call.

After all your settings are in place, the sequence of numbers appears at the bottom of the Dialing Properties dialog box for that location. Click OK. Your new location entry appears in the I am dialing from drop-down list.

Microsoft's ISDN Accelerator Pack (Stuck in the Slow Lane)

The Microsoft ISDN Accelerator Pack enables you to make Dial-Up Networking connections for ISDN adapter cards. This software program is available free from Microsoft's Web site at:

```
http://www.microsoft.com/windows/software/isdn.htm
```

The current version of Microsoft's ISDN Accelerator Pack doesn't support PPP/MP. Instead, it supports only PPP, which means it allows only one B channel for ISDN communications.

For most ISDN adapter cards, however, you don't need the ISDN Accelerator Pack. Most ISDN adapter card vendors include their own solutions that support the PPP/MP protocol so that you can use both B channels.

WinISDN for your ISDN cards

The WinISDN specification was completed in January 1995. ISDN*Tek, an ISDN adapter card vendor; NetManage, a leading TCP/IP software company; and PSI, a national Internet service provider, teamed up to design the WinISDN specification for plugging in ISDN adapter cards.

Many ISDN CPE vendors support the WinISDN standard. The WinISDN protocol operates as a software layer between the TCP/IP protocol stack on your PC and the ISDN adapter card.

The TCP/IP stack in Windows 95 doesn't support WinISDN. WinISDN is used by third-party Internet access software, however, including NetManage's Internet Chameleon and FTP's Explore OnNet. Typically, ISDN CPE vendors also include software to make their ISDN adapter cards work with the Windows 95 Dial-Up Networking facility.

Chapter 8

ISDN Meets Windows NT 4.0

● ●

In This Chapter

▶ Understanding Windows NT 4.0

▶ Setting up Dial-Up Networking connections in NT

▶ Making connections using the NT 4.0 Dial-Up Networking

▶ Managing Dial-Up Networking connections

● ●

*W*indows NT 4.0 is the latest version of Microsoft's industrial-strength version of Windows. It delivers more computing power, better security, and enhanced networking capabilities for the enterprise computing environment. This chapter explains working with NT in the context of making ISDN connections.

About Windows NT 4.0

Windows NT 4.0 comes in two flavors: Windows NT Server and Windows NT Workstation. As their respective names imply, the Server version is for running a dedicated server to provide services to the network, and the Workstation version is for client computers. You can use NT Workstation as a peer-to-peer networking solution without NT Server for up to ten PCs. NT Workstation lists for $319, and NT Server lists for $699.

Windows NT is true 32-bit, whereas Windows 95 still has a lot of 16-bit code for backward compatibility. The NT 32-bit operating system greatly improves its reliability and performance over Windows 95. Windows 95, however, is still a big improvement over Windows 3.1 and Windows for Workgroups 3.11. Windows 95 represents a halfway point between Windows for Workgroups and Windows NT.

A lot of the power of Windows NT comes from its sophisticated architecture for managing CPU processing. It is capable of running more tasks more efficiently than Windows 95 because it doesn't have the Windows 95 16-bit baggage. NT is best used for multitasking.

Although the performance edge of Windows NT is noticeably better than Windows 95, these enhanced capabilities come at a price of more expensive computer resources. Windows NT requires 32 MB RAM to work effectively. The Microsoft minimum is 16 MB. You need to use a Pentium processor and have lots of hard disk space.

NT is also a lot more disk intensive, so hard disk speed becomes a factor. This means you need the latest disk controllers. If you're moving a lot of data-intensive information across an NT network, you'll also need a 32-bit network adapter card.

Finally, NT doesn't provide the high level of backward compatibility that Windows 95 does. This means it doesn't work well with older hardware and applications.

Windows NT 4.0 is the latest upgrade of Windows NT. One of the biggest changes in Windows NT 4.0 over NT 3.51 is the addition of the Windows 95 interface. NT.4.0 also improved its dial-up connectivity features.

The focus of this chapter is on Windows NT 4.0 Workstation. Many functions, however, are the same for both the Server and Workstation versions of NT.

Windows NT 4.0 and Remote Access

Windows NT 4.0 has improved the NT handling of remote access. It added a Dial-Up Networking facility that is similar to Windows 95, although it has differences in its implementation. The NT 4.0 Dial-Up Networking facility was fused to the previous version's dial-up facility, which is called *remote access service* (RAS). Dial-Up Networking has replaced the general communications functions of RAS in NT 4.0.

In Windows NT, RAS enables NT users at remote sites to connect to an NT network as though their computer were directly connected to the network. This is a Microsoft solution for telecommuting to a Windows NT network. RAS requires setting up an NT computer as a server at the LAN side and setting up each remote PC as a RAS client.

A discussion of RAS is beyond the scope of this book. This chapter focuses on working with Dial-Up Networking.

As of the writing of this book, most ISDN devices did not support Windows NT 4.0 because NT 4.0 was still in beta. ISDN CPE vendors will be soon offering drivers for Windows NT. Many of these software updates will be available for downloading from the Web sites of ISDN CPE vendors.

Installing TCP/IP

The first step in working with NT for ISDN connections is to install TCP/IP. Installing TCP/IP support before you install Dial-Up Networking will save you extra steps later. The Dial-Up Networking installation routine automatically installs the required protocols if you install TCP/IP support first.

1. *Right-click* the Network Neighborhood icon and then choose Properties.

2. On the Protocols page, click Add.

   The Select Network Protocol dialog box appears.

3. Select TCP/IP Protocol and then click OK.

   Windows NT tells you that it's configuring the TCP/IP protocol.

4. When NT asks whether you want to use the *Dynamic Host Configuration Protocol* (DHCP) when using TCP/IP, click No (in most cases).

5. Answer the prompts about the location of your NT distribution media.

   Windows NT proceeds with the installation.

6. If you have RAS installed, click Yes when Windows NT asks whether you want to configure it to use TCP/IP.

7. Click Close.

   This completes the installation process. Windows NT asks whether you want it to restart the computer.

8. Click Yes.

Adding ISDN Remote-Access Devices

In Windows NT, as in Windows 95, you first must install your ISDN remote-access device before setting up Windows NT to use the device and make connections. To install ISDN serial devices in Windows NT, click Modem Properties in the Control Panel. The Modem Properties dialog box is similar to the one in Windows 95.

Adapter cards are installed in the same way in Windows NT and Windows 95. You install the adapter card in your PC and then use the setup software that came with the card. The setup program installs the card as a network adapter card. Keep in mind that Windows NT 4.0 doesn't support Plug and Play.

After you set up your ISDN remote-access device, you're ready to work with Windows NT Dial-Up Networking to create a connection profile. If you're using a serial ISDN device, your need to create a Modem Properties profile.

To install an ISDN serial device as a modem for NT, do the following:

1. Double-click the Modems icon in the Control Panel.

The Modems Properties window appears.

2. Click Add.

The Install New Modem wizard appears.

3. Select the check box labeled Don't detect my modem; I'll select it from a list.

4. Click Next.

The list of modem manufacturers and models appears.

5. Click the Have Disk button.

The Install from Disk page appears.

6. Insert the disk from your ISDN remote-access device that contains the driver for Windows NT and then click OK.

7. Select the device from the list and then click Next.

A page appears for specifying the communications (COM) port.

8. Choose the COM port your ISDN serial device is connected to and then click Next.

The ISDN device driver is installed, and then the final Wizard page appears.

9. Click Finish.

You return to the Modems Properties dialog box with the new ISDN device listed.

Installing Dial-Up Networking

You should install any ISDN remote-access device before you install Dial-Up Networking. Then, before you can use the Windows NT Dial-Up Networking, you must install it.

To install Dial-Up Networking, do the following:

1. Double-click the Dial-Up Networking icon in the My Computer folder on the desktop.

You're prompted to click the Install button to install Dial-Up Networking.

2. Click Install.

3. Type the path to your Windows NT CD-ROM and the I386 folder (for example, D:\I386**).**

4. Click Continue.

The remote-access software is installed. If you did not previously install a modem, RAS will prompt you to install one now. You can install a modem even if it is not attached. Just make sure that you check the Don't Detect modem setting. As you may recall, RAS and Dial-Up Networking share the same facilities.

5. When prompted, restart Windows NT.

Creating a Connection Using the Wizard

After you install Dial-Up Networking, you can use it to create your connection profiles in a similar manner to Windows 95. The first time you open Dial-Up Networking, you see a dialog box that says the phone book is empty. Click OK, and the New Phonebook Entry Wizard appears (Figure 8-1). You can bypass the wizard and fill in the Phonebook entry manually, as explained later. But for now, use the Wizard.

Figure 8-1:
The New
Phonebook
Entry
Wizard
makes
creating a
dial-up
networking
profile easy.

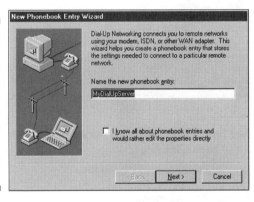

1. In the New Phonebook Entry Wizard page, type the name of the connection.

Leave the check box blank (the default setting).

2. Click Next.

The Server page appears, as shown in Figure 8-2.

3. Click all the connection options that apply for the connection profile you're creating and then Click Next.

The Phone Number page appears (Figure 8-3).

Figure 8-2:
Use the
Server page
to specify
the type of
connection
you want to
make with
the dial-up
networking
profile.

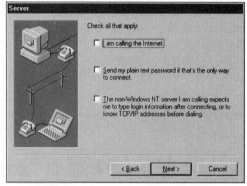

Figure 8-3:
Use the
Phone
Number
page to
enter the
number to
call for your
connection.

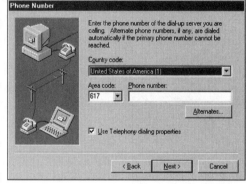

4. **In the Phone number field, type the telephone number for the host you want to connect to and then click Next.**

The Serial Line Protocol page appears (Figure 8-4).

Figure 8-4:
Serial Line
Protocol
page
defines the
protocol to
use for the
connection.

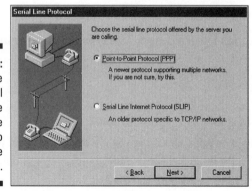

5. **Make sure that the Point-to-Point Protocol check box is selected (the default) and then click Next.**

   The Login Script page appears (Figure 8-5). In most cases, you won't need to create a login script.

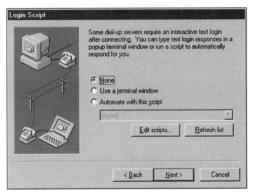

Figure 8-5:
Login Script
page lets
you define a
sequence of
commands
called
scripts for
logging in to
a remote
host.

6. **Leave the default None setting and then click Next.**

   The IP Address page appears (Figure 8-6).

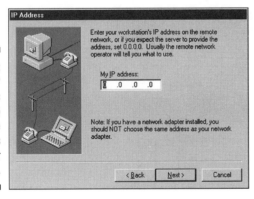

Figure 8-6:
Use the IP
Address
page to
specify the
IP address
of your
computer.

7. **If your Internet account uses a static IP address, type your IP address.**
   If your account uses a dynamic IP address, leave the zeros in the My IP address field (the default).

8. **Click Next.**

   The Name Server Addresses page appears (Figure 8-7).

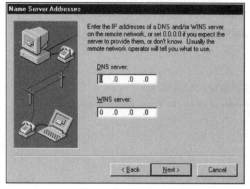

Figure 8-7:
Use the
Name
Server
Addresses
page to
specify the
DNS server
IP
addresses
of the
remote host.

9. **In the DNS server field, type the Domain Name System (DNS) server IP address and then click Next.**

The final Wizard page appears.

10. **Click Finish.**

The Wizard displays the Dial-Up Networking page with your new entry information entered (Figure 8-8).

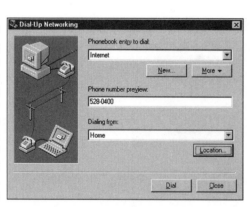

Figure 8-8:
The Dial-Up
Networking
dialog box is
your
gateway to
managing
your Dial-Up
Networking
connections.

11. **Click Close to exit Dial-Up Networking, or make further edits from the Dial-Up Networking profile.**

Shutting Off the New Phonebook Entry Wizard

The New Phonebook Entry Wizard makes the process of setting up Dial-Up Networking smooth. However, you can shut off the Wizard to create your Dial-Up Networking entries manually using the New Phonebook Entry dialog box (Figure 8-9).

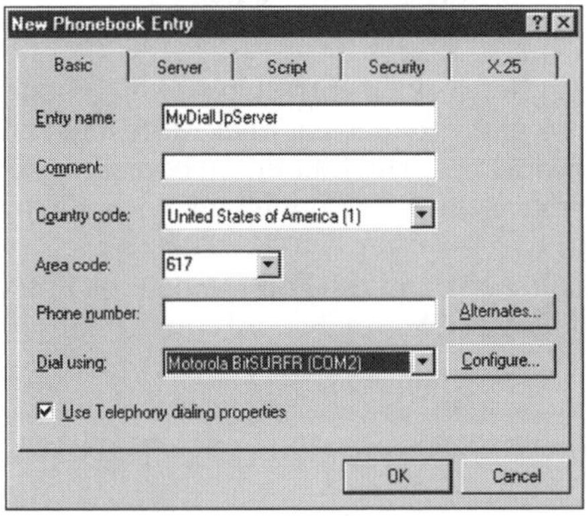

Figure 8-9: The New Phonebook Entry dialog box lets you create your Phonebook entries manually.

After you create your first Dial-Up Networking entry, the next time you double-click the Dial-Up Networking icon in the My Computer folder, the Dial-Up Networking dialog box appears instead of the New Phonebook Entry Wizard. When you click the New button, the Wizard appears.

You can shut off the Wizard in two ways. The first is from the page that appears in the Wizard after you click the New button. Enter the name for your entry and then select the check box labeled I know all about phonebook entries and would rather edit the properties directly. The Next button changes to Finish. Click Finish to display the New Phonebook Entry dialog box (see Figure 8-9).

The second method is from the Dial-Up Networking dialog box. Click the More button to display a drop-down menu. Choose User preferences and click the Appearance tab. Uncheck the option titled Use Wizard to create new phonebook entries. Click OK. You can reactivate the Wizard by using the same procedure, except you select the option titled Use Wizard to create new phonebook entries setting.

Creating and Editing Phonebook Entries Manually

You use the New Phonebook Entry dialog box to manually create or edit a Dial-Up Networking connection profile. The following explains how to create or edit a Phonebook entry manually:

- ✔ To create a new Dial-Up Networking entry with the New Phonebook Entry Wizard shut off, click the New button. The manual New Phonebook Entry dialog box appears.

- ✔ To edit an existing Dial-Up Networking entry, choose the Phonebook entry from the Phonebook entry to dial list. Click More and choose the Edit entry and modem properties. The Edit Phonebook Entry dialog box appears, which is the same as the New Phonebook Entry dialog box.

The New Phonebook Entry dialog box and the Edit Phonebook Entry dialog box include five tabs labeled Basic, Server, Script, Security, and X.25.

Basic properties

The Basic properties page (Figure 8-10) contains the connection name, a comment, the phone number you want to dial, and the device you want to use to dial it. With a modem or ISDN remote-access device selected from the Dial using drop-down list, click the Configure button. The Modem Configuration dialog box (Figure 8-11) appears. This dialog box varies depending on the selected device. In the Dial using list (Figure 8-10), the Multiple Lines item lets you combine multiple lines to act as a single line for more bandwidth.

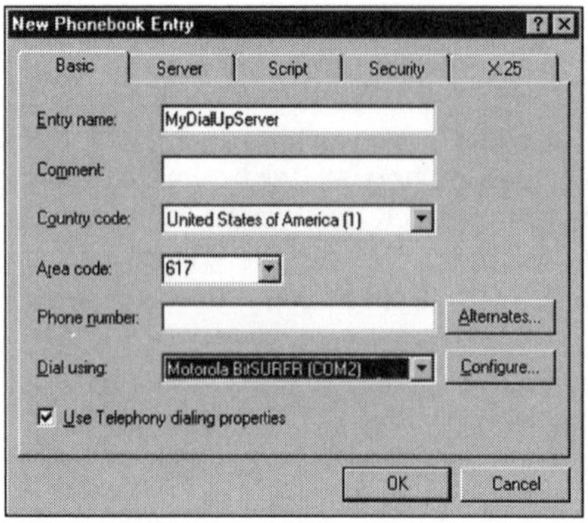

Figure 8-10: The Basic Properties page includes entries for naming your connection, telephone numbers to call, and the device you want to use.

Figure 8-11:
The Modem
Configuration
dialog box
allows you
to make
adjustments
on your
ISDN
device.

The Alternates button displays the Phone Numbers page (Figure 8-12), where you can enter multiple access numbers for the same host computer. Dial-Up Networking automatically goes through the list until it makes a connection using one of the telephone numbers.

Figure 8-12:
The Phone
Numbers
dialog box
allows you
to enter
multiple
numbers for
connecting
to a specific
host.

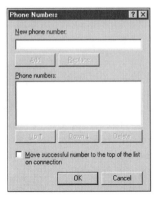

Server properties

The Server properties page (Figure 8-13) includes a list for Dial-up server type. This allows you to choose the kind of connection you want to make. You use the default — PPP, Windows NT, Windows 95 Plus, Internet — most of the time. You can also specify a SLIP Internet server connection or a Windows NT 3.1, Windows for Workgroups connection.

In the Network protocols area, you define the protocols you want to use. To connect to the Internet, you use just the TCP/IP setting. Clicking the TCP/IP Settings button displays the PPP TCP/IP page for entering the IP address for your Internet connection.

The last two check boxes on the Server properties page allow you to use newer communications features. The first check box, Enable software compression, allows you to reduce network traffic and speed packet transmission using compression. The Enable PPP LCP extensions check box allows you to use special tracking features supported by your server. For example, your PC can use this feature to request time remaining and identification packets from the server.

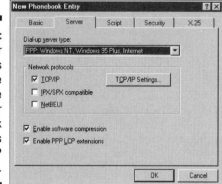

Figure 8-13: The Server properties page includes the settings for network protocols and IP addresses.

Script properties

The Script properties page (Figure 8-14) lets you specify scripts to run that execute a connection. It also lets you tell Dial-Up Networking to display a terminal window after a connection is made. This terminal window enables you to work at the command prompt of a host computer. *Scripts* are a collection of commands executed in a sequence between a client and host computer. Think of scripts as macros for communications.

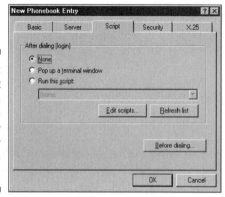

Figure 8-14: The Script properties page lets you specify a script for logging in to a host.

The following describes the settings in the Scripts properties page:

- ✔ The None option is used if you don't want to run a script.

- ✔ The Pop up a terminal window option displays a terminal window so that you can type in any required commands manually. One way that you might use this option is to enter a name and password when required to access the server.

- ✔ The Run this script option enables the associated list box. You simply select the script you want to run from the list. Microsoft supplies a Generic Login script that you can modify to meet your needs.

- ✔ The Edit scripts button enables you to edit any existing scripts or to save them under a new name.

- ✔ The Refresh list button enables you to see any new scripts you create.

Security properties

The Security properties page (Figure 8-15) enables you to select security options that affect only the current connection. Dial-Up Networking offers three levels of security. The first is the least secure; it accepts any form of authentication, including clear text. Unfortunately, this is the option you need to use with most Internet connections. The second option allows only encrypted authentication. This option works with newer servers from a variety of sources. The third option likely works only with Windows 95 and Windows NT Internet servers. It requires the use of Microsoft encryption technology. You'll find it very safe, but also very limiting.

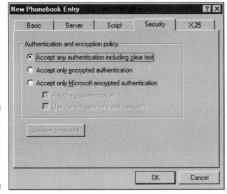

Figure 8-15:
The Security
properties
page.

X.25 properties

You use the X.25 properties page (Figure 8-16) to establish connections over an X.25 network. For example, if you use the CompuServe X.25 network for your communications, you would set up your connection in the X.25 properties page. In the Network list, you select an X.25 network. In the Address box, you type the X.25 address. The User Data and Facilities boxes enable you to enter specific information supplied by the X.25 provider.

Figure 8-16:
The X.25
properties
page lets
you
establish
connections
over an X.25
network.

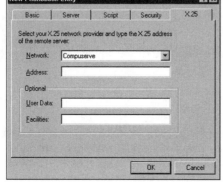

Managing Your Connections

Beyond using the New or Edit Phonebook Entry dialog boxes to create connections, the key to managing connections is the More button in the Dial-Up Networking dialog box. Start by selecting the connection you want to work with from the Phonebook entry to dial list. Click More, and you see a menu of options. The following sections explain the entries on this menu.

Edit entry and modem properties

The Edit entry and modem properties menu item displays the Edit Phonebook Entry dialog box. You change the properties using the same criteria used to create a new entry.

Clone entry and modem properties

You can save time in creating new entries by choosing the Clone entry and modem properties menu item. This creates a new entry with the previous settings, which you can then tweak instead of entering all the information individually.

Delete entry

The Delete entry menu item enables you to remove a connection that you no longer need. Select Phonebook from the Phonebook entry to dial list; then choose the More | Delete entry.

Create shortcut to entry

The Create shortcut to entry menu item lets you place a shortcut to the connection on the desktop (the default) or any location. When you choose Create shortcut, the Create Dial-Up Shortcut dialog box appears for navigating directories and files (Figure 8-17). Find the folder that you want to hold the connection shortcut and then click OK.

Figure 8-17:
The Create Dial-Up Shortcut dialog box lets you create a shortcut icon on the NT desktop for easy access.

Monitor status

The Monitor status menu item displays the Dial-Up Networking Monitor dialog box (Figure 8-18), which provides a status report of any active connection in the Status and Summary pages.

On the Status page, the Hang-Up button is active whenever you're connected. Clicking the Hang-Up button ends your connection. The Summary page displays information for multiple line connections.

The Preferences page (Figure 8-19) enables you to specify audio notification when a particular connection event occurs. For example, when a connection is made, Windows NT will beep. Four options are available.

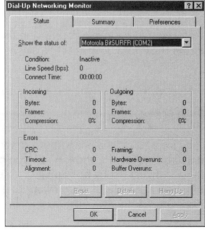

Figure 8-18:
The Dial-Up Networking Monitor dialog box keeps track of what is going on with your connection.

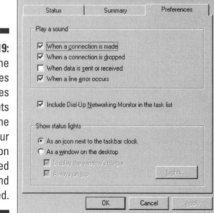

Figure 8-19:
The Preferences properties page lets you define how your connection is handled and monitored.

Checking the Include Dial-Up Networking Monitor in the task list automatically places the Dial-Up Networking Monitor on the taskbar whenever you make a connection. In most cases, you'll want to do this because to hang up a connection requires the Monitor dialog box.

The final group is Show status lights. The default — As an icon next to the taskbar clock — displays status lights showing data movement across your connection, similar to the way status lights work on a modem. Double-clicking the icon displays the Monitor dialog box. Choosing the As a window on the desktop option displays a dialog box showing status lights. When you select this option, the following become active: the Display the window's titlebar option, the Always on top option, and the Lights button.

Operator-assisted or manual dialing

The Operator-assisted or manual dialing menu item forces the connection to ask you to dial the number. This is a good option to choose for numbers that change frequently or numbers that you don't want to compromise by placing them on your computer.

User preferences

The User preferences menu item displays the User Preferences dialog box (Figure 8-20) so that you can define the connection for your individual requirements. This feature is handy for using a laptop, where you may end up calling the same host from different locations.

The following describes the four properties pages in the User Preferences dialog box:

- ✔ On the Dialing tab, the Enable auto-dial by location list contains the locations you've defined. (Locations are explained later.) Just select the locations you want to use with this connection. The next three fields define how Dial-Up Networking will try to complete the phone call. They are the number of retries (0, if you want to try only once); the time you want to wait between retries; and the idle time (the amount of time to wait before the connection is considered unusable even if the remote phone answers).

- ✔ The Callback tab has a feature that enables you to call the server, tell it where to reach you, and then wait for the server to call you back. Although this saves you telephone charges, it's actually a security option. A remote server has the option of ignoring your request for access by not calling you back. Dial-Up Networking provides three levels of callback. You can ignore callback altogether, have the program ask you about callback when it makes the connection, or use callback all the time. If you select the third option, Dial-Up Networking also allows you to enter a number where you can be reached — saving you the trouble of entering it manually.

✔ Use the Appearance tab to change the way connection information is presented. The default settings enable all the options shown. The first option, for example, displays a dialog box containing the connection's phone number before you dial. Also included is a check box that enables the New Connection Entry Wizard.

✔ The Phonebook tab lets you select one of two standard phonebooks: Personal or System. You can also create custom phonebooks by selecting the third option. Simply type the name of the custom phonebook, and Dial-Up Networking will use it to store any connections you create.

Login preferences

The Login preferences menu item defines the setup used when you log on to a server. The Login Preferences dialog box provides a subset of the settings in the User Preferences dialog box.

Changing Locations

The Windows NT Dial-Up Networking, like its Windows 95 counterpart, adapts to the needs of the mobile user. Dial-Up Networking enables you to create new locations for the same dial-up connection as you move around. Just click the Location button in the Dial-Up Networking dialog box to display the Dialing Properties dialog box (Figure 8-21).

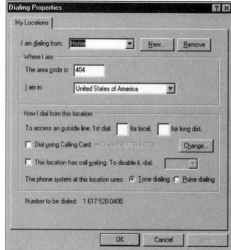

Figure 8-21: The Dialing Properties dialog box lets you define multiple locations for calling into a host computer.

Clicking the New button in the Dialing Properties dialog box creates a new location entry in the I am dialing from field. Type a new location name over the new location entry. Enter the area code you are currently calling from, if it is different from the one you call from.

After you create your new location, specify how Dial-Up Networking makes the call in the area titled How I dial from this location. You can add prefixes to get an outside line and to make a long-distance call using the To access an outside line settings.

Checking the Dial using calling card option enables you to charge your call to a telephone company credit card. You can specify multiple calling cards for a single location entry. Clicking the Change button displays a Change Calling Card dialog box. The Calling card use list displays telephone calling card options from leading telephone companies (such as AT&T, MCI, and Sprint) and their telephone access numbers. Use the Calling Card number field to enter your PIN number.

If the location has call waiting, which disrupts modem communications, you can shut it off using the This location has call waiting setting of the Dialing Properties dialog box. The list includes common codes for shutting off call waiting before making an outbound call.

After all your settings are in place, the sequence of numbers appears at the bottom of the Dialing Properties dialog box for that location. Click OK. Your new location entry appears in the I am dialing from list.

Chapter 9

Going the ISDN Serial Route

··

In This Chapter

▶ Understanding the serial option

▶ Setting up and using the BitSURFR Pro

▶ Setting up and using the 3ComImpactIQ

▶ Exploring other serial ISDN remote-access devices

··

*G*oing the serial route is one of the easiest ways to get up and running with ISDN. All you need is Windows 95 and an available COM port on your PC. The leading serial devices for ISDN are the Motorola BitSURFR Pro and the 3ComImpactIQ.

This chapter takes you on a hands-on tour of setting up and using the BitSURFR Pro and 3ComImpactIQ. You also look at other serial ISDN products.

ISDN via the PC Serial Port

External, serial-based ISDN remote-access devices are stand-alone units that look like modems. They are commonly referred to as *digital modems* or *ISDN modems*. These are marketing terms that make the idea of connecting your PC to ISDN appear like connecting your PC to a modem.

A serial ISDN device typically includes its own power supply and connects to your PC's serial port using a standard RS-232 cable. An advantage of stand-alone ISDN serial devices is that you can connect them to a PC or Macintosh serial port.

Setting up and using serial ISDN modems is typically easier than setting up and operating other ISDN remote-access devices. It's a lot easier to work with ISDN serial devices in Windows 95 than in Windows 3.1 and Windows for Workgroups 3.11, which support serial data rates up to only 19,200 bps. Windows 95 supports up to 921,600 bps.

To take advantage of data rates higher than 115,200 bps, you need a high-speed COM port card. The 115,200 bps limitation is due to the 16550A UART (universal asynchronous receiver/transmitter) chip used in most PCs today. UART chips are the part of the PC's COM port that handles communications between the CPU and any device connected to the COM port.

The major disadvantage of serial ISDN modems is the reduced data communications speed due to their reliance on the asynchronous form of serial communications. PCs can use two forms of serial communications: asynchronous and synchronous. ISDN can support both. Asynchronous communications uses a start bit and a stop bit to define each chunk of 8-bit data being sent, which reduces the amount of data actually transferred by 20 percent. Although asynchronous communications can transfer data at speeds of up to 115.2 Kbps via ISDN, or 57.6 Kbps for each B channel, the extra start and stop bits result in a true data transfer rate of about 92 Kbps for both B channels.

The new generation of faster COM port cards is being incorporated into PCs. As these faster COM ports become available, ISDN serial devices will reach the full 128 Kbps speeds of other ISDN remote-access devices. PCs with built-in COM ports on the motherboard usually allow you to swap out the UART chip. If your PC is using the 16550 UART in a COM port card, you can swap out the card for a high-speed serial card, such as the Lava Link-650 card, which supports up to 460.8 Kbps. For more information on the Lava Link-650, see Appendix B.

The price of external serial ISDN devices ranges from $399 to $699. I've already mentioned the Motorola BitSURFR Pro and 3ComImpactIQ. Following is a list of other serial ISDN devices:

✔ Farallon's Netopia ISDN modem, which is being upgraded as I write this book. The older Netopia is actually the same hardware as the older 3ComImpact. The new version of the Netopia ISDN modem will include all the features of the 3ComImpactIQ as well as some other features.

✔ The U.S. Robotics External Courier I-Modem combines ISDN serial-based access with a V.34 analog fax modem. The I-Modem is easy to install and configure, and the latest version of the product supports PPP/MP. It includes a solid collection of features that makes it a good option if you want a combined V.34 fax/modem with an ISDN serial modem.

✔ The ADTRAN Express XR and Express XRT ISDN modems are the same devices, except the XRT includes two POTS ports. ADTRAN is a supplier of ISDN telecommunications equipment to telephone companies.

For more information on serial-based ISDN CPE vendors, see Appendix B.

Surfing with the BitSURFR Pro

The Motorola BitSURFR Pro, at $399, is an affordably priced serial-based ISDN modem. It connects to your PC by way of a RS-232 cable to a serial port. Thanks to a new installation and configuration utility, the BitSURFR Pro is easy to set up. Motorola BitSURFR Pro has the following features:

- ✔ ISDN SURFR Set for Windows installation and configuration program
- ✔ Built-in NT1
- ✔ Two standard RJ-11 jacks to add analog telephones, faxes, or modems
- ✔ Asynchronous data transfer rates of up to 115.2 Kbps
- ✔ Caller ID delivery, call waiting, conference calling, and security features for telephone service
- ✔ Full ringing support to inform you of incoming calls
- ✔ V.120 rate adaption for asychronous to synchronous communications
- ✔ PPP and PPP/MP support
- ✔ Dynamic bandwidth allocation for dropping one data channel to handle a phone call, and then re-establishing the two-data channel connection after the phone call is completed

One negative aspect of the BitSURFR Pro is that the installation program does not include an uninstall program.

The BitSURFR Pro comes with a copy of Internet Chameleon, the leading third-party TCP/IP package from NetManage. To use it, however, you must pay a licensing fee. You don't need to use Chameleon because Windows 95 includes dial-up networking for making Internet and other network connections.

The BitSURFR also comes with TurboCom/2, which allows Windows 3.1 and Windows for Workgroups to work with serial port speeds higher than 19,200 bps. You don't need to use this software for Windows 95.

Familiarizing yourself with the BitSURFR Pro

The BitSURFR Pro looks like a stand-alone modem, as you can see in Figure 9-1. Figure 9-2 shows the back panel of the BitSURFR Pro.

Figure 9-1:
The
BitSURFR
Pro looks
like a stand-
alone
modem.

Photo courtesy of Motorola.

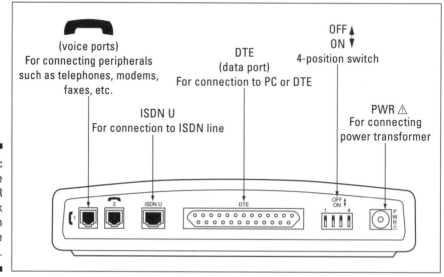

(voice ports)
For connecting peripherals
such as telephones, modems,
faxes, etc.

ISDN U
For connection to ISDN line

DTE
(data port)
For connection to PC or DTE

OFF ▲
ON ▼
4-position switch

PWR ⚠
For connecting
power transformer

Figure 9-2:
The
BitSURFR
Pro back
panel with
available
ports.

Table 9-1 explains the function of the LEDs on the front panel of the BitSURFR Pro. Table 9-2 describes the ports on the back panel of the BitSURFR Pro.

Table 9-1	LED Status Display
LED	*Description*
LS	ISDN Link Status. Red when power is applied; green (not flashing) when all ports are synchronized.
Voice Ports 1 and 2	Call Status. Off when no voice call is in progress. Flashes while a call is being connected. On (not flashing) when the call is connected.
DTE	Data Port Call Status. Off when no data call is in progress. Flashes while a call is being connected. On (not flashing) when the call is connected.
RD	Receive Data. Flashes when the DTE is receiving data.
TD	Transmit Data. Flashes when the DTE is sending data.

Table 9-2	The BitSURFR Pro Ports and Other Back Panel Settings
Port/Setting	*Description*
Analog RJ-11 ports	For connecting a telephone, a fax, and a modem.
ISDN U	For connecting an ISDN line (U interface) using an RJ-45 jack.
DTE	For RS-232 cable to connect the BitSURFR Pro to the PC serial (COM) port.
Power connector	For connecting a power transformer to the BitSURFR Pro.

Before you install the BitSURFR Pro

Before you install the BitSURFR Pro, make sure that your ISDN line is installed and configured for the BitSURFR Pro. You need the following information:

- ✔ One or two DNs *(directory numbers)*
- ✔ One or two SPIDs *(service profile identifiers)*
- ✔ Switch type and software
- ✔ Bearer channel service type (voice/data or data)
- ✔ A 16550 UART serial COM port in your PC

Because the Motorola BitSURFR is so widely used, most telephone companies that offer ISDN service have worked with it. You can tell the telephone company that you're using a Motorola BitSURFR Pro, and it will typically know the correct line configuration. You can also specify the correct configuration for the BitSURFR Pro by requesting the Capability P or S ISDN ordering codes, or Motorola Access 3 when you order your ISDN line. The Motorola BitSURFR Pro package includes handy sheets to fill out for configuring your ISDN service.

If you have any questions about ISDN line ordering or configuration for the BitSURFR Pro, you can call Motorola's ISDN LifeGUARD service at 800-894-ISDN (4736). Folks at this number can help you get the right ISDN service. Don't confuse this service with specific technical support for the BitSURFR Pro, which is a different service group.

Motorola's Information Systems Group offers a toll-free, call-back help desk for the BitSURFR Pro. You call the center at 800-221-4380, and give the operator your name, telephone number, and a brief description of the problem. You are assigned a case number. A Motorola technician then calls you back. It's not instant gratification, but usually someone calls back the same day. Motorola also maintains a support Web site at

```
http:www.mot.com/MIMS/ISG/
```

Connecting the BitSURFR Pro

The following steps explain how to connect the BitSURFR Pro to your ISDN line and PC, as well as how to connect any analog devices to the two RJ-11 ports. Make sure that you have a serial cable because the BitSURFR Pro doesn't come with one.

Before connecting the BitSURFR Pro, you must install TCP/IP and dial-up networking in Windows 95. See Chapter 7 for more information on setting up these facilities, if necessary.

1. **Connect one end of your serial cable to the BitSURFR Pro port labeled DTE Port. Connect the other end to the appropriate COM port on your PC.**

2. **Make sure that all positions of the 4-position switch on the rear of the BitSURFR Pro are off (up position).**

   This is the factory setting.

3. **Connect any analog device such as a telephone, a modem, or a fax to each RJ-11 jack labeled with a telephone handset.**

4. **Plug one end of the power cord into the BitSURFR Pro jack labeled PWR, and plug the other into a surge-protected outlet.**

   Within 20 seconds, the LS LED should come on and remain red and unblinking.

5. **Connect the RJ-11 connector into your ISDN wall jack. Connect the other end (RJ-45 jack) to the ISDN U port at the back of the BitSURFR Pro.**

   If the wall jack is an RJ-45 rather than an RJ-11, don't worry — the RJ-11 connector will snap in.

ISDN SURFR Setup for Windows

You use the ISDN SURFR Setup for Windows program to configure Windows to work with the BitSURFR Pro and to configure the BitSURFR Pro to work with your ISDN line. ISDN SURFR Setup for Windows supersedes the older Configuration Manager program and documentation that may be included in your package.

Disregard the *Getting Started* guide if it doesn't include specific instructions for the ISDN SURFR Setup program. If the unit has the old guide, it includes an insert with instructions for the ISDN SURFR Setup program.

ISDN SURFR Setup works with Windows 3.1, Windows for Workgroups 3.11, Windows 95, and Windows NT 3.51(x86). While I was writing this book, the BitSURFR Pro did not include drivers to work with Windows NT 4.0.

Installing ISDN SURFR Setup

The following steps explain how to install the ISDN SURFR Setup for Windows program on your PC. After you install the setup program, you use it to configure the BitSURFR Pro for your ISDN line from your PC.

The BitSURFR Pro includes a disk labeled Configuration Manager. Do not use this to install your BitSURFR Pro. Use only the ISDN SURFR Setup disks.

1. **Make sure that the serial cable and ISDN line are connected to the BitSURFR Pro and that the power adapter is plugged into a power outlet.**

2. **Insert Disk 1 of the ISDN SURFR Setup into your PC's floppy disk drive.**

3. **Choose RUN from the Start menu, type the command** A:\SETUP, **and click OK.**

4. **Follow the instructions presented on the screen to complete the installation of ISDN SURFR Setup for Windows.**

   After the installation is complete, the ISDN SURFR Setup folder appears with three icons in it, as shown in Figure 9-3.

Figure 9-3:
The ISDN
SURFR
Setup folder
includes the
ISDN SURFR
Setup,
SURFR
Setup Help,
and Read
Me icons.

Figure 9-3:
The ISDN
SURFR
Setup folder
includes the
ISDN SURFR
Setup,
SURFR
Setup Help,
and Read
Me icons.

Configuring the BitSURFR Pro

After you install the ISDN SURFR Setup program and you have your ISDN line information, you're ready to configure the BitSURFR Pro. The configuration program writes your configuration information to the BitSURFR Pro.

1. Double-click the ISDN SURFR icon in the ISDN SURFR Setup folder.

When ISDN SURFR Setup runs for the first time, it looks to see whether your BitSURFR is connected to one of your COM ports. After ISDN SURFR Setup finds your BitSURFR, it checks the configuration data stored in the unit. If ISDN SURFR Setup finds any missing configuration data, which is the case when you first start it, the setup program displays the Configure dialog box, as shown in Figure 9-4.

Figure 9-4:
The
Configure
dialog box is
where you
configure
the
BitSURFR
Pro for
working
with your
ISDN line.

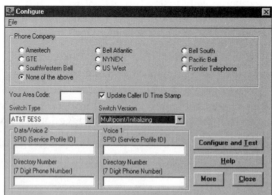

2. In the Phone Company area, select the telephone company that is providing your ISDN service.

ISDN SURFR Setup uses this information to match the BitSURFR Pro to your telephone company's services.

3. **In the Your Area Code box, type your area code.**

   This information is used to make additional entries.

4. **If you're using the Caller ID service with your analog phone attached to the BitSURFR Pro, make sure that the Update Caller ID Time Stamp option is checked.**

   This will set the Caller ID clock, which the BitSURFR Pro uses to tell you what time a call came in on the Caller ID equipment.

5. **In the Switch Type list, select the switch type provided by your phone company.**

   (Switch types represent the kind of software the phone company uses for your ISDN line.)

6. **If the telephone company provided you with a switch version type (for the version of software the phone company is using for your ISDN line), enter that information in the Switch Version box. If you weren't given a switch version, just leave the value that was displayed after you selected your switch type.**

7. **Type the first of the two SPID values that the phone company gave you in the SPID text boxes. Enter the SPID for the B channel that is configured for data and voice in the Data/Voice2 group.**

   The SPID usually looks like a ten-digit phone number with some extra digits at the beginning or end (for example, 61764346880000).

8. **Enter the second SPID for your second B channel in the Voice 1 group, even if you don't have it configured for voice.**

   ISDN SURFR Setup attempts to determine the directory number *(DN)* from the SPID value you just entered.

9. **If the phone company provided you with a DN that is different from what appears in the Directory Number box, type the number the phone company gave you.**

   The DN usually appears as a seven-digit phone number, but this may vary depending on your ISDN service provider.

10. **If ISDN SURFR Setup was unable to determine the appropriate DN, the Directory Number field will be blank; enter the number provided by your phone company.**

11. **In the Voice 1 area, repeat steps 7 to 10 for the second SPID value and DN.**

12. **Click the More button to specify further details if needed.**

    The options presented when you click More typically should not be changed except in special circumstances. Leave these settings as displayed unless your phone company gives you specific instructions otherwise. The More button toggles to the Less button when the expanded dialog box appears.

13. **With your ISDN line connected to the BitSURFR, click the Configure and Test button in the Configure dialog box.**

ISDN SURFR Setup transmits the configuration information to your BitSURFR and then monitors the BitSURFR's progress. After a few moments (up to two minutes), you will see the message

```
Your BitSURFR appears to be properly configured. Your
BitSURFR is ready for use.
```

If ISDN SURFR Setup determined that there is a problem with the configuration, a message informing you of this will be shown and you will have the option to run the Diagnose function. Press Yes to display a listing of possible errors. You should open the Configure dialog box (see Figure 9-4) and correct these errors. The Configure window may have certain fields highlighted in yellow to show which item is most likely causing a problem. Check the displayed information against that provided by your phone company. Correct any errors and then click Configure and Test to update the BitSURFR Pro with the correct information.

ISDN SURFR Setup program features

BitSURFR Pro Setup includes a collection of other features for managing your ISDN connection. The following describes the functions of each button at the top of the ISDN SURFR Setup window:

✔ The Configure button displays the Configure dialog box, which you used to set up the BitSURFR Pro. You can make changes at any time to your configuration using the Configure window.

✔ The Diagnose button displays the Diagnose dialog box, which automatically checks to make sure that your ISDN line is working properly. If any errors are found, they are displayed at the bottom of the dialog box (Figure 9-5).

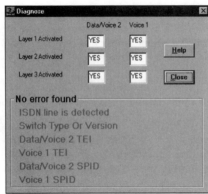

Figure 9-5:
The Diagnose dialog box checks your ISDN line to make sure that it is working properly.

✔ The Phone Monitor button lets you check the status of your voice ports. Clicking the Phone Monitor button displays the Analog Phone Port Monitor dialog box (Figure 9-6). Information is displayed in a window as you make and receive voice calls. Make sure that you are using the same voice port as that selected at the bottom of the window. The Analog Phone Port Monitor dialog box also includes a telephone dialer feature for making and receiving calls from your PC.

Figure 9-6:
The Analog
Phone Port
Monitor
dialog box
lets you test
and manage
the analog
equipment
connected
to the
BitSURFR
Pro.

✔ The Terminal button displays a standard terminal window that enables you to manually enter AT commands. This can be a handy feature if you're troubleshooting a connection between your PC and a host computer.

✔ The COM Port button enables you to change the PC COM port that your BitSURFR is connected to. This is useful when you use a different COM port than the one originally chosen.

✔ The Help button gives you information about using ISDN SURFR Setup as well as some helpful information about ISDN.

✔ The About button provides information regarding which version of ISDN SURFR Setup you are using as well as the firmware version of your BitSURFR Pro.

✔ The Exit button is used to close the ISDN SURFR Setup utility.

Setting up Windows 95 for the BitSURFR Pro

Before you can set up Windows 95 to work with the BitSURFR Pro, make sure that you have the Windows 95 TCP/IP dial-up adapter and Dial-Up Networking installed, as I explain in Chapter 7. Also have Disk 1 of the ISDN SURFR Setup program handy to install INF files for your BitSURFR Pro. The INF files are used when you install the BitSURFR Pro as a modem in Windows 95.

You also need the following information from your Internet service provider to set up Windows Dial-Up Networking.

- An IP address for your PC, if your ISP is using a static IP address. If your ISP uses dynamic IP addressing, an IP address is assigned each time you log on.
- IP addresses for the domain name system servers. Typically two are provided.
- Your username and password. Your username is also called the hostname.
- The domain name of your ISP (for example, zipnet.net).

The following steps explain how to install the BitSURFR Pro as a modem in Windows 95, and then how to set up the Windows 95 Dial-Up Networking to make a connection.

You can set up the BitSURFR Pro also using the Internet Setup Wizard, as I explain in Chapter 7.

1. **Double-click the Modems icon in the Control Panel.**

   The Modems Properties dialog box appears.

2. **Click the Add button.**

   The Install New Modem Wizard appears.

3. **Select the box labeled Don't detect my modem; I'll select it from a list.**

4. **Click Next.**

   The page containing lists of modem manufacturers and models appears.

5. **Click the Have Disk button.**

   A dialog box appears prompting you for the disk.

6. **Insert Disk 1 of the ISDN SURFR Setup program in your floppy drive and then click OK.**

7. **Select the Motorola BitSURFR Pro driver and then click Next.**

A page appears for specifying the communications port that your BitSURFR Pro is connected to.

8. **Select the communications port and then click Next.**

9. **If this is the first time that you've added a communications device to Windows 95, Location Information is displayed for entering the area code that you're calling from and any prefix you may use to call out. Type the information and then click Next.**

10. **Click Finish when the final wizard page appears.**

You're returned to the Modems Properties dialog box, and the Motorola BitSURFR Pro is added to the list of modems installed on your PC.

11. **Open the My Computer icon on the desktop, double-click Dial Up Networking, and then double-click Make New Connection.**

The Make New Connection Wizard appears.

12. **Click Next to begin.**

13. **Type a name to identify your connection, for example,** BitSURFR Pro **or** ISDN Internet.

14. **Make sure that the BitSURFR Pro name appears in the Select a modem setting; then click Next.**

A page appears for entering the telephone number of your Internet service provider's host computer.

15. **Type the area code and telephone number.**

(Type the area code even if you don't use it.) The default country code is the United States of America (1).

16. **Click Next, and then click Finish.**

In the Dial-Up Networking folder, you see a new icon with the name you entered for your connection.

17. **Right-click the BitSURFR Pro connection icon in the Dial-Up Networking folder.**

A menu appears.

18. **Select the Properties item.**

The Properties dialog box (Figure 9-7) appears.

19. **Make sure that the BitSURFR Pro appears in the Connect using list; then click the Configure button.**

20. **Select 115,200 bps from the Maximum speed list; then click OK.**

21. **Click the Server Type button.**

The Server Types dialog box (Figure 9-8) appears.

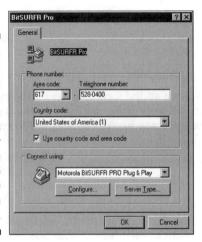

Figure 9-7:
The
BitSURFR
Pro
Properties
dialog box is
your
gateway to
setting up
the
connection
profile.

22. **Make sure that PPP, Windows 95, Windows NT 3.5, Internet is selected, and check only TCP/IP in the Allowed network protocols area.**

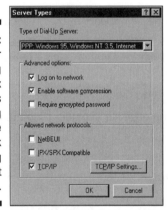

Figure 9-8:
The Server
Types dialog
box
specifies
the setting
for the
network
you're going
to connect
to.

23. **Click the TCP/IP Settings button.**

    The TCP/IP Settings dialog box (Figure 9-9) appears.

24. **If your service provider has assigned you a specific IP address, select the Specify an IP address option, and then type the IP address. In addition, select the Specify name server addresses option; then type the IP addresses supplied by your ISP in the Primary DNS and Secondary DNS boxes.**

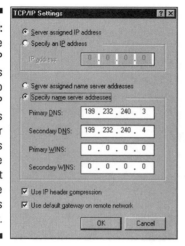

Figure 9-9:
Use the
TCP/IP
Settings
dialog box to
specify IP
addresses
for your
computer as
well as the
Internet
service
provider's
host.

25. **If your service provider uses dynamic IP addressing, select the Server assigned IP address option. In addition, select the Server assigned name server addresses option.**

26. **Click OK three times.**

You've completed the configuration of the dial-up networking profile. Now you're ready to make a connection to the Internet.

Making the connection with the BitSURFR Pro

After you create a dial-up networking connection profile, you can make a connection. Here's how to make a connection using the BitSURFR Pro connection profile you created in the preceding section:

1. **Double-click the My Computer icon on the desktop.**

2. **Double-click the Dial-Up Networking icon.**

   The Connect To dialog box (Figure 9-10) appears.

3. **Double-click the connection profile name you created for the BitSURFR.**

4. **The first time you use the Dial-Up Networking connection, you must enter your username (also known as your hostname), your password, and the telephone number for your Internet service provider.**

5. **Select the Save password check box so that you don't have to enter your password every time.**

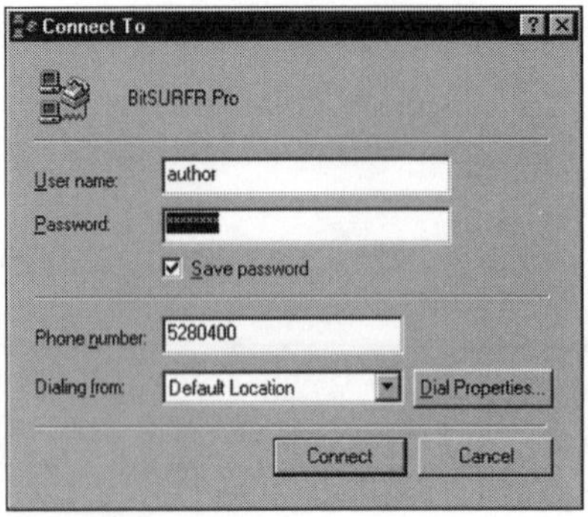

Figure 9-10:
The Connect
To dialog
box is ready
for you to
make your
connection.

6. **Click the Connect button to make your connection.**

   Status dialog boxes appear to indicate dialing, to verify the username and
   password, and to display

   ```
   Connected
   ```

7. **Minimize the Connected To window to the taskbar.**

   You're ready to use a Web browser or other Internet tools.

Smooth Sailing with the 3ComImpactIQ

The 3ComImpactIQ is the latest incarnation of the popular 3ComImpact ISDN
modem. At a street price of $350, the IQ includes an impressive collection of
features, including

- An easy-to-use setup Wizard that automatically detects your telephone
  company switch type and configures the SPIDs

- Multilink PPP support

- Toll-saving data over voice support, which allows you to initiate a 56 Kbps
  call as a POTS call so that you don't pay the higher ISDN rate. This option
  is useful only in areas where telephone companies offer standard POTS
  charges for voice calls over ISDN lines.

- Compression support for the PPP Compression Control Protocol and PPP
  Stacker LZS Compression Protocol

- PAP and CHAP security support

✔ Two analog (RJ-11) ports

✔ Dynamic bandwidth allocation

✔ Flash memory for easy firmware updates

You can order your ISDN service through 3Com by calling 800-572-3Com.

Installing the IQ

As with other ISDN devices, to configure the IQ you need to have the ISDN switch type, directory numbers, and any SPID numbers for your ISDN line. Then follow these steps:

1. **Connect one end of the serial cable to the RS-232 port on the IQ (25-pin connector) and the other end to your PC (9-pin connector).**

2. **Connect your ISDN line to the ISDN U port (RJ-45) on the IQ.**

3. **Connect any analog devices to the RJ-11 ports on the IQ.**

4. **Connect the power cable.**

5. **Insert the 3ComImpactIQ Windows & DOS Installation Diagnostic Utilities disk in your floppy drive.**

6. **Choose Start⇨Run, type** A:\setup, **and click OK.**

   After the configuration program is copied to your hard drive, the readme file opens.

7. **Review the information in the readme file and then close the file.**

   The software is installed.

8. **Double-click the 3ComImpactIQ icon in the 3ComImpactIQ window.**

   The Wizard starts and then displays a dialog box for entering your first telephone number.

9. **Type your first ISDN directory number and then click Next.**

   The Wizard verifies the number and the SPID and displays the dialog box for the second directory number.

10. **Type the directory number and then click Next.**

    The Wizard verifies the number and SPID, and the Finish dialog box appears.

11. **Click Finish.**

    The User registration window appears.

12. **Click Skip Registration (stop reminding) for now.**

   A message appears telling you that the IQ is correctly configured.

13. **Click OK.**

   The Wizard closes.

You're now ready to set up Windows 95 for the IQ.

Setting up Windows 95 for the IQ

Before you start, make sure that the TCP/IP dialup adapter and Dial-Up Networking are installed, as I explain in Chapter 7. Also have the 3ComImpactIQ Windows & DOS Installation Diagnostic Utilities disk handy to install INF files for your 3ComImpactIQ.

You also need the following information from your Internet service provider to set up Windows Dial-Up Networking:

✔ An IP address for your PC, if your ISP is using a static IP address. If your ISP uses dynamic IP addressing, an IP address is assigned every time you log on.

✔ IP addresses for the domain name system servers. Typically two are provided.

✔ Your username and password. Your username is also called your hostname.

✔ The domain name of your ISP (for example, zipnet.net).

The following steps explain how to install the 3ComImpactIQ in Windows 95:

1. **Reboot your PC with the IQ modem powered up and connected to your PC.**

   The New Hardware dialog box appears.

2. **Click the Select the Driver from disk provided by hardware manufacturer option; then click OK.**

   The Install From Disk dialog box appears.

3. **Insert the 3ComImpactIQ Windows & DOS Installation Diagnostic Utilities disk in your floppy drive and then click OK.**

   The Select Device dialog box appears.

4. **With the 3ComImpactIQ device selected, click OK.**

   The 3ComImpactIQ driver is installed and automatically appears in the Modem Properties dialog box.

5. **Double-click the My Computer icon on the desktop, double-click Dial-Up Networking, and then double-click Make New Connection.**

   The Make New Connection Wizard appears.

6. **Click Next to begin.**

7. **Type a name to identify your connection (for example, 3ComImpactIQ or ISDN Internet).**

8. **Make sure that the 3ComImpactIQ name appears in the list titled Select a modem setting; then click Next.**

   A page appears for entering the telephone number of your Internet service provider's host computer.

9. **Type the area code (even if you don't use it) and telephone number.**

   The default country code is the United States of America (1).

10. **Click Next and then click Finish.**

    In the Dial-Up Networking folder, you see a new icon with the name you entered for your connection.

11. **Right-click the 3ComImpactIQ connection icon in the Dial-Up Networking folder.**

    A menu appears.

12. **Select the Properties item.**

    The Properties dialog box appears.

13. **Make sure that the 3ComImpactIQ appears in the Connect using list; then click the Configure button.**

14. **In the Maximum speed list, select 115,200 bps; then click OK.**

15. **Click the Server Type button.**

    The Server Types dialog box appears.

16. **Make sure that PPP, Windows 95, Windows NT 3.5, Internet is selected from the Type of Dial-Up Server list. Also make sure that only TCP/IP is checked in the Allowed network protocols area.**

17. **Click the TCP/IP Settings button.**

    The TCP/IP Settings dialog box appears (refer back to Figure 9-9).

18. **If your service provider has assigned you a specific IP address, select the Specify an IP address option; then type the IP address. In addition, select the Specify name server addresses option; then type the IP addresses supplied by your ISP in the Primary DNS and Secondary DNS boxes.**

19. **If your service provider uses dynamic IP addressing, select the Server assigned IP address option. In addition, select the Server assigned name server addresses option.**

20. **Click OK three times.**

You've completed the configuration of the Dial-Up Networking profile. Now you're ready to make a connection to the Internet.

Making the connection with the IQ

After you create a Dial-Up Networking connection profile, you can make a connection. Here's how to make a connection using the 3ComImpactIQ Pro connection profile you created in the preceding section:

1. **Double-click the My Computer icon on the desktop.**

2. **Double-click the Dial-Up Networking icon.**

   The Connect To dialog box appears.

3. **Double-click the connection profile name you created for the 3ComImpactIQ.**

4. **The first time you use the Dial-Up Networking connection, you must enter your username (also known as your hostname), your password, and the telephone number for your Internet service provider.**

5. **Select the Save password check box so that you don't have to enter the password every time.**

6. **Click the Connect button to make your connection.**

   Status dialog boxes appear to indicate dialing, to verifying the user name and password, and to display

   ```
   Connected
   ```

7. **Minimize the Connected To window to the taskbar.**

   You're ready to use a Web browser or other Internet tools.

The 3ComImpactIQ configuration window

The 3ComImpactIQ configuration window (Figure 9-11) enables you to make changes to your IQ settings. Choose Start⇨Programs⇨3ComImpactIQ⇨ 3ComImpactIQ to open the window. The Tools button at the bottom of the window displays a button bar that includes buttons for updating the IQ's firmware and running diagnostics on your ISDN line. To exit the 3ComImpactIQ configuration window, click the Exit button.

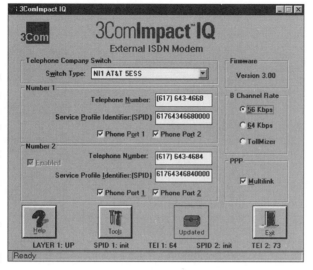

Figure 9-11:
The
3ComImpactIQ
configuration
dialog box
provides all
the settings
for configuring
and testing
your
3ComImpactIQ.

Chapter 10
Playing with ISDN Adapter Cards

● ●

In This Chapter

▶ Installing and using the U.S. Robotics Sportster ISDN 128K adapter card

▶ Installing and using Diamond Multimedia's Supra NetCommander

▶ Taking a look at other ISDN adapter cards

● ●

*T*his chapter covers working with the two leading ISDN adapter cards: the U.S. Robotics Sportster ISDN 128K and Diamond Multimedia's Supra NetCommander. Thanks to Microsoft's Plug and Play, adding adapter cards to your PC is relatively painless compared to installing them in Windows 3.1 or Windows for Workgroups.

ISDN Is in the Cards

ISDN adapter cards fit into an ISA slot in your PC. Because these adapter cards use your PC bus to communicate with ISDN, they deliver data faster than serial devices. Typically, these cards come in both U-interface and S/T-interface models and include an RJ-11 port for connecting a telephone, a modem, or a fax. Most of these products come with easy-to-install programs.

ISDN is fast, except when compared to PC buses — so you don't need to worry about which bus card to get. ISA (*Industry Standard Architecture*) is the current standard supported by most ISDN adapter cards. PCI (*Peripheral Component Interconnect*) offers the most potential for future ISDN adapter cards. At the time I write this, ISDN PCMCIA (*Personal Computer Memory Card International Association*) cards (for laptops) are not available, although a number of vendors, including Xircom, are planning to come out with them.

Windows 95 has improved the process of installing and working with adapter cards. Windows 95's Plug-and-Play feature simplifies installation by automatically avoiding conflicts with other devices connected to your PC. (There's more on this feature in Chapter 7.) Windows 95 handles an ISDN adapter card as a network adapter card because most ISDN adapter cards use an NDIS driver.

The ISDN adapter card market

The price of ISDN adapter cards ranges from $169 to $695. The leading ISDN PC adapter cards are the U.S. Robotics Sportster ISDN 128 Kbps and Diamond Multimedia's NetCommander ISDN. Here are some other vendors that offer ISDN adapter cards:

- ✔ Alpha Telecom's CyberJet ISDN adapter card, in S/T-interface and U-interface models
- ✔ Eicon Technology's DIVA for Windows 95
- ✔ The Motorola BitSURFR Pro ISA for ISDN
- ✔ Cardinal Technologies ISDN Internal Basic Rate ISA Adapter
- ✔ ISDN*tek's Cyberspace Internet+Card

ISDN adapter cards for laptops

At the time I write this book, a few vendors are in the process of releasing PCMCIA ISDN adapter cards for nomadic laptop users. The two PCMCIA ISDN adapters are the I-Bahn from Angia Communications and the DIVA PCM from Eicon Technologies. These cards will cost $495 to $695.

The PCMCIA bus uses credit card-sized cards that connect to external slots on a laptop. Windows 95's Plug and Play makes working with PCMCIA cards easy; Windows 95 automatically changes configurations to match the plugged-in PCMCIA card. Additionally, Dial-Up Networking in Windows 95 allows you to create multiple dialing profiles for connecting to a host. This means that you can quickly connect to a host computer from any location.

For more information on ISDN ISA and PCMCIA adapter card vendors, see Appendix B.

Cruising with the Sportster ISDN 128K

The U.S. Robotics Sportster ISDN 128K, with a price around $399, delivers a smooth ISDN ride. It uses your PC's bus to communicate with ISDN; as a result, data moves faster than with an ISDN serial device.

The Sportster ISDN uses Turbo PPP software to get around the Microsoft ISDN Accelerator Pack's current limitation for internal cards, so you get the full 128 Kbps speed. The Sportster ISDN card supports both Windows 95 Dial-Up Networking and WinISDN applications, such as NetManage Chameleon.

The Sportster ISDN 128K is available with built-in NT1 (U interface) or without (S/T interface). Both products include a single RJ-11 port to connect a telephone, a fax, or a modem to your ISDN line. The Sportster supports dynamic bandwidth allocation, which allows data to be retrieved while you talk on the phone or send a fax. When someone calls you, the Sportster speaker rings instead of the phone itself. This means you won't be able to receive a fax unless you get the $95 external ring generator to give you full ringing support.

You can also get a backup NT1 power supply kit ($18) to keep power to the NT1 when your PC is turned off. This is required if you plan to connect a telephone or a fax machine to the line and make it available all the time. As you may recall, an ISDN line does not have any power; the user must power the line. Combining the backup NT1 power supply kit with the external ring generator enables you to hook up a telephone and fax to receive and make calls even if your PC is turned off.

Getting help from the U.S. Robotics I-Team

The I-Team is a part of the U.S. Robotics Customer Support department that provides free help with the ISDN ordering and configuring process. The I-Team can help you determine the availability and pricing of ISDN service in your location, installation costs, and lead time for installation. The I-Team coordinates the configuration of the telephone company's switches so that your adapter works properly. You can contact the I-Team by any of the following methods:

World Wide Web	http://www.usr.com/Courier/iteam.html
Fax on Demand	800-762-6163
Voice	888-USR-ISDN (888-877-4736)

Check out the U.S. Robotics Web page for any new drivers for the Sportster ISDN 128K. Drivers are usually placed at the site for free downloading.

Ordering ISDN service for the Sportster

Before you can set up the Sportster, you must make sure that your ISDN service requirements are in place. To configure your ISDN correctly, you need to give some information to your telephone company as well as get some information from your telephone company. The following sections explain what information you need to exchange.

If you would like assistance with the ordering process, call the U.S. Robotics I-Team at 888-877-4736 before you call the telephone company.

What to tell your telephone company

You can use two ordering codes for provisioning your ISDN service to match the Sportster. The first is Intel Blue. If your telephone company doesn't recognize the Intel Blue ordering code, request Capability Package M, which has configuration characteristics nearly identical to Intel Blue. Either package will provide 128 Kbps transmission potential, enabling you to take full advantage of your Sportster adapter's PPP/MP as well as voice communications.

If your telephone company doesn't recognize the Bellcore Compatibility Package M or Intel Blue service package, request the following specific ISDN services:

- ISDN BRI service
- Two B channels: one with circuit-switched voice and data (CSV/D) call types and the other with circuit-switched data call type
- No packet mode (X.25) data on the B or D channel
- No EKTS or CACH EKTS service
- Terminal type A
- Dynamic TEI assignments
- Low- and high-layer compatibility information transfer ON
- Called and calling party subaddress information ON
- Idle call appearance
- No additional call appearances
- No flexible calling features or buttons for voice, such as automatic callback, call forwarding, hold, conferencing, pickup, CNI, Caller ID, Multiline hunt groups, or voice mail
- 2B1Q line coding
- Multipoint attachment
- RJ45/RJ61X or RJ11 connector

What to get from the telephone company

Make sure that your local telephone company provides you with the following information:

- The type of switch your ISDN line will terminate at, and which protocol will be controlling your calls.
- The directory numbers. If the line is provisioned for voice and data, there may be a separate number for the B channel that carries voice.
- The *service profile identifiers* (SPIDs). Not all phone companies use SPIDs. If yours does, there should be one SPID for each phone number.

Installing the ISDN Sportster card

After your ISDN line provisioning is completed, you're ready to install the Sportster. The following steps explain how to install the ISDN Sportster adapter card into an ISA slot in your PC:

1. **Turn off and unplug your computer, remove the cover, and remove the metal bracket covering an unused 16-bit expansion slot.**

2. **Check the (JP1 and JP2) jumpers on the adapter card located near the middle of the top edge of the board.**

   Each shunt should cover only one prong of each pin. These jumper settings allow software to automatically set the I/O base address and IRQ values for the card.

3. **If you are using an S/T-interface version of Sportster, you also need to check the JP4 and JP5 jumpers, which are located next to the LED.**

   Make sure the shunt on each jumper covers both pins on each jumper.

4. **Insert the Sportster adapter into the expansion slot and fasten the metal retaining bracket with a screw.**

5. **If you have a U-interface adapter, plug one end of the cable in the RJ-45 jack on the adapter and the other end into your RJ-45 ISDN wall jack, which connects to your ISDN line.**

6. **If you have an S/T interface adapter, plug one end of the cable in the RJ-45 jack on the adapter and the other end into the RJ-45 jack on the external NT1 or NT1 Plus device.**

7. **Connect a telephone to the RJ-11 analog port at the back of the Sportster.**

8. **If you are connecting a fax or modem and are using the telephone ring generator, plug it into the analog port on the Sporster first and then plug the fax or modem into the ring generator.**

   Figure 10-1 shows how the ring generator connects.

9. **If you are connecting a fax or modem and are not using the telephone ring generator, connect the analog device directly to the to the RJ-11 analog port at the back of the Sportster.**

10. **Replace the cover and plug your computer back in.**

Setting up Sportster

After you install your adapter card, you're ready to install the Sportster Setup program. Setup installs the Sportster Manager program, prompts you for basic information about your ISDN line configuration and connection, and runs tests to ensure that the adapter and your ISDN line are working.

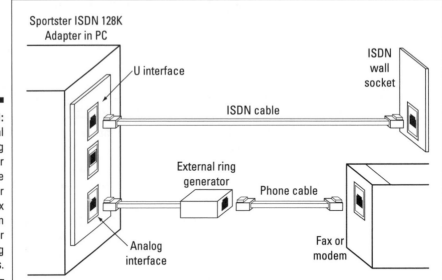

Figure 10-1:
The External
ring
generator
lets you use
a modem or
a fax
machine on
your line for
receiving
calls.

In the following steps, I assume that you've installed Dial-Up Networking and TCP/IP in Windows 95. See Chapter 7 for more information on setting up these facilities, if necessary.

1. **Insert Disk 1 in your floppy disk drive.**

2. **Choose Start⇨Run in Windows 95.**

3. **Type** A:\SETUP **and then click OK.**

   The Sportster ISDN 128K Setup dialog box appears (Figure 10-2).

Figure 10-2:
The
Sportster
ISDN 128K
Setup
Wizard
walks you
through the
installation
and
configuration
process.

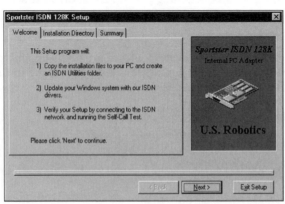

4. Click Next.

The Installation Directory page appears.

5. Specify another drive and directory, if necessary.

6. Click Next.

The Summary page appears.

7. Click the Start Copy button.

The setup program copies files and then displays the Installed Components Configuration Settings dialog box (Figure 10-3).

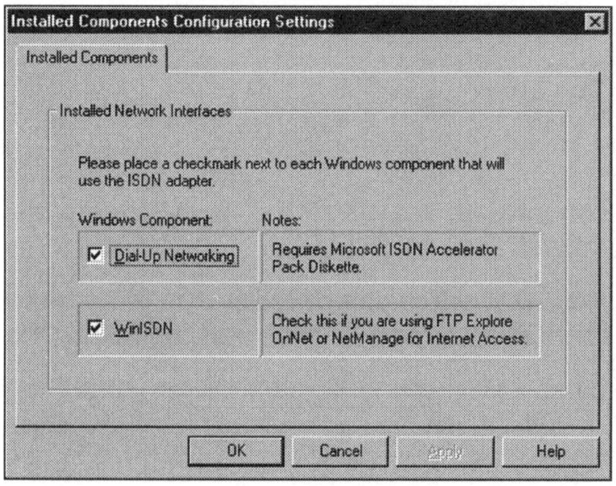

Figure 10-3:
Use the
Installed
Components
Configuration
Settings
dialog box
to specify
the TCP/IP
stack you're
using
with the
Sportster.

**8. If you plan to use Windows 95 Dial-Up Networking, uncheck the WinISDN
setting and make sure that the Dial-Up Networking setting is checked.**

**9. If you are using a third-party TCP/IP program, uncheck Dial-Up Networking
and make sure that the WinISDN setting is checked.**

10. Click OK.

The Setup program displays the Internal Properties dialog box (Figure 10-4),
which shows the IRQ and I/O address range for the Sportster card. If a
conflict exists, an asterisk appears before the setting in the text box.

**11. If there's an asterisk before the setting in the text box, click the arrows
to the right of the setting until a setting appears without an asterisk.**

12. Click OK.

The ISDN Configuration Wizard page appears. This Wizard walks you
through the configuration of the Sportster for your ISDN provisioning.

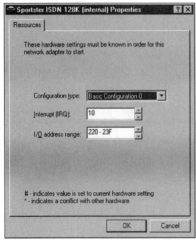

Figure 10-4:
Use the
Internal
Properties
dialog box to
make
hardware
setting
changes if
there is a
clash with
another
adapter in
your PC.

13. **Make sure that you have all your ISDN line-provisioning information handy and then click Next.**

14. **Choose the type of ISDN switch you're connected to at the telephone company from the Switch protocol switch and then click Next.**

    A page appears for entering your ISDN line directory numbers and SPIDs (Figure 10-5).

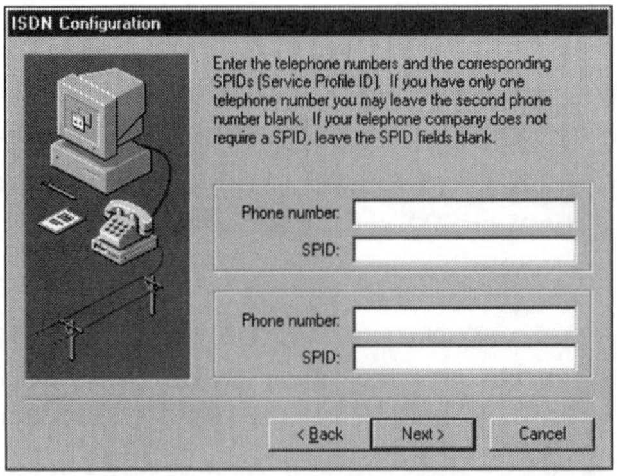

Figure 10-5:
The page for
entering
your ISDN
directory
numbers
and SPIDs.

15. **Type the telephone number (including area code) and SPID for each B channel. If your telephone company didn't assign SPIDs, leave the fields blank.**

16. **Click Next.**

The final Wizard page appears.

17. **Click Finish.**

The Setup program installs the Sportster software, configures Windows 95, and displays a dialog box asking whether you want to install Microsoft Internet Explorer.

If you already have the latest version of Internet Explorer, click No.

If your version of Internet Explorer is older than the current version released with the Sportster

- Click Yes.

- Click Yes again. Internet Explorer is installed, and a License Agreement dialog box appears.

- Click I Agree.

- After Setup installs the Internet Explorer, click OK. A Notepad window appears with release notes.

- Close the Notepad window.

18. **When the dialog box appears prompting you to restart Windows, click Restart Windows.**

After Windows 95 restarts, the Sportster automatically runs a diagnostics of your setup and ISDN line. If your adapter board and ISDN are working properly, the Starting Sportster window looks like the one in Figure 10-6. If any of the tests fails, you can make any necessary configuration changes and restart the adapter software using the Sportster Manager.

Figure 10-6:
The Starting
Sportster
dialog box
showing
that your
adapter
card and
ISDN line
are working
properly.

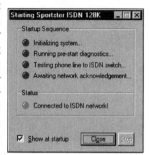

Each time you load the Sportster ISDN drivers, the adapter and line are tested to confirm that they are working. If you don't want to see the diagnostics window at system startup, uncheck the Show at startup check box in the Starting Sportster dialog box. The diagnostics are still performed, but the process happens in the background. (When the diagnostics are being run, the sports car icon next to the clock display on the taskbar appears with an X over it.)

When the Sportster diagnostics program checks your ISDN connection, it checks your ISDN line through to the switch. It is not a billed call because the Sportster dials the number, waits for a ring, and then disconnects.

If you don't want the Sportster Manager and diagnostics program to execute automatically every time you run Windows 95, you must remove them from the StartUp folder, as follows:

1. **Choose Start⇨Settings⇨Taskbar.**

   The Taskbar Properties dialog box appears.

2. **Click the Start Menu Programs tab and then click the Remove button.**

   The Remove Shortcuts/Folders dialog box appears.

3. **Double-click StartUp.**

4. **Select the Sportster ISDN 128K Startup item and then click Remove.**

5. **Click Close and then click OK.**

6. **Restart Windows.**

Working with the Sportster Manager

Before setting up Windows 95 Dial-Up Networking, you should familiarize yourself with the Sportster Manager program that is installed on your Windows 95 PC. To run the Sportster Manager, choose Start⇨Programs⇨USR ISDN Utilities⇨Sportster Manager. The Sportster ISDN 128K Manager window appears (Figure 10-7).

A quick way to display Sportster Manager is to double-click the sports car icon at the far right of the taskbar.

The Sportster Manager includes a collection of menus and buttons. The File menu includes items for displaying the Configuration Settings dialog box (which is also accessible from the toolbar), always displaying the Sportster Manager window on top, and exiting the program. The Tools menu includes items for accessing the System Diagnostics, Call Logger, and Protocol Monitor screens, which are all available from the toolbar. The Advanced item in the Tools menu has commands for disconnecting from and connecting to the ISDN network.

Figure 10-7:
The
Sportster
ISDN 128K
Manager
window
accesses all
the tools
you need to
manage the
Sportster.

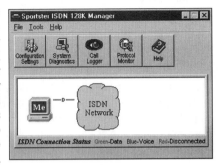

When you're connected to your ISDN line properly, the Sportster Manager window displays the graphic shown in Figure 10-7. The line between Me and the ISDN Network cloud is green, indicating that you're connected as a data call. A blue line indicates a voice connection, and a red line means you're disconnected but ready to make a connection.

Choosing Tools⇨Advanced⇨Disconnect from ISDN Network disconnects you from the ISDN network. When you choose this command, Sportster Manager removes the ISDN drivers from your system. Click Yes to confirm, and the graphic in the Sportster Manager window changes to a large button labeled Connect to ISDN Network, as shown in Figure 10-8. Clicking the button starts the same process as when you start Windows 95 with the Sportster Manager.

Figure 10-8:
When the
Sportster
Manager is
disconnected
from the
ISDN line,
the Connect
to ISDN
Network
button is
displayed.

The following describes the functions of the five buttons on the Sportster Manager button bar:

✔ The Configuration Settings button displays the Configuration Settings dialog box (Figure 10-9). The General tab lets you make changes to the way the Sportster handles calls. The Telephone Company tab contains the settings for your ISDN line, including switch type, telephone numbers, and SPIDs. The Adapter Board tab lets you change the IRQ and I/O addresses for your Sportster adapter card. The Installed Components tab lets you change between using Windows 95 Dial-Up Networking and WinISDN.

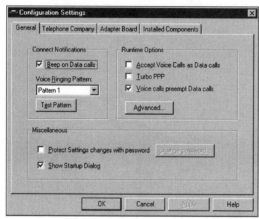

Figure 10-9:
Use the
Configuration
Settings
dialog box to
change the
Sportster's
settings.

✔ The System Diagnostics button displays the System Diagnostics dialog box (Figure 10-10), which has features to check the status of your system, the adapter board, and telephone company settings. The System Integrity and Adapter Board tests are performed automatically when you start Windows 95.

✔ The Call Logger button displays the Call Log window (Figure 10-11). This window shows a log of your connections, which can be useful for tracking down any problems you have making your ISDN connection.

✔ The Protocol Monitor button displays the D Channel Protocol Monitor dialog box. As you may recall, the D channel carries all the signaling for your ISDN line. Checking this dialog box can help you track down any problems you have with your ISDN line provisioning.

✔ The Help button displays the Sportster's online Reference Guide and help system. All the features of the Sportster Manager are described in the online Reference Guide.

Figure 10-10:
The System
Diagnostics
dialog box
lets you
perform
tests on
your adapter
board and
ISDN line to
troubleshoot
any
problems.

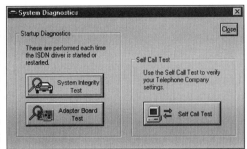

Figure 10-11:
The Call Log
window
keeps a
running log
of your
connection
activities so
that you can
pinpoint the
source of
any
problems.

The Sportster Manager program includes its own un-install program, so you can easily remove it from your PC at any time. This is handy if you encounter a problem during installation and want to start over. To execute the program, choose Start⇨Programs⇨U.S. Robotics ISDN Utilities⇨Un-Install Utility for Sportster ISDN 128K.

Setting up Sportster ISDN for Dial-Up Networking

After you've successfully installed the Sportster ISDN 128K, you're ready to create a Dial-Up Networking connection. Unlike adding an ISDN serial device, you don't add the Sportster ISDN 128K as a modem before creating a Dial-Up Networking connection. Instead, the Sportster ISDN 128K appears as a network adapter. The following steps explain how to set up a Dial-Up Networking connection to connect to an Internet service provider.

You can also use the Internet Setup Wizard to create a Dial-Up Networking connection by choosing Start➪Programs➪Accessories➪Internet Tools➪ Internet Setup Wizard.

1. **Double-click the Make New Connection icon in the Dial-Up Networking group.**

2. **Type a name for your connection, select Sportster ISDN 128K Dial-Up from the Select a modem drop-down list, and then click Next.**

3. **Type the telephone number for your Internet access provider and then click Next.**

4. **Click Finish.**

5. *Right-click* **the new connection icon in the Dial-Up Networking folder and select the Properties item.**

   The Properties dialog box appears.

6. *Right-click* **the connection icon. From the menu that appears, select Properties.**

   The Modem Properties dialog box appears with your ISDN device name.

7. **Click the Server Type button to display the Server Types dialog box.**

8. **Make sure that PPP, Windows 95, Windows NT 3.5, Internet is selected from the Type of Dial-Up Server list. In the Allowed network protocols area, make sure that only TCP/IP is checked.**

9. **Click the TCP/IP Settings button.**

   The TCP/IP Settings dialog box appears.

10. **If your service provider has assigned you a specific IP address, select the Specify an IP address option; then type the IP address. In addition, select the Specify name server addresses option; then type the IP addresses supplied by your ISP in the Primary DNS and Secondary DNS boxes.**

11. **If your service provider uses dynamic IP addressing, select the Server assigned IP address option. In addition, select the Server assigned name server addresses option.**

12. **Click OK two times.**

You've created your Dial-Up Networking profile for the Sportster.

Now you're ready to make a connection to your Internet service provider or another computer:

1. **Make sure that you activate the Sportster connection from the Sportster Manager before you open the Dial-Up Networking profile.**

2. **Double-click the Dial-Up Networking icon you created.**

   The Connect To dialog box appears.

3. **Type your username (also known as your hostname) and password for logging on to the Internet.**

4. **Click the Connect button to make your connection.**

   Status dialog boxes appear to indicate dialing, to verify the username and password, and to display

   `Connected`

Now that you are connected to the Internet, you can use your Web browser or other Internet applications.

An Internet item appears minimized on the taskbar while you are connected to the Internet. You can open this at any time to display the Connect To dialog box, which shows the bps rate and duration of your connection.

To end your connection, click the Disconnect button in the Connect To dialog box.

Taking Command of ISDN with the Supra NetCommander

At $299, Diamond Multimedia's Supra NetCommander is a great ISDN remote-access buy that includes an impressive set of features. One of the most significant is its support of true dynamic bandwidth allocation. Unlike many other ISDN remote-access devices, the NetCommander determines the bandwidth it needs for a particular session and adjusts the channel allocation accordingly. In low traffic sessions, such as surfing the Web without large graphics files, it uses only one B channel. When you go into file download mode, it kicks in both B channels for overdrive speed. This feature saves you money in connection charges. Additionally, the NetCommander works with all the leading bandwidth allocation protocols, so it works with most Internet service providers.

The Supra NetCommander provides full ringing support, which means your regular telephone will ring on the ISDN line. You can assign a Distinctive Ring capability for up to three analog devices connected to your line. NetCommander includes PPP/MP and user-programmable bandwidth on demand. It also includes built-in NT1 and voice and data capability on both B channels.

Installing the NetCommander adapter card is easy because it uses the Windows 95 Plug-and-Play feature to automatically set the interrupt (IRQ) and I/O base address to avoid conflicts. A Windows AutoISDN application provides easy ISDN service configuration and support. You can upgrade the NetCommander by software. NetCommander supports Stac and Microsoft compression.

Diamond includes an ISDN Service Activation Request Form with the Diamond AutoISDN installation and line-monitoring application. Use this form as a reference for ordering ISDN service from your telephone company, or fax it to the telephone company to make ISDN service acquisition easier. Diamond Multimedia technical support for the Supra NetCommander is available for voice at 408-325-7110. You can also access the Diamond Multimedia Web site at `http://www.diamondmm.com/` for technical support information and new software drivers.

Ordering ISDN service for the NetCommander

With most telephone companies, you can simply request the Intel Blue ordering code or Capability Package M, which has configuration characteristics nearly identical to Intel Blue. Either package provides 128 Kbps transmission potential, which enables you to take full advantage of the NetCommander PPP/MP and analog voice communications features.

If your telephone company doesn't recognize the Bellcore Compatibility Package M or Intel Blue service packages, request the following specific ISDN services:

- ISDN BRI service
- Two B channels, both with *circuit-switched voice and* data (CSV/D) call types
- No packet mode (X.25) data on the D channel
- No EKTS or CACH EKTS service

✔ Terminal type A

✔ Dynamic TEI assignments

✔ Multipoint attachment

What you need from the telephone company are the switch type, the directory number or numbers, and any SPIDs.

Installing the Supra NetCommander ISDN card

The following steps explain how to install the Supra NetCommander in an ISA slot in your PC. The Windows 95 TCP/IP stack and Dial-Up Networking must be installed, however, before you can install NetCommander.

1. **Turn off the power to the computer and any related equipment.**

2. **Remove the cover from your computer.**

3. **Touch the power supply box on your computer with one hand while the computer is plugged in.**

   This will ground you and discharge any static electricity, allowing you to safely handle your Supra NetCommander card.

4. **Unscrew and remove the slot cover from the 16-bit ISA expansion slot you have chosen for the NetCommander card.**

5. **Insert the NetCommander card into the ISA expansion slot. Replace the screw that originally held the slot cover in place and tighten the screw into the metal lip of NetCommander's metal bracket.**

6. **Put the cover back on your computer.**

7. **Plug your ISDN phone line into the ISDN port on your NetCommander.**

   The ISDN port is the RJ-45 on the back of the NetCommander board, labeled ISDN to Wall.

8. **Plug in any analog device you want to connect to your ISDN line by connecting the RJ-11 jack into the port labeled Analog Phone on your NetCommander.**

   Diamond recommends connecting analog devices in the following order: analog modem, fax machine, and then telephone. There are two connections on your modem — one marked phone and the other marked line or wall. Use the included phone cable to connect your fax machine or modem to the analog phone port on NetCommander.

If your computer is turned off, analog devices will not work on the ISDN line.

Installing NetCommander software

After you've installed your Supra NetCommander adapter card, you need to install the supporting software. This software includes the AutoISDN program for configuring and managing your ISDN connection.

The following steps explain how to install and configure the NetCommander. Make sure that you have all your ISDN line-provisioning information available before you install the software.

1. **Restart your PC and Windows 95.**

   The New Hardware Found dialog box is displayed.

2. **Choose Drivers from disk provided by the hardware manufacturer (the default), and click OK.**

3. **Insert the NetCommander ISDN Setup diskette in your floppy drive and click OK.**

   The drivers are copied to a new directory, and the NetCommander ISDN Installation Setup Wizard appears.

4. **Click Next.**

   The Select Directory dialog box appears.

5. **To accept the default directory, click Next. If you want to use a different directory, type the path and then click Next.**

   The Configure ISDN Service page appears.

6. **Click Next.**

   The SPID page appears.

7. **Type one SPID in each of the spaces provided. Or if your telephone company didn't provide any SPIDs, select the No SPID Required check box.**

8. **Click Next.**

   The Switch Type page appears.

9. **Select the Switch Type used by your telephone company at the central office providing your ISDN service and then click Next.**

   The Phone Numbers page appears.

10. **Enter the last seven digits (everything but the area code) of the ISDN phone numbers (directory numbers) and then click Next.**

    The Save Configuration page appears.

11. **Click Next.**

   You've completed the NetCommander installation. Setup displays a Helpful Hints page.

12. **Click Next.**

   The Congratulations page appears telling you that the setup is complete.

13. **Click Finish.**

   Setup prompts you to restart Windows 95.

14. **Remove any disk in your floppy drive and then click OK.**

NetCommander's AutoISDN program

The NetCommander's AutoISDN program provides a collection of tools for managing the NetCommander and your ISDN connection. To open the program, choose Start➪Programs➪NetCommander➪AutoISDN. The Supra NetCommander AutoISDN dialog box appears (Figure 10-12).

You can open the AutoISDN window also by clicking the Diamond AutoISDN icon on the Windows 95 taskbar. (The Diamond AutoISDN icon is next to the time indicator.)

Figure 10-12:
The Supra Net-Commander AutoISDN dialog box is where you make all your configuration changes and run ISDN line diagnostics.

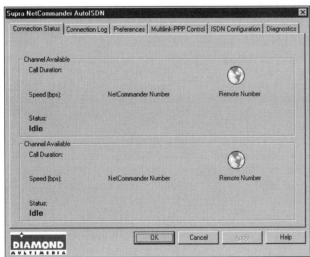

The following describes the pages in the AutoISDN dialog box:

✔ The Connection Status tab (see Figure 10-12) shows the status of your ISDN connection. When you're connected, it provides status information for each B channel.

✔ The Connection Log tab provides a listing of your ISDN calls. Entries can be sorted, and you can produce a printout.

✔ The Preferences tab (Figure 10-13) has settings that control how incoming calls are handled, determine whether the connection log is enabled or disabled, determine whether the AutoISDN icon is always displayed on the taskbar or only when the ISDN line is active, and adjust phone volume control.

Figure 10-13: The Preferences properties page includes settings for specifying how you want Net-Commander to act when it is active or receiving calls.

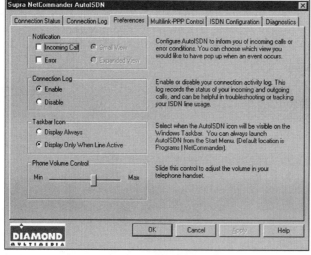

✔ The MultiLink-PPP Control tab (Figure 10-14) lets you enable MultiLink-PPP for two B-channel connections and flexing, which is the capability to use both B channels to aggregate data to handle larger data transfers. To activate the MultiLink PPP protocol, check the Enable Diamond MultiLink-PPP option.

✔ The ISDN Configuration tab (Figure 10-15) includes the settings for the telephone company side of your ISDN connections, including SPIDs, switch types, and settings for any analog devices connected to the NetCommander's analog (RJ-11) port. If you select a telephone number from the list at the bottom of the page and then click the Edit NetCommander Number button, the Phone Number dialog box (Figure 10-16) appears. This window lets you specify the type of analog device you're connecting to the telephone number. The ringing pattern specifies the type of ringing pattern you want for the line.

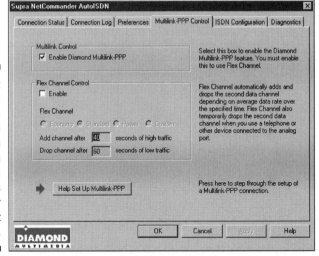

Figure 10-14: The MultiLink-PPP Control properties page lets you use both B channels for your Internet connection.

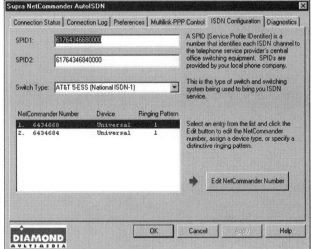

Figure 10-15: Use the ISDN Configuration properties page to make changes to your ISDN directory number and SPID settings.

✔ The Diagnostics tab (Figure 10-17) provides a collection of tools to test the NetCommander card and the telephone ringing. In addition, a troubleshooting log file can keep track of your activities and record them, along with responses from Windows, your ISDN line, and the adapter card.

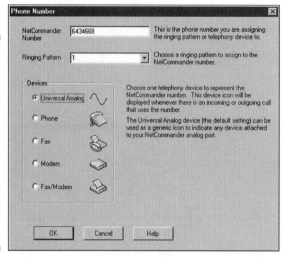

Figure 10-16:
Use the
Phone
Number
dialog box to
assign
ringing
patterns to
specific
devices
receiving an
incoming
call.

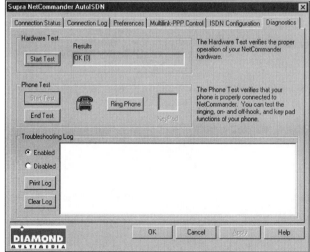

Figure 10-17:
The
Diagnostics
properties
page lets
you test
the Net-
Commander
card and
your ISDN
line.

Creating a Dial-Up Networking connection

Because the NetCommander is an adapter card, you don't need to add it as a modem. You just need to create a Dial-Up Networking connection profile. The following steps explain this process:

1. **Double-click the Make New Connection icon in the Dial-Up Networking group.**

2. **Type a name for your connection.**

3. **Select Supra NetCommander ISDN Line 1 from the Select a modem drop-down list; then click Next.**

4. **Type the telephone number for your Internet service provider.**

   If you're using the MultiLink PPP setting, which is enabled in the AutoISDN program, enter two asterisks (*) after the telephone number (for example, 528-0400**). This instructs the number to be dialed twice, once for each B channel.

5. **Click Next.**

6. **Click Finish.**

7. *Right-click* **the connection icon, and a menu appears.**

8. **Select Properties.**

   The Modem Properties dialog box appears with your ISDN device name.

9. **Click the Server Type button to display the Server Types dialog box.**

10. **Make sure that PPP, Windows 95, Windows NT 3.5, Internet is selected from the Type of Dial-Up Server list. In the Allowed network protocols area, make sure that only TCP/IP is checked.**

11. **Click the TCP/IP Settings button.**

    The TCP/IP Settings dialog box appears.

12. **If your service provider has assigned you a specific IP address, select the Specify an IP address option; then type the IP address. In addition, select the Specify name server addresses option; then type the IP addresses supplied by your ISP in the Primary DNS and Secondary DNS boxes.**

13. **If your service provider uses dynamic IP addressing, select the Server assigned IP address option. In addition, select the Server assigned name server addresses option.**

14. **Click OK three times.**

You've finished creating your Dial-Up Networking profile for the NetCommander. Now you're ready to make your connection to your Internet service provider or another computer:

1. **Double-click the Dial-Up Networking icon you created.**

   The Connect To dialog box appears.

2. **Enter your username (also known as your hostname) and password for logging on to the Internet.**

3. **Click the Connect button to make your connection.**

Status dialog boxes appear to indicate dialing, to verify the username and password, and to display

Connected

Now that you are connected to the Internet, you can use your Web browser or other Internet applications.

An Internet item appears minimized on the taskbar while you are connected to the Internet. You can open this at any time to display the Connect To dialog box, which shows the bps rate and duration of your connection.

To end your connection, click on the Disconnect button in the Connect To dialog box.

Chapter 11

Going the ISDN Router Route for LAN Connections

· ·

In This Chapter

▶ Understanding the Zen of ISDN routers

▶ Surveying the ISDN router market

▶ Making LAN connections to ISDN routers

▶ Taking the Ascend Pipeline 75 for a test spin

▶ Cruising with Farallon's Netopia Internet router

· ·

*I*SDN routers enable you to connect a *local area network* (LAN) via an ISDN line to the Internet or other networks. When the router is connected as a device on your LAN, you can share an ISDN line across the PCs on your network. ISDN routers also make connecting to the Internet faster and easier than using Windows Dial-Up Networking with an ISDN serial device or adapter card.

A new generation of ISDN routers is now both affordable and easy to install. These devices offer a cost-effective way to connect two or more PCs to the Internet or another network. This chapter introduces you to how routers work and takes you on a hands-on tour of two leading ISDN routers.

The Zen of ISDN Routers

Routers form the basis of *inter-networking,* the connecting of different networks over wide area networks (WANs). Internetworking is what the Internet is all about. In the case of ISDN access to the Internet, the router routes data from your local network via the ISDN to the Internet; ISDN is the WAN. Because routers are Ethernet-based devices, you can support multiple platforms, including PCs running Microsoft Windows, UNIX workstations, and Apple Macintosh computers.

Routers deliver more intelligence than bridges because they can route data by looking at packet addressing and protocol to route it accordingly. *Bridges* are basically dumb devices that connect two networks of the same type, routing all information indiscriminately between the two networks. Routers let you define routing tables for handling connections to different types of networks at different locations, all based on information in the data packets.

Routers support *filtering,* which allows the router to monitor and selectively choose packets as they enter or leave it. With filtering, a router can protect your network from undesired intrusion and prevent selected local network traffic from leaving your LAN through the router. This is a powerful feature for managing incoming and outgoing data for your site.

ISDN routers provide a cost-effective way to connect two or more computers to the Internet or another network. Using a router connected to your LAN lets you share your ISDN line across several PCs. Keep in mind, though, that the 128 Kbps of bandwidth is shared among all the LAN users, which can reduce the speed of each user's connection during heavy use.

Another benefit of using a router is that you bypass using Windows 95 or the Windows NT Dial-Up Networking. Instead, all you have to do to make an Internet connection is double-click your Web browser or any TCP/IP application.

You can use a router with a dial-up or dedicated ISDN connection. Typically, the difference in cost for a LAN Internet access account is for the use of added IP addresses. As your Internet traffic increases, you may find a dedicated ISDN connection cheaper. But for many smaller LANs, a dial-up ISDN Internet account is the way to go.

The changing ISDN router scene

The router marketplace has traditionally been a technical market made up of ISPs and large enterprise computing organizations. ISDN routers are a subset of the larger router networking market and are easier to use than other types of routers. As the Internet continues to explode and Windows 95 and Windows NT continue to make PC networking easier, ISDN routers can provide the exploding SOHO *(small office/home office)* market with a smooth linkup to the Internet.

ISDN routers come in all types of configurations. Internet access via the IP *(Internet Protocol)* represents the largest market for ISDN routers. Most routers, however, offer routing support for other network protocols (such as IPX for Novell networks). Router technology has dramatically improved, and the cost of routers continues to fall. ISDN routers now cost in the range of $695 to $1,195. Although a router is more expensive than a single PC serial device or ISDN adapter card, if you want to connect more than one PC to the Internet, a router is actually the better value.

Survey of ISDN router vendors

Ascend Communications is the leader in the ISDN router market. The majority of ISPs use high-end versions of Ascend routers. More than 90 percent of the central site ISDN routers sold to Internet service providers (ISPs) are manufactured by Ascend. Ascend also captured 46.5 percent of the worldwide ISDN remote networking equipment market in 1995. The Ascend Pipeline series remains the leader in ISDN routers and is the benchmark for all ISDN routers. However, Ascend is facing growing competition from a host of other vendors.

Another leader in the ISDN router market is Farallon Computing. Its Netopia Internet router family is impressive, with an easy-to-use interface, a great price, and the right mix of router features. The Netopia Internet router continues to gain wide acceptance.

Later sections in this chapter cover working with the Ascend Pipeline 75 and the Netopia Internet router.

Enterprise-computing router vendors, including Cisco Systems, 3Com, Bay Networks, and Cabletron, are entering the ISDN router market with a steady stream of new offerings. Cisco Systems offers a line of ISDN routers called the 760 Series; 3Com offers the OfficeConnect Series; Bay Networks offers the NETGEAR Series; and Cabletron offers the CyberSwitch 100 Series.

For more information on ISDN router vendors, see Appendix B.

Making the LAN to ISDN router connection

Routers can connect to your Ethernet network in different ways. The most common way is using 10Base-T cabling, which is a twisted-pair version of Ethernet. A 10Base-T network uses a device called a hub, and the cabling uses RJ-45 connectors. A *hub* is a simple device that acts as a central spoke for your network traffic. Hubs are inexpensive, with some costing less than $100, and are available at many computer stores.

Each PC on your network has an Ethernet card with a 10Base-T port. The 10Base-T cable connects via RJ-45 connectors to the PC and a port on the hub. (The typical small LAN hub has eight to ten ports.)

Trancell Systems offers an ISDN router called WebRamp IP Router for $695, which includes a built-in eight-port Ethernet hub as well as an IP router. The WebRamp also includes a friendly Windows setup Wizard that makes installation easy.

You plug in the ISDN router to the hub in the same way you do for a PC. Figure 11-1 shows a typical 10Base-T network with an ISDN router.

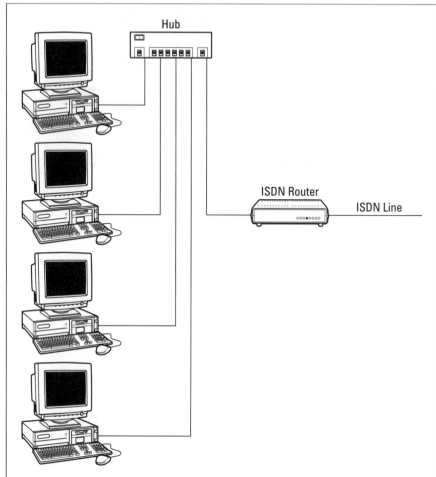

Figure 11-1:
A typical
10Base-T
LAN
configuration
with an
ISDN router
added.

The 10Base-T cabling contrasts with the commonly used Ethernet cabling referred to as Thinnet or 10Base-2. This form of Ethernet networking doesn't use a hub. Instead, each device is connected by a BNC connector. Figure 11-2 shows a 10Base-2 network configuration with an ISDN router added. You can use an ISDN router with this type of Ethernet network, but you may need to use the AUI (attachment unit interface) port on the ISDN router. (An AUI port allows you to connect a 10Base-2 network via a transceiver unit and cable. This transceiver unit is required to use the AUI port.)

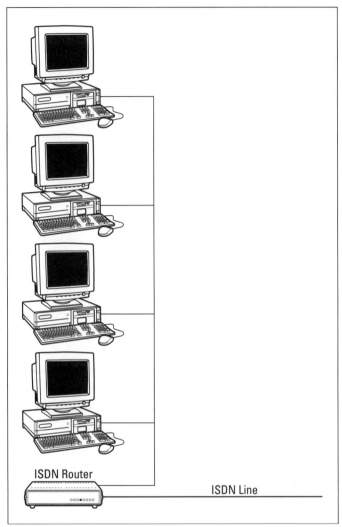

Figure 11-2:
A typical
10Base-2
LAN
configuration
with an
ISDN router
added.

ISDN Router

ISDN Line

If you have a Thinnet (10Base-2) type of Ethernet network, you can use an inexpensive hub that includes both a BNC connector as well as 10Base-T ports (RJ-45). LinkSys makes an inexpensive (under $100) ten-port Ethernet hub that includes a single BNC connector as well as nine 10Base-T ports. This way, you can connect your 10Base-2 network to the BNC port and your ISDN router to any of the 10Base-T ports. You can add other PCs to the remaining eight 10Base-T ports to expand your network. For more information on the LinkSys hub, check out its Web site at http://www.linksys.com/.

Anatomy of an ISDN router

An ISDN router is about the size of an external modem. It usually includes a series of status lights for monitoring network and ISDN line traffic. Configuring an ISDN router typically involves connecting the device to a COM port on your PC via an RS-232 cable, and then using a communications program called a *terminal program.*

Most ISDN routers use a text-based menu system for configuration. You can use the HyperTerminal program that comes with Windows 95. You can also use the telnet program to access an ISDN router to configure it. The telnet program is a simple remote login program that lets you connect to a remote device via a network. Windows 95 includes a DOS version of the telnet program.

More and more ISDN routers are using friendlier Windows interfaces — including Wizards — to help guide users through the configuration process. With these Windows setup programs, you configure the device via Ethernet instead of using the communications program method.

At the back of the ISDN router are several ports for connecting your network and the ISDN line. Figure 11-3 shows the ports panel for the Ascend Pipeline 75.

Figure 11-3:
The Ascend
Pipeline 75
ports panel.

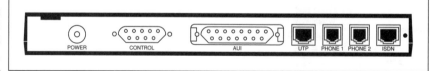

Different routers may have a different mix of ports. The typical ISDN router includes the following ports:

- ✔ A serial config port for connecting an RS-232 DB9 cable from the router to a COM port on a PC. This connection is used to configure the device via a terminal program.

- ✔ A U-interface port (RJ-45) for your ISDN line or an S/T-interface port for connecting the router to an NT1 device. Some routers with built-in NT1 (U interface) include an extra S/T-interface port for plugging in another ISDN device, such as a desktop video-conferencing system.

- ✔ A 10Base-T port (RJ-45) for connecting to a 10Base-T network via a hub. Most vendors also include a special 10Base-T cable that lets you connect the router directly to a single PC's network adapter card.

- ✔ An AUI *(attachment unit interface)* port allows you to connect a Thinnet (10Base-2) network cable via a transceiver unit and cable.

✔ One or two RJ-11 ports for adding analog telephones or faxes to your ISDN line. Not all ISDN routers include these ports.

✔ A power supply port.

ISDN routers, IP addresses, and Internet access

Until recently, using an ISDN router required getting a LAN Internet access account. For connecting a LAN to the Internet, an ISP assigned IP addresses for every machine on the local area network, including one for the router itself. This required an ISP to relinquish IP addresses and a subnet mask for each LAN.

The subnet mask indicates to TCP/IP which part of the IP address is used to identify your network and which part is used to identify each device on that network. A subnet mask is composed of the numbers 255 or 0. Typically, the subnet mask is 255.255.255.0.

Because of the growing scarcity of IP addresses, many ISPs offering ISDN service were reluctant to offer LAN accounts with static IP addresses, or offered them at much higher rates than single-user Internet access accounts. This limited the deployment of ISDN routers. In response to the difficulty in getting affordable LAN accounts with multiple static IP addresses, a growing number of ISDN routers now support dynamic IP addressing.

With a dynamic IP address, you are not assigned a specific IP address. Instead, IP addresses are automatically assigned for each connection session, on an as-needed basis. This allows you to access the Internet via an ISDN router without a static IP address for each computer and the router.

While I am writing this book, a number of ISDN router vendors are announcing support for dynamic IP addressing. Using an ISDN router that supports dynamic IP addressing, you can connect a LAN to the Internet using a dynamic IP addressing scheme that allocates IP addresses from a pool of available IP addresses at the ISP. The result is that you can use the same low-cost, dial-up Internet access accounts used by individuals to connect a LAN. In addition, you don't need assigned IP addresses from your ISP for each machine on your network.

Taking the Ascend Pipeline 75 for a Test Spin

Ascend Communications rules the ISDN router market. The Ascend Pipeline product line includes several models and different configuration options within models. The Pipeline 75 and Pipeline 50 are the workhorses of the Ascend Pipeline family of ISDN routers. The only difference between the two is that the Pipeline 75 includes two POTS ports for connecting telephones, faxes, and modems to your ISDN line.

The Pipeline 75, which is the model used in this chapter, has the following key features:

- Bandwidth-on-demand for instant connections only when you need to connect

- Support for both bridging and routing, including simultaneous bridging and routing to multiple destinations

- Two analog ports for adding telephones, fax machines, and modems

- SNMP *(Simple Network Management Protocol)* based LAN and WAN network management

- Support for 4:1 data compression

- U interface or S/T interface

- Authentication support for PAP, CHAP, and *Calling Line ID* (CLID)

- Support for an unlimited number of users

- Support for standard routing protocols: *Internet Protocol* (IP), *Point-to-Point Protocol* (PPP), *PPP/Multilink Protocol* (PPP/MP), and *Multilink Protocol Plus* (MP+)

- Five status LEDs (power, activity, collision, WAN, and condition)

- Management interface accessible through a serial cable and communications software or via Ethernet using telnet or the Pipeline Console program (a Windows 95 configuration program)

- User-definable transmit and receive packet filtering

Getting started

The Pipeline 75 includes both 10Base-T and AUI Ethernet connectors, so you can hook up any type of Ethernet cabling system. To use the AUI, you have to add a transceiver to connect through the AUI port. The Pipeline 75 also has the RJ-45 jack for connection to your ISDN.

If you're connecting the Pipeline 75 via a hub for 10Base-T, use any RJ-45 Ethernet cables wired straight through, which means the same color wire goes to the same pin number on each end. If you are connecting the Pipeline directly to an Ethernet card for a single PC connection, you need to use the special 10Base-T cable supplied with your Pipeline 75.

You can configure the Pipeline 75 using an RS-232 cable connected to a COM port and the Windows 95 HyperTerminal program (or any communications program). The Pipeline uses a DB9 connector, so it includes a DB9 male to DB25 female adapter if you need to convert a DB25 connector to a DB9 connector.

To set up the Pipeline 75, connect the Ethernet cable, the ISDN line, and the terminal cable. Hook up the Ascend to the power supply. The Pipeline 75 has no power switch. The little switch on the back is reserved for future use.

Before you can use the Pipeline 75, all the PCs on your Windows 95 or Windows NT network must be configured for TCP/IP. The configuration of PCs for TCP/IP is handled by Windows 95 Network Properties in the Control Panel. You establish your LAN IP addressing scheme based on the addresses provided by the ISP. Typically, this involves specifying a unique IP address for each PC as well as a unique IP address for the ISDN router.

You need the following information from your ISP to configure your network and the Pipeline 75:

- ISP's ISDN phone number
- ISP's IP gateway address
- ISP's IP subnet mask
- IP addresses for each PC on your network and one for the Pipeline unit, plus a subnet mask IP address for your LAN
- Authentication information, including authentication type (PPP or CHAP), username, and password
- *Domain name server* (DNS) IP addresses
- Your domain name

From the telephone company, you need the ISDN provisioning information, including the directory numbers, SPIDs, and switch types.

Configuring the Pipeline 75

The following steps explain how to access the Pipeline 75 using the Windows 95 HyperTerminal program.

At the time that I write this book, a Windows 95 program for configuring the Pipeline 75 is in early beta. This Java-based program, called the Pipeline Console, will configure the Pipeline via Ethernet. I describe the Pipeline Console program briefly later in this chapter.

1. **Choose Start⇨Accessories⇨HyperTerminal. In the HyperTerminal window, double-click the Hypertm icon.**

   The Connection Description window appears.

2. **Type the name of the connection (such as Ascend), choose an icon, and click OK.**

   The Phone Number screen appears.

3. **In the Connect using list, choose the Direct to Com port for the port you're using to connect the PC to the Ascend. Click OK.**

   The Com Properties dialog box appears.

4. **Change the Bits per second to 9600, and choose None for the Flow control setting.**

5. **Click OK.**

   The HyperTerminal screen appears.

6. **Press Ctrl-L to redraw the screen.**

   The Ascend Pipeline 75 Configuration Profile screen appears (Figure 11-4).

You traverse the configuration list in the Edit menu by selecting the item and then toggling through entries or entering strings of characters. The greater-than (>) symbol appears to the left of the item you're working with. On some items,

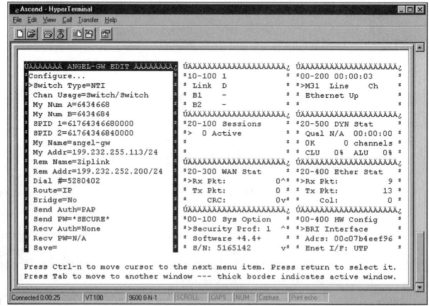

Figure 11-4:
The Pipeline 75 Configuration Profile screen.

you toggle by pressing Enter until you get the right item. When you enter a string, brackets ([]) appear, and you insert the characters within them. After you are finished, you press Enter.

To configure your Pipeline 75 for basic IP routing, fill in the essential settings in the Edit menu (see Figure 11-4). Table 11-1 explains each of these settings.

Table 11-1	Basic Settings for the Pipeline 75
Setting	*Description*
My Num A	Field for entering the directory number of your first ISDN B channel
My Num B	Field for entering the directory number of your second ISDN B channel
SPID 1	Field for entering any SPID assigned to the My Num A entry
SPID 2	Field for entering any SPID assigned to the My Num B entry
My Name	Assigns your Pipeline 75 a name (Use any domain name given by your ISP. If none was assigned, enter any name you want.)
My Addr	Assigns the IP address for your Pipeline 75
Rem Name	Assigns the remote host name of your ISP's server or any name you like to identify the host network
Rem Addr	Assigns the IP address of the ISP's remote host
Dial #	Field for entering the phone number to dial to reach the remote network, as you would dial it
Route	Defines whether the Pipeline 75 will be routing IP or IPX
Bridge	Defines whether the Pipeline 75 will be bridging
Send Auth	Defines the authentication required on the remote network, such as PAP or CHAP
Send PW	Assigns the password required to log on to the remote network
Recv Auth	Assigns any authentication you may use for incoming calls into the Pipeline 75
Recv PW	Assigns the password required for incoming calls to the Pipeline 75

The following steps walk you through the basic configuration of the Ascend Pipeline 75 to connect to an Internet service provider's machine:

1. **Using the HyperTerminal program, open the Configure Profile menu from the Ascend configuration menu (see Figure 11-4). If necessary, press Esc until the main Edit menu appears, select Configure, and press Enter.**

2. **Select Switch type and press Enter until the switch type for your ISDN line appears.**

   Depending on the switch type you select, certain parameters become N/A, which means they are not required for your switch type.

3. **Type the Chan Usage setting for your ISDN line.**

   The typical setting is Switch/Switch.

4. **Type the phone number for your first ISDN B channel in the My Num A field.**

   Press Enter to open a text field, type the phone number, and then press Enter again to accept the entry.

5. **Repeat Step 4 for the second ISDN B channel in the My Num B field.**

6. **Enter the SPID associated with your first ISDN B channel in the SPID 1 field.**

7. **Do the same for the second SPID associated with the second ISDN B channel in the SPID 2 field.**

8. **Select the Data Usage for the B channel, which is typically A+B.**

9. **Select the Phone 1 Usage setting for the first B channel.**

10. **Do the same for the Phone 2 Usage setting.**

11. **Select the Phone Num Binding for each B channel you're using for voice communications.**

12. **Type the name of your Pipeline 75 in the My Name field.**

13. **Type the IP address of the Pipeline in the My Addr field.**

14. **Type the name of the remote computer you will be connecting to in the Rem Name field.**

15. **Type the IP address in the Rem Addr field.**

16. **Type the phone number used to access the remote network in the Dial # field.**

17. **Select the IP address routing option in the Route field and then select No in the Bridge field.**

18. **Enter the type of authentication used on the remote network in the Send Auth field.**

19. **Type the password required to log on to the remote network in the Send P/W field.**

20. **Select Save and then press Enter to save your changes.**

After you configure the Pipeline 75's IP address using a terminal communications program, you can use telnet to access it from a local or remote site. The telnet method displays the same configuration menus as the terminal communications connection.

Performing a self-test

Now that you have finished filling out the Configure Profile, you can perform a self-test to verify the configuration of the WAN interface and the Pipeline configuration. To perform a self-test, do the following:

1. **From the main Edit menu, select System, and then press Enter.**

2. **Select Sys Diag, select Term Serv, and then press Enter.**

   The Ascend Pipeline Terminal Server interface appears.

3. **At the ascend% prompt, type** test [My Num], **where [My Num] is the number you entered for My Num A.**

4. **Press Enter.**

   The Pipeline displays the progress of the call. If the line is correctly configured, the following message is displayed:

   ```
   calling......answering...testing...end
   100 packets sent, 100 packets received
   ```

5. **Repeat Steps 3 and 4 for the number you entered in My Num B.**

6. **Type quit at the ascend% prompt to return to the configuration interface.**

7. **In the Configure Profile, press Ctrl-D.**

   The Do menu appears.

8. **Select 1, Dial.**

   The Pipeline 75 makes an outgoing call. Watch the status window in the upper right corner. If you see the message LAN Session Up, your call was successful.

You are now ready to use the Ascend Pipeline router. Simply execute a TCP/IP program, such as the Netscape Navigator, on any PC connected to your LAN and the Pipeline 75. The IP packets are detected by the Pipeline 75, and the connection is automatically made to your Internet service provider via ISDN.

If you set up Dial-Up Networking for making connections, you need to turn off the AutoDial feature so that you're not prompted with the Connect To window every time you open a TCP/IP application. Double-click the Internet icon in the Control Panel to display the Internet Properties window. Click Use AutoDial and then click OK.

Using telnet to configure the Pipeline 75

You can use the telnet program to access the Ascend 75 configuration program through your Ethernet network. However, you can use telnet only after you have configured the Pipeline 75 with its own IP address. You must have the Pipeline 75 hooked up to your network via a hub or connected directly to a PC's Ethernet card using the special 10Base-T cable included.

The telnet method is faster than the terminal method and doesn't require connecting the serial cable to the Pipeline 75. Here's how to access the configuration screen using telnet:

1. **Choose Start⇨Programs⇨MS-DOS Prompt.**

   The MS-DOS Prompt window appears.

2. **At the DOS prompt, type** telnet **[IP Address] (for example,** telnet 199.232.252.113**).**

3. **Press Enter.**

   The Pipeline 75 configuration screen appears in the telnet window.

Using the Windows 95 Pipeline Console

As I write this book, Ascend's Pipeline Console program is in beta. (The *Pipeline Console* is a Windows program written in Java that improves the configuration of all Ascend Pipeline ISDN routers.) By the time you read this, the Pipeline Console is probably shipping with all Pipeline products, or you can probably download it from the Ascend Web site at http://www.ascend.com/.

The Pipeline Console program works through your Ethernet connection, so you don't need to use the terminal connection. Double-click the Console icon or choose Start⇨Programs⇨Ascend⇨Pipeline Console. The Ascend Pipeline window appears (Figure 11-5).

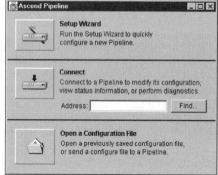

Figure 11-5:
The Ascend
Pipeline
window is a
friendly
Windows
interface for
configuring
the Ascend
Pipeline 75.

The Pipeline Console includes a Wizard (which is unavailable at the time I write this) for configuring the Pipeline 75 for the first time. You can modify an existing configuration by entering the IP address in the Address field (the second option in the Ascend Pipeline window) and then clicking Find.

The Console program finds your Pipeline 75 and displays the Pipeline 75 Configuration screen (Figure 11-6). This screen enables you to change existing settings or add some new ones. The Open a Configuration File button (Figure 11-5) lets you use different existing profiles by sending the selected profile to the Pipeline 75.

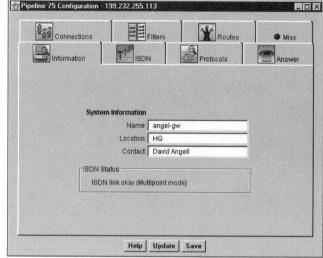

Figure 11-6:
The Pipeline
Configuration
window lets
you change
existing
settings or
add new
ones.

Cruising with the Netopia Internet Router

Farallon's Netopia Internet router is another leading ISDN router in the SOHO market. It includes a number of impressive features and has a cool design (Figure 11-7). Although you use a terminal program to configure the Netopia, it has a friendly, step-by-step menu system that makes the process easy. Farallon is adding a Web interface to the Netopia Internet router to give it a Windows 95 interface. Like the Ascend Pipeline, Netopia Internet can be accessed over the network using telnet (after you configure it with an IP address).

The Netopia Internet router product line includes a five-user unit (model PN630, $749), an unlimited user device (model PN640, $995), and an unlimited user device with Macintosh LocalTalk support (model PN440, $1195). For a PC network, the PN640 model is the best buy for Windows-only networks. You can get this unit from many ISPs or computer stores for as low as $799.

At the time that I am writing this book, Farallon is upgrading the Netopia Internet router to include several enhancements that are sure to make it an even better buy. The Netopia PN640 includes the following features:

Figure 11-7:
The Netopia Internet router has a cool design.

(Photo courtesy of Farallon Computing.)

✔ Data-Over-Voice, which allows data calls to be placed or answered using ISDN speech grade capabilities instead of circuit-switched data grade capabilities. In many areas, this feature enables Netopia customers to avoid paying higher ISDN per-minute charges.

✔ DHCP (Dynamic Host Configuration Protocol) support for simple, automated TCP/IP addressing. The Netopia can be configured to hold a range of IP addresses and then provide them to PCs as needed. By entering all the DHCP parameters in the Netopia, the only TCP/IP setup that is required in Windows 95 is to set the TCP/IP network control panel to obtain an IP address automatically. Normally, configuring each desktop requires filling in the IP address, subnet mask, default gateway, and Domain Name Server.

✔ Support for Dynamic IP addressing, which allows the router to work with a single ISDN dial-up account from an ISP that uses dynamic IP addresses. Most lower-cost ISDN dial-up accounts use dynamic IP addresses.

✔ Built-in firewall filter for security. The preconfigured firewall blocks undesirable traffic originating from the Internet (or any remote network), but passes all traffic originating on the local area network side. You can also deploy more customized filters using Netopia's extensive custom filtering capabilities.

✔ Scheduled connections based on preset times. The Netopia enables you to schedule connections at specified times. This feature is perfect for businesses that want outsiders to have access to their network (that is, for WWW access) during specific times of the day or for schools that want students to have access during certain times of the day.

✔ PCMCIA card slot for remote configuration over POTS. The Netopia ships with on-board PC Card (PCMCIA) capability. By adding a PC Card modem, you can configure and troubleshoot Netopia over an analog phone line. You can use the telnet program to access the Netopia over ISDN.

✔ Firmware upgrade and configuration via software uploads and downloads.

✔ Data compression support for STAC and Ascend's proprietary CCP.

✔ Support for up to 16 connection profiles.

✔ Support for Farallon's Etherwave daisy-chain technology to support up to eight 10Base-T devices without a hub.

✔ IPX routing to allow connections to Novell networks.

Getting started

The Netopia includes both 10Base-T and AUI Ethernet connectors, so you can hook up any type of Ethernet cabling system. To use the AUI, you have to add a transceiver to connect through the AUI port.

The Netopia includes two 10Base-T ports. You can connect the Netopia to a hub for using any 10Base-T Ethernet cables. You can also daisy chain the Netopia to a Farallon EtherWave 10Base-T network.

Before you can use the Netopia, all the PCs on your Windows 95 or Windows NT network must be configured for TCP/IP. The configuration of PCs for TCP/IP is handled by Windows 95 Network Properties in the Control Panel. You establish your LAN IP addressing scheme based on the addresses provided by the ISP. Typically, this involves specifying a unique IP address for each PC as well as a unique IP address for the ISDN router.

You need the following information from your ISP to configure your network and the Netopia Internet router:

- ISP's ISDN phone number
- ISP's IP gateway address
- ISP's IP subnet mask
- IP addresses for each PC on your network, IP address for the Netopia unit, and subnet mask IP address for your LAN
- Authentication information, including authentication type (PPP or CHAP), username, and password
- Domain Name Server (DNS) IP addresses
- Your domain name service name

From the telephone company, you need the ISDN provisioning information, including directory numbers, SPIDs, and switch types.

You can configure the Netopia using the Windows 95 HyperTerminal program (or any communications program) and an RS-232 cable connected to a COM port. (The Netopia includes the RS-232 cable.)

After you configure the Netopia by giving it its IP address using the terminal method, you can use telnet to access it from a local site or a remote site. The telnet method displays the same configuration menus as the terminal communications connection.

Configuring the Netopia

The following steps explain how to configure the Netopia using the HyperTerminal program in Windows 95:

1. **Choose Start⁄Accessories⁄HyperTerminal. In the HyperTerminal window, double-click the Hypertrm icon.**

   The Connection Description screen appears.

2. **Type the name of the connection (such as** Netopia**), choose an icon, and click OK.**

The Phone Number window appears.

3. **In the Connect using list, choose the Direct to Com port for the port you're using to connect the PC to the Netopia. Click OK.**

4. **In the Com Properties window, change Bits per second to 9600, and choose None for the Flow control setting.**

5. **Click OK.**

The HyperTerminal window appears.

6. **Choose CallÍConnect and then press Ctrl-L to redraw the screen.**

The Netopia Main menu screen appears (Figure 11-8).

7. **Choose Easy Setup and press Enter.**

The ISDN Line Configuration screen appears (Figure 11-9).

8. **Type your ISDN provisioning information by using the up and down arrow keys to highlight the setting, entering the information, and then pressing Enter.**

9. **After entering your ISDN information, choose NEXT SCREEN and press Enter.**

The Connection Profile 1 screen appears (Figure 11-10).

Figure 11-8:
The Netopia Main menu lists the main submenus for configuring the Netopia.

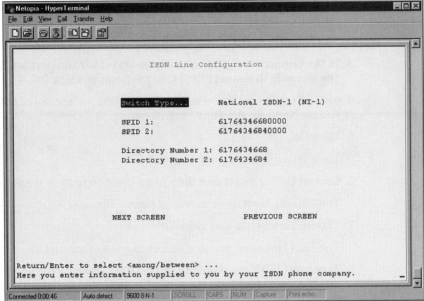

Figure 11-9:
Use the ISDN Line Configuration screen to enter your ISDN line directory numbers and SPIDs.

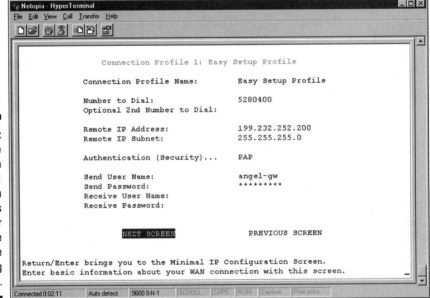

Figure 11-10:
The Connection Profile 1 screen includes settings for the remote host you're connecting to.

10. **Type the ISP information in the screen by using the up and down arrow keys to highlight the setting, entering the information, and then pressing Enter.**

11. **After entering your ISP information, choose NEXT SCREEN and press Enter.**

    The IP Setup screen appears (Figure 11-11).

12. **Type the IP address of your Netopia in the Ethernet IP Address and Ethernet IP Subnet Mask settings.**

13. **Type your ISP's default gateway and domain server IP addresses.**

14. **Choose RESET DEVICE and press Enter.**

15. **In the next screen, choose Continue and press Enter.**

    The Netopia router is reset according to the information you entered, and the Main menu screen appears.

16. **Exit the HyperTerminal window.**

    You're now ready to use the Netopia.

With the Netopia operating, you can automatically connect to the Internet by executing any TCP/IP program. For example, double-clicking the Internet Explorer icon on the desktop opens the program and makes the connection to the Internet. You don't need to use Dial-Up Networking — the connection is made through your Ethernet card.

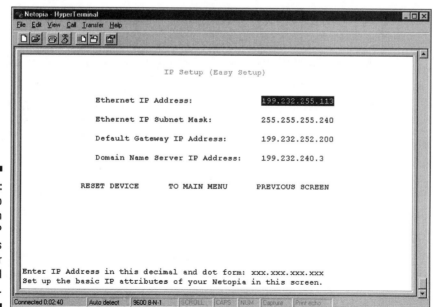

Figure 11-11:
The IP Setup screen includes IP address entries for your local network.

If you set up Dial-Up Networking for making connections, you need to turn off the AutoDial feature so that you're not prompted with the Connect To window every time you open a TCP/IP application. Double-click the Internet icon in the Control Panel to display the Internet Properties window. Click Use AutoDial; then click OK.

Using telnet to configure the Netopia

After you have initially configured Netopia with its own IP address, you can connect to the Netopia using the telnet program. The Netopia must be hooked up to your network via a hub or connected directly to a PC's Ethernet card. The telnet method is faster than the terminal method and doesn't require connecting the serial cable to the Netopia.

Here's how to access the Netopia configuration program using telnet:

1. **Choose StartÍProgramsÍMS-DOS Prompt.**

   The MS-DOS Prompt screen appears.

2. **At the DOS prompt, type** telnet **[IP Address] (for example, telnet 199.232.252.113).**

3. **Press Enter.**

   The Netopia Main menu configuration screen appears in the telnet window.

Netopia configuration options

Beyond the basic setup, the Netopia includes menus for a variety of configuration options. This section gives you a quick tour of the options in the Main menu.

The Advanced Configuration menu item displays the Advanced Configuration menu screen (Figure 11-12). This menu provides a gateway to a collection of manual configuration options. Many of these features are accessible also using Quick Menus, which the nontechnical user may find easy to use.

The Statistics, Utilities, and Tests menu item displays the menu shown in Figure 11-13. This menu accesses diagnostic information and utilities. For example, you can use the Ping option in the Utilities group to ping another computer, or you can force a manual connection using the Establish Connection item. The Ping program sends packets out to the IP address you specify to verify whether the remote computer is up and running and connected to the network.

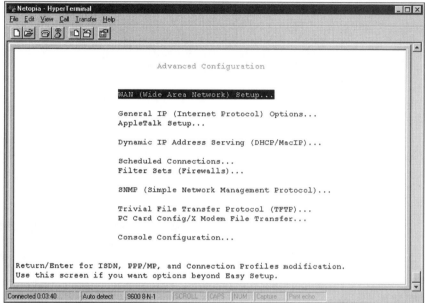

Figure 11-12:
The Advanced Configuration screen includes a variety of settings for more advanced router functions.

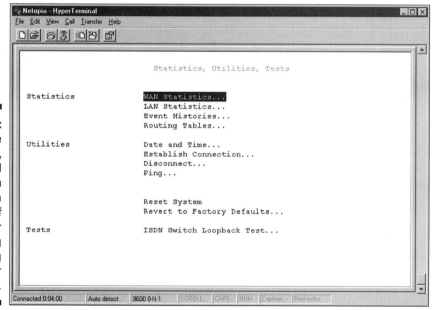

Figure 11-13:
The Statistics, Utilities, and Tests screen includes a collection of programs for monitoring and testing your connection.

The Quick Menu item displays a Quick Menu screen (Figure 11-14). This is the gateway for using friendly step-by-step guides that walk you through configuring the Netopia. For many, this is the screen that will be used most often. It includes access to menu screens for working with connection profiles, filters, scheduled connections, and static routes.

The Quick View item displays the Quick View screen (Figure 11-15), which displays the current status of your ISDN line.

Finally, the Security item displays the Security Options screen (Figure 11-16). This screen enables you to specify security parameters for the Netopia, including password settings for restricting remote access into the Netopia and for adding or removing users.

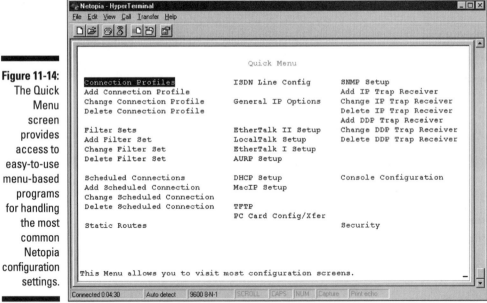

Figure 11-14: The Quick Menu screen provides access to easy-to-use menu-based programs for handling the most common Netopia configuration settings.

Figure 11-15:
The Quick View screen displays the current status of your connection.

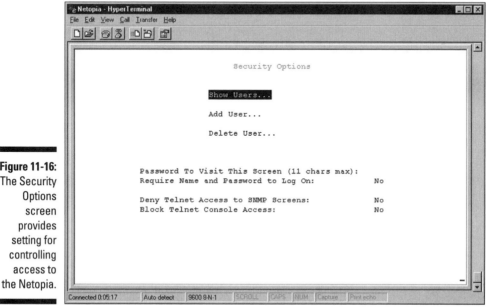

Figure 11-16:
The Security Options screen provides setting for controlling access to the Netopia.

Part III
Face to Face with Desktop Video Conferencing

The 5th Wave   By Rich Tennant

In response to video-phone technology, Technuts Corp. releases a phone system fitted with a continuous-action flash camera linked through the caller's fax machine.

In this part . . .

1t's time to discover desktop video conferencing via ISDN. Desktop video-conferencing systems use a video/audio capture board, an ISDN adapter, and software to turn your PC into a visual communications medium. In the following chapters, you discover how video conferencing works and how to use it effectively. You then experience desktop video conferencing over the ISDN system and Internet by taking a walk-through of three leading systems.

Chapter 12

I Want My DVC (Desktop Video Conferencing)

- -

In This Chapter

▶ Discovering how desktop video conferencing works

▶ Figuring out what you need for ISDN-based video conferencing

▶ Surveying the leading DVC systems

▶ Understanding the elements of video-conferencing style

- -

*O*f all the ISDN applications, desktop video conferencing (DVC) is the sexiest. It adds the powerful visual (and audio) dimension to communications. The convergence of video-conferencing standards, affordable desktop DVC systems, and ISDN makes DVC an exciting communications tool that is available right now. This chapter covers the fundamentals of desktop video conferencing.

The Downsizing of Video Conferencing

Video conferencing isn't new. Expensive, room-size systems incorporating specialized hardware and software components have been around for years. Large companies recognize them as productive tools and use them in everyday business. What *is* new is that a new generation of video-conferencing technology has downsized these expensive, room-size systems into inexpensive, desktop systems.

These desktop video-conferencing systems work with the large systems to allow individuals to participate in meetings conducted in the room-size systems. Desktop video-conferencing systems support both one-on-one conferences as well as multiperson meetings.

The technology that allows desktop video conferencing to make a fast trek from the boardroom to the desktop includes the advancement of data compression technology, the implementation of video-conferencing standards, and ISDN. Developments in compression and standards helped make desktop video conferencing a reality; ISDN delivers it at speeds that make it viable for the mass market.

Seeing Is Believing

Video conferencing brings a valuable strategic tool to millions of individuals and small businesses for face-to-face meetings, team collaboration, brainstorming, training, and more, regardless of the proximity of the participants. The affordable cost of desktop video conferencing means that many people from all walks of life can benefit from it. Figure 12-1 shows what a video-conferencing session might look like on your PC screen.

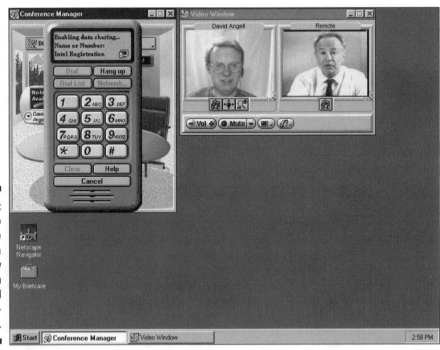

Figure 12-1:
A video conference can add a new dimension to critical communications.

DVC is an option in any activity where a face-to-face meeting is important. All types of business and professional functions can use DVC, including remote expert support, customer service, recruiting, distance learning and training, telemedicine, telecommuting, and even video surveillance. Desktop video conferencing delivers a number of benefits, including the following:

✔ Extends people's expertise and presence beyond the bounds of their physical location

✔ Speeds decision making and problem resolution because of its show-and-tell capabilities

✔ Allows specialists and experts to communicate with clients and team members regardless of their location

✔ Makes meetings more productive because each person at a video meeting has immediate access to both computer and paper documents, and can quickly involve other people who have special expertise

✔ Enhances brainstorming and collaboration because there's less formality with DVC than with traditional in-person meetings

✔ Creates flexibility in the work schedule by allowing people to work wherever there is an ISDN connection and a PC

✔ Allows telecommuters to attend meetings from home and generally stay in the loop at the office

✔ Empowers virtual companies and organizations by enhancing the management of geographically dispersed people

✔ Saves money by reducing both travel and travel time costs

DVC Systems Primer

Two types of ISDN-based desktop video-conferencing systems are available. The first group includes complete systems that you can connect to other DVC users via the ISDN system. ISDN is the WAN (wide area network) that is the global telephone system. For this group of DVC systems, you can dial up other DVC users by calling their ISDN number directly. This system includes the ISDN adapter as part of the package (Figure 12-2).

The second group consists of DVC systems that work on only the Internet or any TCP/IP network. They don't support connections to other DVC users via the ISDN WAN. For these systems, participants use ISDN connections to the Internet as the conduit for video conferencing. These systems do not include an ISDN adapter, but instead rely on your ISDN remote-access device to make the video-conferencing connection. Figure 12-3 shows the layout of this type of DVC

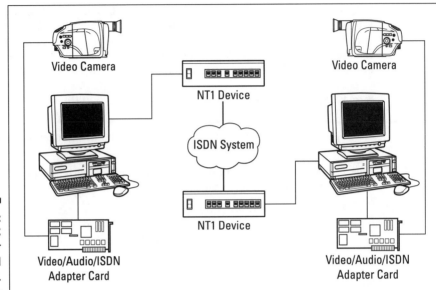

Figure 12-2:
A DVC
system for
the ISDN
WAN.

system. These Internet-only DVC systems are considerably less expensive than
the systems that support dial-up and Internet video conferencing. They are also
considerably cheaper to use because they require a local telephone call,
instead of a long-distance ISDN call.

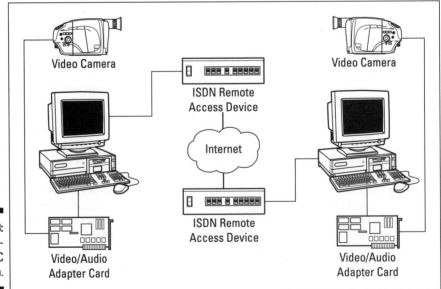

Figure 12-3:
An Internet-
only DVC
system.

Internet DVC systems are less expensive, but a downside to their use is that you may experience a latency problem if Internet traffic is heavy. Also, if the person on the other end is using a POTS connection, there will be added latency and video and audio degradation.

Anatomy of a video-conferencing system

The configuration of components varies depending on the type of DVC system and how the vendor packages the product. A complete ISDN desktop video-conferencing system for the PC typically includes the following elements:

- ✔ A video/audio card: The card includes ports for connecting the video camera, audio devices (microphone, headphones, speakers), and an S/T-interface (RJ-45) port for connecting to an NT1 device. A network-only (Internet and LAN) DVC system doesn't include the S/T-interface port because access is through your ISDN remote-access device.

- ✔ A small digital video camera: It typically mounts on top of your monitor or has its own stand.

- ✔ Video-conferencing software: Beyond software to make the DVC system work, DVC programs typically include collaborative computing tools. These tools enable you to display and share applications across all the participants' screens.

ISDN video-conferencing systems that enable you to make dial-up connections via the ISDN system include a built-in ISDN adapter with an S/T interface. This functionality is built into the video/audio card or as a separate card. The ISDN adapter allows your desktop video-conferencing system to communicate via ISDN. If you use a desktop video-conferencing system with an ISDN remote-access device, in most cases you'll need to use a separate NT1 device. Both the ISDN remote-access device and the DVC system must have an S/T interface, unless the U-interface remote-access device has an S/T-interface port.

Most video systems include a color video camera. The standard for digital cameras and video capture cards is the NTSC standard. Different video capture cards support different types of video cameras. Typically DVC systems support composite video via an RCA connector and S-VHS via a four-pin mini-DIN connector. The significance of the S-VHS port is that it enables you to connect a camcorder to your video-conferencing system. In most cases, an S-VHS camcorder offers a better quality image as well as sophisticated camera features.

If you have an S-VHS camcorder, get a video-conferencing system with a video capture card that supports S-VHS.

Software tools of the video-conferencing trade

Video-conferencing systems typically include software for managing the video conference as well as for collaborative computing. The systems include tools for managing a video conference, such as video and audio adjustments, address books for making automatic connections, and file-transfer programs for uploading and downloading files.

Many DVC systems include whiteboard programs that let people communicate while sharing the same whiteboard across their screens. Participants can illustrate points or develop ideas in the same way they would in a conference room. Whiteboard features typically include annotation tools and file import tools for bringing in information from other Microsoft Windows applications. Figure 12-4 shows a whiteboard application.

Application-sharing software enables participants to work interactively by sharing the same application such as Word for Windows or Excel (Figure 12-5).

Figure 12-4: A whiteboard application lets video conference participants have a common "chalkboard" space for sharing information.

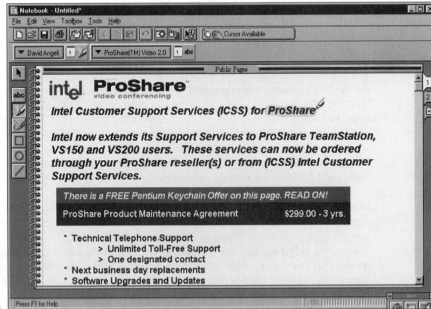

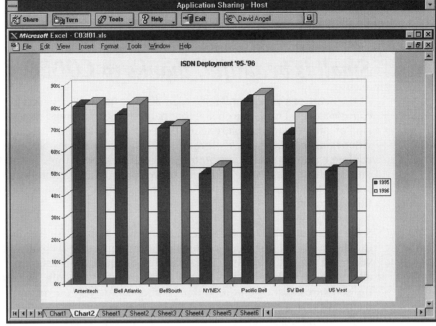

Figure 12-5:
Working
interactively
with an
Excel
spreadsheet
during a
video
conference
allows both
participants
to play with
the
numbers.

Support your local standards

For a video-conferencing system from one vendor to work with another
vendor's system, both systems must comply with the H.320 standard. This
standard, established by the International Telephone Union (ITU), defines the
interoperability between video and voice for video conferencing over ISDN.
Most desktop video-conferencing systems comply with this standard, as do
many room-size video-conferencing systems. This means that desktop video-
conferencing systems can work with room-size video-conferencing systems.

The H.320 standard actually consists of a subset of other standards that fall
within the H.320 classification. The H.323 is the standard for desktop video
conferencing over LANs; H.324 is the standard for POTS connections.

Beyond the visual element of desktop video conferencing, much of the interaction during a conference involves reviewing and marking up documents,
sharing information via files and applications, and exchanging faxes. The T.120
standard covers these functions. It's a general multimedia-conferencing standard. Using this standard in desktop video-conferencing systems enables you to
use whiteboard and application-sharing programs across different products.
Like the H.320 standard, the T.120 also includes a subset of other standards. For
example, T.127 establishes a way for DVC users to execute simultaneous
multipoint file transfers. For a vendor to claim T.120 compliance, the DVC
system must support the T.124 (Generic Conference Control), T.122 (Multipoint

Communications Service), and T.123 (Network Specific Transport Protocols) standards.

Small is beautiful, thanks to CODEC

At the heart of a video-conferencing system is the *CODEC,* which is short for *coder/decoder.* This is the engine that handles the compression and decompression of data for video conferencing. Data compression allows data-intensive video images to flow quickly through ISDN and your PC. PC-based video-conferencing systems incorporate the CODEC engine in three forms: a software-only solution, a hardware and software combination, or a purely hardware solution. Most current desktop video-conferencing systems use the combination approach.

Software solutions depend on the CPU power of your PC for handling the CODEC functions. For video-conferencing systems using the software option, you need a Pentium system. The software-only package is less expensive and allows for upgrading capabilities via software improvements. The downside of the software CODEC solution is that it relies exclusively on your CPU. If you're using a CPU that's slower than a Pentium, the quality and speed of your video conferencing will suffer.

The combination hardware and software CODEC solution shares the burden of compression between a processor on the video capture card and software. This middle-of-the-road approach takes pressure off a PC's CPU. It is less flexible in terms of future upgrades, however, because the CODEC functions are in a processor on the video capture board. The purely hardware solution delivers the fastest capabilities for CODEC tasks, but it's the least flexible in terms of upgrading.

What's behind a pretty picture?

The differences in the quality of desktop video-conferencing systems largely boil down to frames per second (fps) rate, resolution, and color bits per pixel. The higher the frame rate, resolution, and color bits per pixel, the better the quality of the video.

A *frame* is a single picture that, when pieced together with other pictures and displayed in a certain order, creates videos. *Frames per second* is the number of pictures flashed in a second to give the image the illusion of motion. Broadcast television presents a moving picture at 30 fps, which is based on the National Television Standards Committee (NTSC) standard. The NTSC standard defines how any television set in North America receives any transmitted broadcast television signal. Most desktop video-conferencing systems deliver a video image at around 20 fps. At about 16 fps, the illusion of motion changes to the perception of a series of frames.

The NTSC standard covers not only the United States, Canada, and Mexico, but also most Asian and South American countries. Much of Western Europe and other countries use the Phase Alteration Line (PAL) video format. Much of Eastern Europe, the former Soviet Union, and other countries use a video format called Séquential Couleur Avec Memoire (SECAM).

Resolution refers to the number of pixels your monitor and card can display. Because of the huge data demands made by video, having a video image the size of your PC's full screen currently is not feasible. Image sizes for most desktop video-conferencing system fit within windows that range from 160 x 120 to 320 x 240 pixels in size. (*Pixels* are picture elements, those little dots on the screen that light up in different colors to make pictures.) Standard video images measured in pixels are 160 x 120, 240 x 180, 320 x 240, and 640 x 480. *Bits per pixel* define the color depth of an image. The more bits supported, the better the color quality. The better graphics cards support 24-bit color.

What You Need for Video Conferencing

You need several key things in place to work with video conferencing. They include a PC that meets certain requirements, a properly configured ISDN line, and an NT1 or an NT1 Plus device. This section explains the PC and ISDN requirements.

The optimum PC configuration for DVC

Here's what you should have in terms of PC capabilities to get the most out of video conferencing. In most cases, you can get by with less, but you'll pay in terms of performance. Your PC should include

- ✔ At least a 486 CPU running at 100MHz or higher; or better yet, a Pentium CPU running at 90MHz or higher

- ✔ An accelerated VESA-bus or PCI-bus graphics card that supports at least SVGA with 800 x 600 resolution with 256 colors recommended

- ✔ A minimum of 16MB of RAM; more is better

- ✔ One or two empty 16-bit ISA bus slots or one PCI slot, depending on the desktop video-conferencing system

- ✔ Microsoft Windows 95 or Windows NT 4.0

- ✔ 20MB of available hard disk space

- ✔ A CD-ROM drive to install the video-conferencing software, although some come on 3 ½-inch diskettes

Graphics cards and monitors

Video-conferencing systems rely on your PC system's graphics card and monitor. A graphics card sends pictures to your monitor. The better the quality of your graphics card and monitor, the better your video display. Here are optimal graphics card and monitor features for working with video conferencing:

- ✔ A 24-bit graphics card that can display 16.7 million colors, often called *true color*. This large number of colors is about the same number of colors that the human eye can differentiate.

- ✔ A dot pitch of .28 or smaller. The *dot pitch* is the distance between the pixel dots on the screen. The smaller the dot pitch, the clearer the picture.

- ✔ A noninterlaced monitor with a 15-inch or larger screen (measured diagonally). A noninterlaced monitor's display has less flicker and looks better than an interlaced monitor.

- ✔ A VESA or PCI graphics card with 2MB of VRAM (video RAM) that supports extended graphics resolutions of 800 x 600, 1024 x 768, or higher. VRAM is a special type of dynamic RAM that is faster than DRAM (dynamic RAM).

ISDN line requirements

Following are the ISDN line requirements for establishing a video-conferencing system. You must have a single BRI line with two B channels. One of your B channels usually needs to have both *circuit-switched data and circuit-switched voice* (CSD/CSV). In most cases, you must use both B channels for video conferencing.

In addition, you need either an AT&T 5ESS Custom, National ISDN-1 compliant, or Nortel DMS 100 telephone company switch. You also need to know the telephone number(s) for your ISDN line and any SPIDs.

NT1 or NT1 Plus device

All the leading DVC systems that support dial-up ISDN and Internet connections don't include built-in NT1s. To use these systems, you need to use an NT1 device, an NT1 Plus device, or have an S/T-interface port on a remote-access device. Typically, you use either an NT1 or an NT1 Plus device that has an S/T-interface port for plugging in the RJ-45 cable from the video-conferencing system's ISDN adapter card.

If you use an Internet-only video-conferencing system, your connection is made through your ISDN remote-access device. The video-conferencing system sends its information to the remote-access device via your PCs bus, so it doesn't connect to the ISDN line directly.

For more information on NT1 and NT1 Plus devices, see Chapter 5.

Leading Desktop Video-Conferencing Systems

The leading complete PC-based video-conferencing systems for dial-up DVC include Intel's ProShare Personal Conferencing Video System 200 and PictureTel's Live 200p. These systems represent the top of the line in ISDN DVC systems.

The ProShare Personal Conferencing Video System 200 sells for between $999 and $1999, depending on the telephone company in your area. The ProShare system also lets you do video-only conferences across a TCP/IP or Novell network. ProShare was the first mass-market ISDN-based DVC system, and it continues to dominate the ISDN DVC market. The latest version, 2.0, offers significant improvements over earlier versions. (Chapter 13 explains working with the ProShare Personal Conferencing Video System 200.)

The PictureTel Live 200p is a new DVC product from PictureTel, which is the leading player in the video-conferencing industry with around 70 percent of the market in mid- to high-end video-conferencing systems. The Live 200p, at $1495, is PictureTel's entry-level product in the ISDN DVC market. (Chapter 14 explains how to work with the PictureTel Live 200p.) The Live200p comes in either a LAN-only version or an ISDN-only version.

Appendix B provides a complete listing of desktop video-conferencing products, vendors, and services.

For Internet access, you can build your own DVC system using video capture and audio cards combined with a digital video camera and desktop video-conferencing system software. A number of á la carte solutions involve the use of a single video/audio card or separate video and audio cards. These video capture and audio cards are available from Creative Labs, Logitech, ATI, Turtle Beach, Pro Audio, and other well-known PC industry vendors. A number of companies sell digital cameras ranging from the inexpensive Connectix QuickCam ($99) to more expensive models from Toshiba, Chinon, Phillips, Sony, and Cannon ($259 to $495). For Internet-based DVC software, the leading package is CU-SeeMe, which has become the de facto standard for the Internet.

WINNOV's VideumConf Pro system, which sells for $499, is a slick Internet-based video-conferencing system that includes the video/audio card, a Phillips digital video camera, and an enhanced version of CU-SeeMe. It also includes a collection of video and audio editing tools. (Chapter 15 describes working with the VideumConf Pro system.)

Lights, Camera, Action

Video conferencing thrusts you in front of a camera. As part of setting up a video-conferencing system, you need to pay attention to lighting, camera placement, and even what color clothing you wear. Additionally, because the video and audio elements of your desktop video conference are delayed by transmission, there are guidelines for interacting. This section presents key concepts for presenting yourself in the best possible light in front of the camera as well as basic DVC etiquette.

Sculpting with light

Three forms of lighting affect how you appear in your video image: key light, back light, and fill light. You can use these to sculpt the subject of a video conference, which is you.

The *key light* is the main source of light that defines the basic shape of the subject. Typically, key light comes from above the subject and in front of the subject but to the side. The *main,* or *back, light* adds definition to the subject to counteract the key light. Typically, this form of lighting is behind the subject. *Fill lighting* is used to fill in any dark areas not covered by the key and back lighting. Figure 12-6 shows the placement of the key, back, and fill lights.

Although you may not be able to control all the lighting elements for your video-conferencing system, here are some basic lighting guidelines:

- ✔ Avoid strong back lighting. For example, avoid directing the camera toward a window or another strong light source.

- ✔ Use only fluorescent or white incandescent lights if possible. Clear incandescent and older fluorescent lights tend to result in yellowish video images.

- ✔ Avoid direct lighting from the front because it creates a flat look. The camera increases the contrast of your scene — dark areas get darker, light areas get lighter. This produces unnatural-looking images.

- ✔ Make sure that the lighting is adequate — too little light results in grainy-looking images.

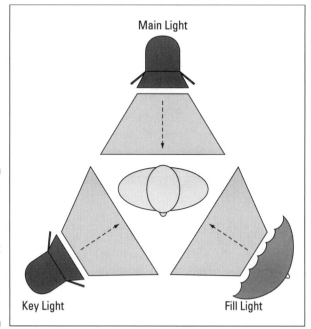

Figure 12-6:
A typical main light, fill light, and key light layout can improve your video image.

Main Light

Key Light

Fill Light

Backing up your image

Beyond lighting, another area to pay attention to is your backdrop or background. Most cameras catch whatever is behind you, so you may want to play around with backdrops to get the best possible environment. One of the best colors to use for a background is blue. You can use two methods to define a background: darken it or lighten it. You can also have fun playing with backdrops to create different views for remote viewers.

Clothes make the video conference

One final area to pay attention to is the color of your clothing. Certain colors and patterns don't come across well on video. Here are some simple clothing guidelines for getting in front of the camera:

✔ Dark or white clothing negatively affects the lighting of your image.

✔ Reds bleed on-screen.

✔ Patterns are difficult for the video-conferencing system because they must be constantly redrawn.

Elements of video-conferencing style

Video conferencing is a visual medium that incorporates new ways for conducting one-on-one or group meetings. As a communications environment, it takes some elements from face-to-face meetings and some from telephone conversations.

Most desktop video-conferencing systems have a delay in the audio and video links. The key thing to remember for video conferencing is to pause often to allow for transmission delays, especially when using application-sharing applications. This takes a little getting used to, but as you work with desktop video conferencing, you'll get into a slower mode of interaction.

Group Conferencing

To participate in a multiple-person DVC session over ISDN, you must connect to a central site with equipment (called an MCU) that supports multiple DVC connections. An MCU (multipoint control unit) is a bridging device that enables multiparty, multichannel voice, video, and data calls.

MCUs, which are available at individual company sites or through a conferencing service provider, enable everyone to connect to each other over ISDN lines. Either all participants call into the central site and are hooked into a conference, or the central site calls the participants (it depends on your conferencing service provider). Before you can start conferencing, you may have to register with a conferencing service provider. Most telephone companies, such as AT&T, MCI, and Sprint, offer DVC services.

The WorldWorx service from AT&T is a video-conferencing service for multipoint video conferencing via ISDN. WorldWorx supports any desktop video-conferencing system that supports the H.320 and T.120 standards. AT&T offers a variety of subscription pricing plans in addition to a basic entry level package. The Entry Level Plan costs $5.00 a month and $1.30 a minute anywhere in the continental USA. WorldWorx has 30-, 60-, and 120-minute plans that reduce the cost of connection time. A one-time Start-Up Package, which costs $50, is required for each subscriber. It includes 45 minutes of free usage, application validation, and technical support for the first two months of service. Contact the WorldWorx Customer Center at 800-843-3646 for more information.

The NetworkMCI Videoconferencing service offers both multipoint and point-to-point video conferencing. It supports DVC standards. The NetworkMCI Videoconferencing service offers two service levels: Premier and Signature. For more information, call 800-475-5000.

Chapter 13

Going Face to Face with ProShare

In This Chapter

▶ Installing the ProShare video-conferencing system

▶ Conducting a video conference using ProShare

▶ Using ProShare's collaboration tools

*T*he Intel ProShare Personal Conferencing Video System 200 was one of the first DVC systems for ISDN. It continues to be the leading desktop video-conferencing system. In this chapter, you can experience desktop video conferencing using Intel's ProShare 2.0.

Meet Intel's ProShare

The Intel ProShare Personal Conferencing Video System 200 is H.320 and T.120 compliant. ProShare 2.0 includes a complete interface overhaul as well a number of new enhancements.

Because the ProShare is an S/T-interface system, you need to use an NT1 or an NT1 Plus device. Remember, you can have only one NT1 on your side of the ISDN line. For more information on NT1 devices, see Chapter 5.

The ProShare video system includes the following components and features:

✔ Support for both a composite RCA and an S-VHS video camera

✔ A digital camera that mounts on your monitor and connects to the video capture card using the composite RCA jack

✔ A whiteboard program for collaboration

✔ Support for three types of connections: ISDN lines, a LAN (IPX or TCP/IP), or over the Internet. Using a modem, you can use ProShare to share data only.

✔ Multipoint conferencing with more than one person over a network or over ISDN lines

✔ A user-friendly Conference Manager and Video Window for handling and managing your video-conferencing tasks

✔ File-transfer capability for transferring files to everyone or to only certain people in a conference

✔ Application-sharing program

Unfortunately, the ProShare has some negatives. It requires two slots, one for the video capture card and the other for the audio/ISDN adapter card. Of the leading DVC systems, this is the only one that requires two cards.

Also, the combination earphone and microphone earpiece is cheap and doesn't fit well. You'll probably want to purchase a better headset to use with the ProShare.

Installing ProShare

Installing ProShare is easy. On the hardware side, ProShare uses two slots, one for the audio/ISDN adapter and another for the video adapter. You also need to connect the headset and the camera.

To install the ProShare hardware, do the following:

1. **With your PC turned off, remove the cover, choose two empty 16- or 32-bit slots, and remove their cover plates.**

   The two slots don't need to be next to each other.

2. **Insert the ISDN adapter card into one of the slots.**

   The ISDN board is the longer of the two boards that come with ProShare.

3. **Insert the video capture card into another slot.**

   The video board is the shorter board.

4. **Attach the camera cable to the back of the video card and camera.**

5. **Plug one end of the camera power cord into the back of the camera, and plug the other end into the wall plug or power strip.**

6. **Attach the headset's speaker and microphone connectors to the HP and MIC jacks on the back of the ISDN board.**

7. **Mount the camera on the top of your monitor and attach the headset holder to the side of your monitor.**

8. **Attach one end of the ISDN line to the Line jack on the ISDN board, and connect the other end to an S/T-interface port in an NT1 or an NT1 Plus device.**

9. **Put the cover back on your PC; turn on your PC and start Windows 95.**

   Windows 95 detects the Intel boards in your system, and displays the New Hardware Found dialog box.

10. **Choose the Do not install a driver option.**

11. **Click OK.**

Before you install the ProShare software, make sure that you have the following information about your ISDN connection. This information is required to answer the prompts during the ProShare's software setup:

✔ Your ISDN line number or numbers

✔ SPID number(s) your telephone company assigned to your ISDN line, if any

✔ The type of switch used at the CO

Here's how to install the ProShare software:

1. **Insert the Enhanced CU-SeeMe CD into your computers CD-ROM drive and double-click the My Computer icon on the desktop.**

2. **Double-click the CD-ROM drive icon.**

   The contents of the CD appear.

3. **Double-click the folder titled Disk1.**

   The contents of the Disk1 folder appear.

4. **Double-click the icon titled Setup.exe and then follow the instructions on your screen.**

   The Setup Wizard walks you through the ISDN configuration process. The default setup option is Typical, which installs all the files with the Add Conference Manager Listening to Startup group option turned off (not checked). Use this default setting.

5. **When the ProShare setup program prompts you to restart Windows, click the Restart Windows button.**

   Windows 95 restarts.

6. **Choose Start⇨Programs⇨ProShare Personal Conferencing⇨ProShare Conferencing.**

   The first time you open the ProShare program, it performs diagnostics and calibration tests of your system. After the tests are successfully performed, the Intel ProShare displays the Welcome dialog box (Figure 13-1). You can check out What's New, a tutorial, a guided tour, or video-conferencing services for multipoint video conferences.

Figure 13-1:
The ProShare Welcome screen offers you access to tutorials and general ProShare information.

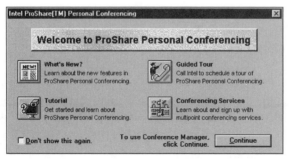

7. **If you don't want this dialog box to appear each time you start ProShare, select the Don't show this again check box.**

8. **Click the Continue button.**

   The Intel Registration dialog box appears.

9. **For now, click the Don't Register Now button.**

   The Conference Manager and the Video Window appear on your screen as shown in Figure 13-2.

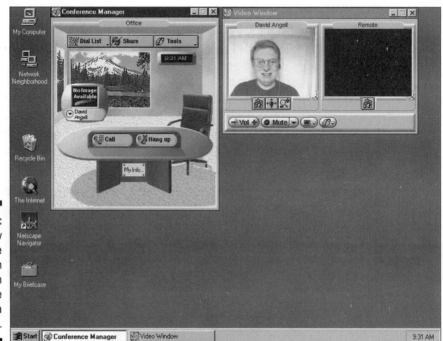

Figure 13-2:
This is how ProShare appears on your screen before making a connection.

The Conference Manager window is the main control area for the ProShare video-conferencing system. The Video Window displays your local video image and the remote video image. When you run ProShare, your image is the only one that appears. After you make a video conference connection, the image of the remote site appears in the remote window.

Making or Answering the DVC Call

You start the ProShare program by choosing Start⇨Programs⇨ProShare Personal Conferencing⇨ProShare Conferencing. Make sure that your video camera is on by sliding the door to the left. A green status light turns on.

An active video in the ProShare Video Window doesn't constitute activity for a screen saver. Therefore, turn off your screen saver to avoid its interruptions during a connection.

To make a video-conferencing call on the fly, you can quickly open the hand-set (Figure 13-3), type in the number, and click on the Call button. The call is made.

To give you an instant desktop video-conferencing experience (and so you can check to make sure that everything is working), the following steps explain how to connect to the Intel ISDN test line:

1. **Click the Call button in the Conference Manager.**

   The hand-set appears in the Conference Manager (Figure 13-3).

Figure 13-3:
The ProShare hand-set looks like a telephone hand-set and works in a similar manner.

2. Type the Intel ISDN test number: 503-264-1368 **or** 503-264-1367.

Don't forget to enter prefix numbers, if necessary. For example, type **1** for long distance.

3. Click the Dial button.

The Unknown Call Type dialog box appears.

4. Double-click on ISDN.

The remote window displays lava lamps (Figure 13-4), and you hear music. You're connected.

Figure 13-4:
The lava lamps at the Intel ProShare test center.

5. Click the Hang Up button in the Hand-set window after finishing your conference.

A dialog box appears asking whether you want to save the participant's information in your Address Book. The default Yes option is selected.

6. Choose OK.

The video conference call is disconnected.

Making speed-dial calls with the Dial List

ProShare's Dial List is the quickest and easiest way to make calls. You can type a name and number directly in the Dial List. Or when you enter a name and number in the handset, the entry is added automatically to the Dial List. If you made the call to the Intel ISDN test line (in the preceding section), you've already created an entry in the Dial List.

To speed dial from the Dial List, click the Dial List button in the Conference Manager window or on the hand-set, which you display by clicking the Call button in the Conference Manager. A drop-down list appears. Clicking a number in the list automatically dials the number.

Creating Dial List entries

You can create entries directly into the Dial List without making a call. You can enter the person's name as well as the telephone number or network address. You can also edit numbers. Here's how to add an entry into the Dial List:

1. **Click the Dial List button in the Conference Manager or the hand-set.**

   A drop-down list of entries appears.

2. **Click Edit Dial List entry.**

   The Edit Dial List dialog box appears (Figure 13-5).

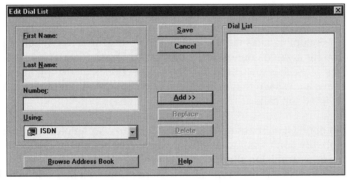

Figure 13-5: Use the Edit Dial List dialog box to change entries in your Dial List.

3. **Enter the first and last name.**

4. **Select the connection type from the Using drop-down list.**

   The default option is ISDN, but you can also choose LAN/IPX for a Novell Network; LAN/TCPIP for TCP/IP for the Internet (or other TCP/IP network); or voice. For now, use the default ISDN setting.

5. **Enter the ISDN number(s) in the Number field.**

   If you call two numbers (one for each B channel), type the first number, type a colon, and then type the second number.

6. Click Add.

The entry appears in the Dial List box on the right side of the Edit Dial List dialog box.

The Browse Address Book button, which works with the Dial List, displays. You can select Address Book entries to make them available in the Dial List. Working with the Address Book is explained later.

7. Repeat Steps 3 tthrough 6 for as many entries as you want and then click Save.

After you create a Dial List entry, you can make a video conference call by simply clicking the name of the entry in the Dial List. You can also edit any Dial List entry using the Edit Dial List. Selecting any item in the Dial List window (on the right side of the dialog box) displays a button for replacing or deleting the entry.

Answering a call

When you are running the ProShare program on your system, it can receive incoming calls to your ISDN telephone number or, if you're connected to the Internet, incoming calls via the Internet to your IP address. When somebody calls you for a video conference, a dialog box appears with two choices. If you click Yes, the call is answered and the connection is made. If you click No, the caller sees a message that the call can't be completed. The caller isn't told that you declined the call.

You can configure ProShare to automatically answer an incoming call. However, you probably don't want to use this feature — what if your camcorder catches you in a compromising situation? This feature, which is available from the Preferences dialog box, is typically used for showing a live video image to anyone who calls the ISDN directory numbers.

Making ProShare listen

ProShare also has a Listening program that places the ProShare program into a state of listening in the background for an incoming call. A minimized icon appears as a button on your taskbar. The ProShare Listening program takes up less memory resources than loading the full-blown version of ProShare.

You can start Listening mode two ways. In the first, you simply choose Listen in the Conference Manager's Control menu. The other way is to choose Start➪ Programs➪ProShare Personal Conferencing➪Conference Manager Listening.

Group Conferencing

You can conference with several people at the same time, which is called *multipoint conferencing*. You can conduct an ISDN multipoint conference in two ways: using a conferencing service from a conferencing service provider or using a company's MCU (multipoint control unit). The MCU is the connecting unit that allows everyone to connect to each other over ISDN lines. Either all participants call into the MCU and are hooked into a conference, or the MCU calls the participants (it depends on your conferencing service provider).

Before you can start conferencing, you may have to register with a conferencing service provider. To use a conferencing service: double-click the Conferencing Services icon (in the ProShare Personal Conferencing program group) to learn more about or sign up with conferencing service providers. If your company has its own MCU, contact your MCU administrator.

How you start an ISDN multipoint conference depends on your conferencing service provider or MCU. In general, a few minutes before the scheduled conference time, you start the ProShare software on your system. When it's time for the conference, either the MCU calls you or you call it (depending on your MCU or service provider). How you end an ISDN conference also depends on your MCU or service provider.

If your multipoint video-conferencing service supports the ProShare Scheduler application, you can use it to request and track your ISDN multipoint conferences. To start the Scheduler program, choose Scheduler from the Control menu in Conference Manager.

Adjusting Your Sights and Sounds

The Audio and Video Preferences button (located to the right of the Mute button) in the Video Window displays a menu of options for managing window arrangements, controlling audio and video quality, adjusting the video camera, and more.

The following describes the commands in the Audio and Video Preferences menu:

- ✔ The Windows Layout item provides a collection of local and remote video window arrangement options.
- ✔ The Use Headset and the Use Speakers settings let you toggle between using one or the other.

✔ The Use Camera 1 and the Use Camera 2 settings let you toggle between two cameras connected to your ProShare video card (RCA or S-VHS).

✔ The Image control command displays the Image Controls dialog box (Figure 13-6), which you use to adjust saturation, contrast, brightness, and tint for the local and remote windows. Here's an explanation of these settings:

- Saturation: Changes the intensity of colors

- Contrast: Adjusts the lightness or darkness of the image

- Brightness: Adjusts the amount of light in the image

- Tint: Affects the depth of colors from pale to deep

Figure 13-6:
Use the Image Controls dialog box to adjust how the video appears in the local and remote video windows.

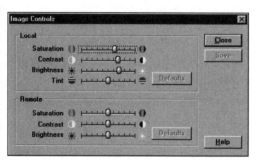

Zooming and panning

The Zoom button (the third button under the local video window) zooms your video image in or out. The Pan button (the middle button under the local video window) displays a Pan & Tilt window (Figure 13-7) to enable you to adjust your image in your local window.

Click the Pan button under your local window (you can pan only your local window). Click the appropriate arrow button to move, or pan, the camera in that direction. You can pan only when you've zoomed in (using the Zoom button). When the window looks the way you want, click OK.

Figure 13-7:
Use the Pan
& Tilt dialog
box to
adjust the
placement
of the
subject in
the local
video
window.

If you're displaying video in Sharper mode (320 x 240), you won't be able to zoom and pan.

Changing your reflection

When you first install the ProShare Video System, your image in your local window is mirrored (it's as if you're looking in a mirror). To switch it so that it's not mirrored, click the Tools button in the Video Window (the button located at the far right, bottom of the window) and then choose Preferences. Under Local Window Mirroring, choose Not Mirrored and then click OK.

The Not Mirrored option also enables you to show written text in readable form. (The Mirrored setting makes the text appear as a reflection, which results in the text appearing backward on the screen.)

Changing the size of the video windows

Unfortunately, you cannot get a video image to full screen in Windows 95. You can, however, drag the local and remote video window handles to change the size of the local or remote video window (see Figure 13-8). Move the pointer to the lower right corner of the local or remote window and then drag the handle outward to enlarge the window. Dragging the handles inward makes the window smaller.

Figure 13-8:
The local
video
window is
the large
window size
and the
remote
window is
the smallest
window
size.

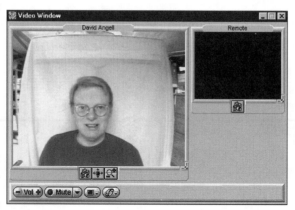

Making other window arrangements

During a DVC session, your desktop can quickly get cluttered. To help you make your windows stay collected and organized, ProShare includes a number of options for window arrangements. Click the Audio and Video Preferences button in the Video Window, and a menu is displayed. In the Windows Layout item, you access commands for arranging the relationships between the local and remote windows. For example, you can hide the local window, or you can place the remote window at the top and the local window below it.

The Select Window Arrangement command in the Tools menu displays the Select Window Arrangement dialog box (Figure 13-9). You can choose from several basic window arrangements for your ProShare application and video windows.

Muting a video conference call

ProShare lets you mute a video conference call. When you mute a call, you can still hear and see the other person, but they can't hear or see you, depending on the settings you choose. The other person sees a Mute notice when you mute the video.

Click the Audio and Video Mute button at the bottom of the Video Window to choose one of the following settings: Mute Audio and Video, Mute Audio, or Mute Video. Click the Mute button to enable the Mute option you choose. When the Mute option is active, a red light appears on the Mute button. To turn off the Mute option, click the Mute button again.

If the other person mutes the video or mutes both the audio and video, you'll see a message that the call is being muted (so you can't see or hear what the other person is doing). The other person can still see and hear you, though.

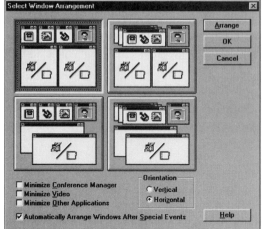

Figure 13-9:
The Select Window Arrangement dialog box provides a collection of window arrangement templates that you can use as default settings.

Changing Preferences

The ProShare program enables you to make all kinds of changes to the initial program settings. The bulk of these configuration settings are in the ProShare Preferences dialog box (Figure 13-10). To access this dialog box, click the Tools button in the Conference Manager or the Tool button (the far left button) on the Video Window toolbar. Then choose Preferences.

Figure 13-10:
ProShare's Preferences dialog box is your gateway to customizing ProShare.

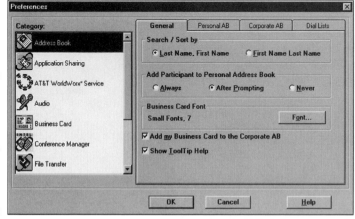

Click a category in the Category list, and the settings for that category appear on the right side of the Preferences dialog box. The 11 preferences categories have configuration settings for the following:

- ✔ The Address Book
- ✔ The Application Sharing program
- ✔ The AT&T WorldWorx Service
- ✔ Audio
- ✔ Business cards
- ✔ The Conference Manager
- ✔ File transfers
- ✔ The Notebook application
- ✔ The Photo Exchange program
- ✔ The Scheduler program
- ✔ Video

The Intel ProShare program also includes a collection of diagnostics utilities programs. Choosing Start⇨Programs⇨ProShare Personal Conferencing⇨ Diagnostics & Utilities displays the Diagnostics & Utilities dialog box (Figure 13-11). Double-clicking an item in the listing runs the respective program. This is where you can change your network IP address and your ISDN line provisioning information.

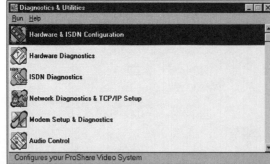

Figure 13-11:
The Diagnostics & Utilities dialog box.

Exchanging Electronic Business Cards

ProShare includes an electronic Business Card feature that you can use to quickly create a business card for contact information. At the end of a video conference, everyone can exchange Business Cards. Then when you disconnect from the conference, you have the option of saving them in your Personal Address Book. (You can edit the electronic Business Cards from other conference participants, but you can't send altered Business Cards anywhere.)

Your electronic Business Card (which has your name, number, and other information) is created automatically when you install the ProShare software. You'll want to complete it, however, for use in your video conferences. To edit your Business Card, double-click the No Image Available box (inside the television) in the Conference Manager window. The Business Card Wizard appears (Figure 13-12). Follow the steps on your screen to create a business card with a snapshot from your local video window. After you've finished, your picture appears in the TV screen in the Conference Manager.

Figure 13-12:
The
Business
Card wizard
makes
creating an
electronic
business
card with
your picture
easy.

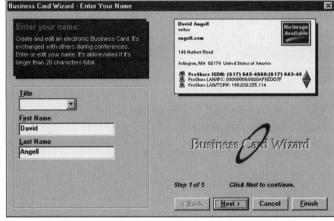

Managing Contacts with the Address Book

ProShare's Address Book is a more powerful version of the Dial List. It lets you add more detailed information about video-conferencing participants as well as link files you want to share. When you use the Address Book to make a video conference call, the files you specified are immediately available for sharing. You can use the Address Book to store and organize names, phone numbers, LAN addresses, street addresses, company names, and so on. You can also start a conference from the Address Book.

ProShare has two types of Address Books. The Personal Address Book is your main Address Book file. You enter all your information in this Address Book. All Business Card information is saved to your Personal Address Book. The Corporate Address Book is usually created and set up by a system administrator. It might list, for example, everyone in a department or company. You can have as many Address Book files as you like, but only *one* Personal Address Book and *one* Corporate Address Book file can be designated at one time.

Adding, editing, or deleting an Address Book entry

Adding a person to your Address Book involves entering optional address information, specifying the video number, and then linking documents to that participant. To create an entry to the Address Book, do the following:

1. In Conference Manager, choose Tools⇨Address Book.

The Address Book dialog box appears (Figure 13-13). Initially, the Address Book list contains Personal (DEFAULT.ab2).

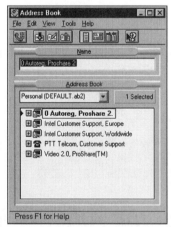

Figure 13-13: The Address Book dialog box lets you create a contact list complete with automatic dialing.

2. Choose Edit⇨Add Entry or press Ctrl-A.

The Add Entry dialog box appears (Figure 13-14).

3. Click New.

The New Connection dialog box appears.

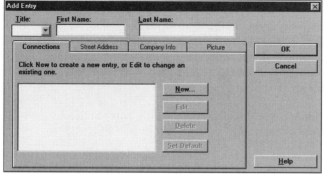

Figure 13-14: Use the Add Entry dialog box to create your address book entries.

4. **Choose how you want to connect with this person. For this example, choose ISDN.**

   You can choose only one connection type at a time in this dialog box.

5. **In the Description field, type a description of the remote site.**

6. **In the # of Lines setting, click One or Two.**

   If you click Two, a second telephone number field appears.

7. **Type a telephone number in the telephone number field(s), including an area code and any additional prefixes, such as 1 for calls outside your area code.**

8. **If you are entering two telephone numbers and you need to specify the order in which they are dialed, click the Dial As setting and arrange the numbers.**

9. **Click OK.**

   Your new connection entry appears in the Connections tab in the Add Entry dialog box.

10. **Type or choose a title in the Title list and then type the first and last name of the person.**

11. **Click the Set Default button to set this as the default number for the person.**

12. **If you want to add street address information click the Street Address tab.**

13. **If you want to enter company information, click the Company Info tab.**

14. **If you want to add a picture to this Address Book entry, click the Picture tab. Click the Browse button until you find the graphic file, and then add it.**

    You get these pictures by using ProShare's snapshot feature. See the section "Taking Snapshots and Exchanging Pictures" later in the chapter.

15. Click OK.

The entry is added to the Address Book.

Editing an Address Book entry is similar to adding an entry. You select the entry and then choose Edit⇨Edit Entry or press Ctrl-E. Click the Edit button to edit the entry.

To delete an Address Book entry, select the entry in the Address Book dialog box and then choose Edit⇨Delete Entry or press Ctrl-D.

Making a call from the Address Book

The Address Book is more than just a contact list; you can use it also to make calls. In the Address Book dialog box, click the name of the person you want to call. Then click the Calls selected person button on the toolbar or choose Tools⇨Call. Proshare prompts you to confirm making the call. Click Yes. The hand-set appears and your call is made. You can make the call also from the Dial List.

Group Collaboration via Sharing Applications

During a conference, any application can be shared as long as it's installed on one of the computers in the conference. When you share an application, everyone in the conference can use it, so everyone can edit a file together. You can have video and audio contact during an application-sharing session. You can share multiple applications at the same time; you're limited only by the amount of memory in your system.

Application sharing has two types of participants: the host and guests. The host is the computer that is running the application locally and sharing it. Any conference participant can be the host, but only one host is allowed during an application-sharing session. Guests are the participants who share the application with the host. The guest participants do not need to have the shared program running on their systems.

To share an application, do the following:

1. In the Conference Manager, click the Share button.

2. Choose Share an Application.

The Application Sharing dialog box appears with the Share dialog box in it. (Figure 13-15).

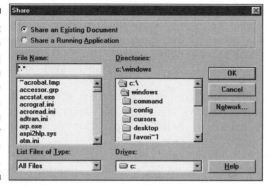

Figure 13-15:
Use the
Share dialog
box to
specify a file
to share or a
program
already
running on
your system.

3. **Click one of the two options at the top of the Share screen.**

   If you click the Share an Existing Document option, you can select the
   document you want to share. The file and the corresponding application
   will be loaded on your screen (see Figure 13-16).

   If you click the Share a Running Application option, you can share
   an application that's currently running on your system. A list of running
   applications appears so that you can select the application you want.

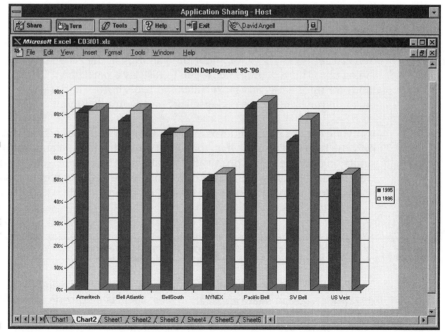

Figure 13-16:
An
application
and its
document
as they
appear in
the
Application
Sharing
window.

If any guest's screen setting is at a lower resolution than the host's, the guest may not be able to see all of the shared application. In this case, the Pan dialog box appears, showing an outline of the shared application area visible on the host's screen and a gray box that outlines the part the guest can see. To display a different part of the screen, the guest needs to drag the gray box.

Within the Application Sharing window, you can access all the commands in the application itself, as well as tools for managing your sharing session. The following describes the main controls in the Application Sharing window's toolbar, which are shown in Figure 13-16:

✔ The Turn Tray (the last button on the Application Sharing toolbar in Figure 13-16) shows either Cursor Available or your name (if you click on the tray). This control enables you to take or give up a turn.

✔ The Turn button lets you take turns editing. The default allows anyone to edit and all edits show up on all screens. Clicking the Turntaking button allows a more orderly editing process, with each participant taking turns. After anyone clicks the Turn button, everyone else is locked out until that person clicks the Turn button again. If one person turns on turntaking, it's on for everyone. You can change how turntaking works in Application Sharing Preferences.

✔ The Tools button displays the menu of ProShare applications and tools. This allows you to continue managing your connection while sharing an application.

✔ The Exit button ends the Sharing session.

You can set preferences for application sharing in the ProShare Preferences dialog box. These settings allow you to display a participant list, specify time limits for turntaking, and more. Click the Tools button and then choose Preferences. In the Preferences dialog, click Sharing Application.

If anyone cuts or copies information from the shared application, it's placed on only the host's Clipboard. If anyone prints from the shared application, the file prints on only the host's printer. If a guest needs a printout, the host can transfer the file using File Transfer. When anyone in the conference saves a shared file, it's saved on only the host's computer.

Taking Notes with the Notebook

The ProShare Notebook application lets you collaborate using the whiteboard metaphor. You can share application files, such as a PowerPoint slide; but instead of sharing the application, you place a copy of the file into your Notebook. Figure 13-17 shows the Notebook application window with an entry.

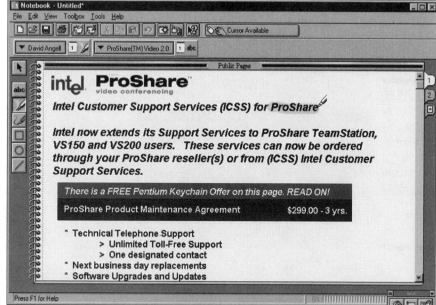

Figure 13-17:
The
Notebook
window lets
you use a
whiteboard
during a
conference.

Using the Notebook, you and other participants can view notebook pages and mark them up. Then each of you can save your markups in a Notebook file (.nbk). The marks you make on that image in the Notebook are marked and saved only in the Notebook file, not in the original file. The marks lay on top of the image, as if you had laid a transparency over it.

The Notebook's toolbar has a collection of tools for collaboration. You can take snapshots of different parts of the screen, import files, embed objects from other Windows applications, enter and highlight text, and draw pictures. You can also transfer a file in the background, which means that you can continue to work in the notebook during the transfer.

You can create different notebooks and save and work on them as ongoing projects. Each notebook has pages that you can leaf through as you would a regular notebook. You can add, delete, copy, and print notebook pages. The shared notebook also lets you take private notes that the other person can't see.

Transferring Information in File Form

You can send a copy of any file on your system to any number of conference participants. To transfer a file, do the following:

1. From any Tools menu, choose File Transfer.

The File Transfer window appears (Figure 13-18). The other participants don't need to start File Transfer; it starts automatically on their system.

Figure 13-18:
The File Transfer window provides all the tools you need to select and transfer files.

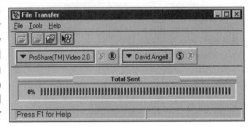

2. Choose File⇨Send Files.

The Send Files dialog box (Figure 13-19) appears.

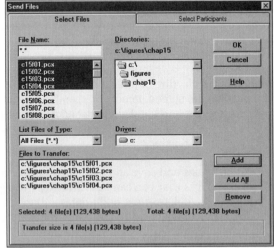

Figure 13-19:
The Send Files dialog box lets you choose one or more files for transferring.

3. Select the files you want to send and then click Add.

The files are added to the Files to Transfer list.

4. **Click the Select Participants tab to choose the people you want to send to.**

5. **Select the names of all the people to whom you want to send the file and then click Add.**

The names are added to the Selected Participants list.

6. **Click OK to start the transfer.**

Shortly after the sender starts the file transfer, the File Transfer Receipt dialog box appears on the receiving side. The receiver then chooses the drive and directory where he or she wants to save the file.

Either the sender or the receiver can cancel a file transfer. If you cancel a transfer before it's completed, none of the file is transferred. (There are no partial transfers.) If there's more than one recipient, the sender cannot cancel a file transfer to only one person; the transfer must be cancelled for all or none.

You have two choices for canceling a file transfer. Choosing File⇨Stop This File stops sending or receiving the current file, and starts sending the next file in the queue (if there is one). Choosing File⇨Stop All Files stops sending or receiving the current file and any other files in the queue.

Taking Snapshots and Exchanging Pictures

The Snapshot button (it looks like a camera) under the local and remote video windows lets you take snapshots of images in the corresponding window. You can use these snapshot in any application that supports the Windows bitmap (.bmp) file format.

To take a snapshot, click the Snapshot button. The Snapshot dialog box appears. You can choose a Normal, Large, or Extra Large format. Click Snap if you want to take multiple pictures, or click on Snap & Close to take a single shot. The Photo Exchange window appears with your captured picture (Figure 13-20). You can send the image, put it in a photo album, or save it as a .bmp file on your system.

You can use Photo Exchange to share high-resolution (high-quality) pictures during a conference. You can share pictures in electronic format as well as snapshots from your video camera. The other people see exactly what you see on your screen, and can save the image to a file on their computer.

Figure 13-20:
The Photo
Exchange
window
with a
snapshot.

From any Tools menu, choose Photo Exchange. Photo Exchange organizes pictures by albums (.pcx files). An album can consist of one picture or several pictures (up to 75, as long as there's space on your hard drive). You can have as many albums as you like. The Album supports all of the following file formats:

BMP (Windows bitmap)

GIF (CompuServe art)

TGA (Targa)

TIF (Tag Image File)

BMP (Windows bitmap)

JPG (Joint Photographic Group)

PCX (PC Paintbrush)

Chapter 14

Doing DVC with the PictureTel 200p

●●●

In This Chapter

▶ How to install the PictureTel Live 200p system

▶ Making and answering a video conference call

▶ Managing your Live 200p system

▶ Sharing applications and ideas

●●●

*T*he PictureTel 200p is a new desktop video-conferencing system from PictureTel, the leader in the mid-to high-end video-conferencing market. The 200p represents PictureTel's serious entry into the ISDN DVC market. This chapter takes you on a 200p joyride.

About the PictureTel 200p

The PictureTel Live 200p is a high-quality video-conferencing system. The Live 200p, at $1495, is more expensive than the ProShare product, but it includes an impressive collection of features:

✔ Operates under the Windows 95 environment as a 32-bit application and is automatically configured using the Windows 95 Plug-and-Play device detection feature.

✔ Real-time access lets you send and receive data simultaneously. (With real-time access, there is virtually no delay in the transmission of audio signals or video images.)

✔ Configuration of hardware from the Windows 95 Control Panel.

✔ Full H.320 compatibility/interoperability to allow you to connect and communicate with anyone who has another H.320 system or PictureTel product, including room systems.

✔ High-quality audio and video, including high-fidelity audio (7 kHz) and high-video resolution (352 x 288 pixels).

✔ Application sharing to allow the sharing of any application with your calling partner even if the application is not installed on your calling partner's computer.

✔ Remote control computing, which lets you access another PictureTel user's desktop automatically. You can also access your office desktop from your home computer (or vice versa), provided you have an ISDN line.

✔ Whiteboard application for collaboration. You can share word-processing files, presentations, and graphics using markup tools. Each Whiteboard file can hold up to 250 pages of information.

✔ Clipboard feature for the quick transfer of data from one computer to another. You and your calling partner can use the clipboard to cut, copy, or paste data.

✔ Transferring any type of file between you and your calling partner. PictureTel LiveWare lets you use the Windows 95 Explorer to drag and drop files into the File Transfer window.

Installing the Live 200p Hardware

This section explains how to install the Live200p board, video camera, and audio equipment, and how to connect the ISDN cable. To install the Live 200p board

1. **Shut down your computer.**

2. **Remove all cables connected to your computer. Open the computer chassis cover, remove the back plate of the PCI expansion slot, and then ground yourself by touching the power supply.**

3. **Insert the Live200p board securely into the PCI slot and then replace the screw that holds the backplate. Attach the peel-off label to your computer chassis on the left of the Live200p board, with the arrows pointing toward the board.**

4. **Replace the chassis cover on the computer. If you have disconnected any cables, reconnect them. Leave your computer turned off.**

5. **Connect the video camera to the adapter card.**

   The video camera end of the cable has four pins, and the other end has eight pins.

6. **Position the video camera on top of your computer monitor.**

7. **Install one of the audio devices included with the Live 200p.**

   To connect the earpiece, plug the red connector into the microphone socket on the Live200p board and plug the black connector into the speaker socket on the board. To connect the microphone and speakers, plug the microphone into the microphone socket on the Live200p board and then connect the speakers.

8. **Connect the ISDN cable to the RJ-45 socket labeled ISDN on the Live200p board. Plug the other end of the cable into an S/T-interface port on an NT1 device or your U-interface ISDN remote-access device.**

You've finished the installation of the Live 200p hardware.

Installing the LiveWare Software

This section explains how to install the PictureTel LiveWare system software and application software. To install the system software

1. **Start your computer.**

   During startup, Windows 95 prompts you to install drivers for the new Plug-and-Play devices, which are needed for running PictureTel LiveWare. The New Hardware Found dialog box appears, displaying PCI Multimedia Device at the top of the dialog box. The Driver from disk provided by hardware manufacturer option is selected by default.

2. **Click OK.**

   The Install From Disk dialog box appears.

3. **Insert the disk labeled Picture Tel Live200p Hardware Setup Disk 1 into your disk drive.**

   In the dialog box, the default source drive is A:\. Change the drive letter if needed.

4. **Click OK.**

   Files are copied to your hard drive. The New Hardware Found dialog box appears and displays PictureTel Virtual Comm Port at the top of the dialog box.

5. **Insert the PictureTel Live200p Hardware Setup disks as prompted and click OK.**

   Files are copied to your local drive.

6. **Click Continue.**

   The Camera Format dialog box appears.

7. **Specify the type of camera you are using and then click OK.**

8. **For North America (or Japan), choose the NTSC (National Television Standards Committee) option. If you're operating PictureTel LiveWare in Europe, choose the PAL (Phase Alternation Line) option.**

   After you make a selection, the Live200p Settings dialog box appears.

9. **Select an ISDN protocol. If SPIDs are required, enter them. Click OK.**

   A dialog box appears for starting the installation of the LiveWare software.

10. **Insert the disk labeled PictureTel LiveWare Disk I into your disk drive and click OK to install the application software.**

   The Welcome to the PictureTel LiveWare Setup Program dialog box appears.

11. **Click Next.**

   The PictureTel Registration dialog box appears.

12. **Type your name, company (optional), and PictureTel LiveWare serial number (located on the diskette envelope). Then click Next.**

   The Verify box appears.

13. **If the information you entered is correct, click Yes. If the information is incorrect, follow the directions on the screen.**

14. **Select the destination folder in which you want to install PictureTel LiveWare.**

   The default folder is C:\PictureTel.

15. **Click Yes to create the folder and then click Next to continue.**

   The ISDN Network Number dialog box appears.

16. **Enter your ISDN dialing number(s) and then click Next.**

17. **Choose the group folder in which you want to install PictureTel LiveWare; then click Next.**

   The default group folder is PictureTel LiveWare. The Site Name dialog box appears.

18. **Type your site name and then click Next.**

   Your site name identifies you during application sharing. A progress indicator appears and displays the status of setup.

19. **Insert the PictureTel Setup disks as instructed.**

20. **Specify whether you want PictureTel LiveWare to be copied to your Startup folder.**

   In most cases, you'll choose No.

21. **Click Yes if you want to view the README file.**

   The README file contains last-minute information that became available after the Installation and User's Guides were printed.

22. Click the Finish button.

Your computer restarts Windows 95.

Getting Started with PictureTel LiveWare

To start the PictureTel 200p LiveWare program, choose Start⇨Programs⇨ PictureTelLiveWare⇨PictureTelLiveWare. The PictureTel LiveWare window appears (Figure 14-1). This is the main control panel for your PictureTel 200p system.

Figure 14-1 identifies the buttons on the PictureTel LiveWare window's toolbar. You can change and customize the Main toolbar buttons at any time. Table 14-1 describes the buttons. You can add several other buttons to the Main toolbar using the Preferences Properties window, as I explain later in this chapter.

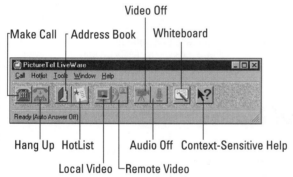

Figure 14-1: The PictureTel LiveWare window.

Table 14-1	The Main Toolbar Buttons
Button	**Description**
Make Call	Makes a video or audio call to your calling partner over a phone line.
Hang Up	Disconnects and ends a video or audio call with your calling partner.
Address Book	Opens the Address Book window, which provides telephone directories for storing phone numbers and other information about your calling partners.
HotList	Provides a speed-dialing list for your most frequently called phone numbers.

(continued)

Table 14-1 *(continued)*

Button	Description
Local Video	Opens the Local Video window, which displays the image you are sending to your calling partner.
Remote Video	Opens the Remote Video window, which displays the image your calling partner is sending you. The Remote Video window is also where you access application sharing.
Audio Off	Turns off your microphone so that your calling partner cannot hear you or local conversations. A red circle means off.
Video Off	Turns off the video image so that your calling partner cannot see you. A red circle means off.
Whiteboard	Opens the Whiteboard before making a video call to prepare a presentation or word-processing file. You can open the Whiteboard also during a video call using the toolbar in the Remote Video window.
Context-Sensitive Help	Turns your pointer into a help icon that you can use to get help on the Main toolbar.

Your Local Video window

The Local Video window displays the image you are sending your calling partner from your video camera (usually yourself). You can view the image you are sending before and during a video call. Figures 14-2a and 14-2b show the types of live video images that you can display in the Local Video window.

The following describes the settings available in the Local Video window:

- ✓ The Image Size list box lets you automatically resize the Local Video window. The choices are Small, Medium, and Large. You can resize this window manually, too, by dragging the bottom right-hand corner. The window dimensions are then displayed in the list box. You can also set the default sizes for Small, Medium, and Large in the Video Window sheet, which is available from the Preferences Properties window.

- ✓ The Increase Brightness button lets you increase the balance of light and dark shades in your image in the Local Video window.

- ✓ The Decrease Brightness button lets you decrease the balance of light and dark shades in the Local Video window.

Figure 14-2a:
The Local
Video
window
typically
shows your
video
image.

Figure 14-2b:
The Local
Video
window can
show any
live video
image.

You can also add the following buttons to the Local Video Toolbar using the
Toolbar tab in the Preferences Properties window (Tools⇨Preferences).

✔ The Increase Contrast button lets you increase the range between the
lightest tones and the darkest tones in your image in the Local Video
window.

✔ The Decrease Contrast button lets you decrease the range between the
lightest tones and the darkest tones in your image in the Local Video
window.

✔ The Increase Color button lets you increase the color mixture of your
image in the Local Video window.

✔ The Decrease Color button lets you decrease the color mixture of your
image in the Local Video window.

Remote Video window (viewing the other half)

When your call connects, the Remote Video window appears with your calling partner's image (Figure 14-3). The Remote Video window lets you open the Whiteboard, share applications, send messages, and transfer files using the menus or toolbar buttons. You can change the size of the Remote Video window by dragging the lower right-hand corner of the window border.

Figure 14-3:
The Remote Video window shows the image of your video-conferencing partner.

You can use the following buttons in the Remote Video window toolbar to immediately access a feature. Each button is a shortcut way of choosing a pull-down menu item.

 ✔ The Hang-up button lets you end the call in progress with your calling partner.

 ✔ The Image Size list box lets you automatically resize the Remote Video window. The choices are Small, Medium, and Large. If you manually resize it by dragging the bottom right-hand corner, the window dimensions are displayed in the list box. You can also set the default sizes for Small, Medium, and Large in the Video Window sheet, which is available from the Preferences menu.

 ✔ The Audio Off button lets you turn off the microphone so that your calling partner cannot hear you or local conversations. A red circle means turned off.

 ✔ The Video Off button lets you turn off the video image so that your calling partner cannot see you. When you turn off your video, the image in the Local Video window is black. A red circle means turned off.

✔ The Whiteboard button lets you open the Whiteboard during a call to annotate a presentation or word-processing file with your calling partner.

✔ The Share Application button lets you share an application or file with your calling partner.

✔ The Unshare Application button lets you stop sharing an application that you are currently sharing. You cannot unshare an application that your calling partner set up to share. When you unshare an application, it disappears from your calling partner's desktop but remains open on your desktop.

✔ The Volume control slider lets you adjust the volume of the audio you are receiving from your calling partner. Sliding the control to the left decreases the volume. Sliding the control to the right increases the volume.

✔ The Call duration counter records the length of time of your video call by displaying the hours, minutes, and seconds.

You can add the following buttons to the Remote Video toolbar using the Toolbar tab in the Preferences Properties window (Tools⇨Preferences). You can also add the Message and File Transfer buttons.

✔ The Control Remote Desktop button lets you remotely control a desktop.

✔ The Detach button lets you disable application sharing while retaining your view of open applications.

✔ The Clipboard button lets you share data from one computer to another using the clipboard.

You can also use the menu bar in the PictureTel LiveWare Remote Video window to access all the options available from the buttons.

Making Your First Video Call

To make your first video call, you can manually enter the ISDN numbers in the Make Call dialog box (see Figure 14-4). As I explain later in the chapter, you can create Address Book entries for speed dialing your video conferences. To make your first video call with PictureTel LiveWare, do the following:

To test your PictureTel 200p LiveWare system, you can call the PictureTel service center at 508-437-9361.

1. Click the Make Call button in the Main toolbar.

The Make Call dialog box appears (Figure 14-4).

2. **Dial the ISDN telephone number twice using the 1st and 2nd Phone Number boxes.**

   If the first and second phone numbers are identical, press the Tab key to automatically enter the 1st phone number into the 2nd Phone Number field.

Figure 14-4:
Use the
Make Call
dialog box to
manually
enter a
video-
conferencing
number and
then place
the call.

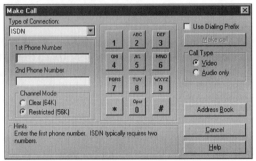

3. **Select the Use Dialing Prefix check box if you want to automatically add one or two digits (for example, 9 and 1) to the ISDN phone number that you are dialing.**

4. **Enter your calling partner's ISDN phone number in the 1st and 2nd Phone Number boxes and then press Enter.**

   You can enter digits using the number pad on your keyboard or by clicking the number buttons on the dialpad in the Make Call dialog box.

5. **Choose a different channel mode, if necessary.**

   You can usually use the Clear (64K) channel mode, which is the default.

6. **Click the Make call button to dial the video call.**

   A dialog box appears and provides a status of your call by highlighting the words *Dialing, Ringing,* and *Connecting.* After your connection is made, the Local Video window appears with your image (unless you opened the window before the video call), and the Remote Video window appears with your calling partner's image (Figure 14-5).

7. **To end your video conference call, click the Hang-up button in the Remote Video window.**

Figure 14-5:
After a
connection
is made, the
Local and
Remote
Video
windows
appear on
your screen.

Answering the Video Call

You can choose to answer a video call manually or automatically. In most cases, you want to answer all your video calls manually. Having the PictureTel answer video-conferencing calls automatically can be dangerous — you never know when it could be your boss calling!

When you receive a video call, your computer rings to notify you. The message *Incoming Call* appears in the status line of the Main toolbar, and the Incoming Call dialog box appears. If the person calling you is listed in your Address Book list, the name of that person is identified in the Incoming Call dialog box (this is called Caller ID). To answer the video call manually, click Answer Call in the Incoming Call dialog box. In a few moments, the video call connects and the Remote Video and Local Video windows appear.

If you do not want to answer a call, click Reject Call in the Incoming Call dialog box or ignore the dialog box. If you let the call ring without clicking Reject Call or Answer, the caller receives a message that you are not available to answer the call. The dialog box on your screen automatically closes when the caller hangs up.

To let your computer automatically answer an incoming video call, choose Tools⇨Preferences and select the Call tab. Select the Auto Answer check box and leave PictureTel LiveWare running (minimized) on your computer. If the person calling you is listed in your Address Book list, the name of that person is identified in the Incoming Call dialog box. In a few moments, the video call automatically connects, and the Local Video and Remote Video windows appear.

Changing Your Preferences

PictureTel LiveWare has preference settings that let you customize the program's working environment to suit your needs. For example, you can customize toolbars so that they contain the buttons that you use most. All these preferences are available from the Preferences Properties dialog box (Figure 14-6), which you can display by choosing Tools⇨Preferences.

Following are the nine tabs in the Preferences Properties window:

- ✔ The General tab lets you retain window sizes and positions and set the PictureTel LiveWare Main toolbar.

- ✔ The Call tab lets you assign yourself a Site Name and set your computer to automatically answer incoming calls. It also includes settings for enabling the ringer and adjusting the volume, as well as setting automatic dialing prefixes.

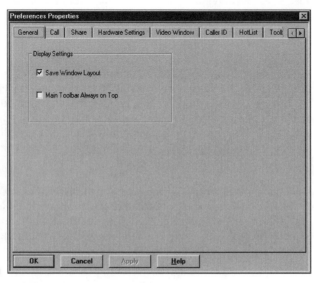

Figure 14-6:
The Preferences Properties dialog box includes a variety of settings for customizing PictureTel LiveWare.

✔ The Share tab lets you set application scrolling and set up your computer for remote control. Application scrolling automatically scrolls a window to follow your calling partner's mouse pointer. If you enable remote control, you can set a password to prevent unauthorized access to your computer.

✔ The Hardware Settings tab lets you adjust your camera settings or change hardware settings that you specified during the setup of PictureTel LiveWire.

✔ The Video Window tab allows you to automatically reposition and size the Local Video and Remote Video windows to optimize your video-conferencing desktop.

✔ The Caller ID tab lets you identify incoming calls with the name of the caller if the caller is listed in an Address Book list.

✔ The HotList tab lets you define the number of calling partners (up to ten) you can make speed-dial calls to using entries in the Address Book list.

✔ The Toolbar tab lets you create custom toolbars for the Main toolbar, the Local Video toolbar, the Remote Video toolbar, and the Audio-Only Call toolbar.

✔ The Menu tab allows you to customize PictureTel LiveWare menus so that they contain the items you use most often.

You may want to add the Preferences button to the PictureTel LiveWire toolbar for easier access.

You can make adjustments also from the Windows 95 Control Panel by double-clicking the Live200p icon. The Live200p Settings dialog box appears (Figure 14-7).

Figure 14-7:
The Live200p Settings dialog box includes additional settings for the PictureTel 200p.

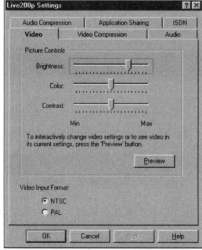

You use this dialog box to change your hardware settings. The following describes the tabs in the Live200P Settings dialog box:

- ✔ The Video tab includes controls for adjusting your video camera settings, which you can preview in the Local Video window.

- ✔ The Video Compression tab allows you to define the quality of your video image.

- ✔ The Audio tab includes settings that affect the sound that your calling partner hears.

- ✔ The Audio Compression tab lets you specify different compression schemes for your audio communications.

- ✔ The ISDN tab lets you make changes in the ISDN line provisioning information, including switch type, SPIDs, and directory numbers.

- ✔ The Application Sharing tab lets you control the performance of application sharing in the context of your total video-conferencing connection. For example, if you want application sharing to take precedence over video images, you select the High setting.

Making Video and Audio Adjustments

As you work with the PictureTel, you may want to make various video and audio adjustments. This section explains how to adjust common settings that affect your audio and video for video conferencing.

Adjusting your ring volume

Your computer notifies you by ringing when you have an incoming video call. You can increase or decrease the volume of your computer's ring or turn it off. To adjust your ring volume, choose Tools⇨Preferences and click the Call tab. Adjust the volume between low and high using the volume control slider.

If you set up your computer to answer a video call manually and you turn off the ringer, you are alerted that you have an incoming call by the Incoming Call dialog box. If you set up your computer to answer a video call automatically and you turn off the ringer, you cannot be alerted that you have an incoming video call.

Adjusting your video camera

During (or before) a video call, you can check your on-camera presence and resize the Local Video window. You can tilt the camera to center the image you are sending. You can increase or decrease the brightness level of your video camera to conform to your lighting conditions using the Local Video toolbar. You can also adjust the color and contrast levels by adding the Color and Contrast buttons to the Local Video toolbar or by adjusting their sliders in the Video tab in the Live200p Settings dialog box.

Turning off your video camera

You can turn off your video camera so that your calling partner cannot see your image. Click the Video Off button in the Remote Video window or choose Call⇨Video Off.

Arranging and resizing your video windows

You can resize and save the position of the Local and Remote Video windows. To resize the Local or Remote Video window automatically, click the Image Size list box and select Small, Medium, or Large. To resize the Local Video or Remote Video window manually, drag the lower right corner of the window border.

You can also save video window positions so that your choice of locations are the defaults each time you run PictureTel LiveWare. Choose Tools⇨Preferences, and then click the Video Window tab. To change the default sizes of the Small, Medium, and Large screens, drag the Default Video Size sliders to the left (decrease) or to the right (increase).

Adjusting audio levels

To adjust the audio level you receive from your calling partner, click the volume control in the Remote Video window. Dragging the pointer to the left decreases the volume. Dragging it to the right increases the volume.

To turn off your audio device so that your calling partner cannot hear you or local conversations, click the Audio Off button in the Remote Video window or choose Call⇨Audio Off.

Managing Your Connections with the Address Book

The Address Book lets you create telephone directories so that you can make calls automatically without having to manually dial numbers each time. You can create one or more Address Book lists. Each list contains entries that have a calling partner's name, address, phone number, and other connection information.

Getting started

To open the Address Book window, click the Address Book button or choose Call⇨Address Book. The Address Book window appears (Figure 14-8). When you open the PictureTel Address Book window for the first time, your first name, last name, and ISDN number (which you entered during setup) are displayed. Later, when you have created one or more Address Book lists, the last address list that you accessed is displayed.

You can use the following buttons in the toolbar of the Address Book window to immediately access a feature. Each button is a shortcut way of choosing a pull-down menu item:

- ✔ The New button lets you create a new Address Book list.
- ✔ The Open button lets you open an existing Address Book list.
- ✔ The Print button lets you print the contents of an Address Book list.

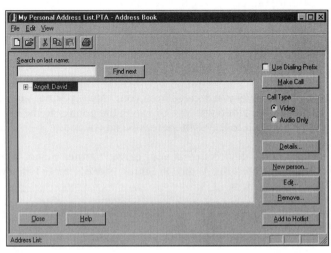

Figure 14-8:
Use the Address Book window to create contact lists for speed dialing.

Creating an Address Book list

After you open the Address Book window, you can create an Address Book list and start adding entries. Information on a specific calling partner in an Address Book list is called an *entry*. Each Address Book list can have an unlimited number of entries.

To create an Address Book list

1. **Choose Call⇨Address Book.**

   The Address Book window is displayed.

2. **Click the New Person button or choose File⇨New Address List.**

   The Create New Address Book List dialog box appears (Figure 14-9).

Figure 14-9:
The Create
New
Address
Book List
dialog box
displays a
list of all
your
address
books for
easy
access.

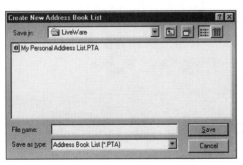

3. **From the Save in list box, choose the location where you want to store the Address Book list.**

   The default directory is C:\PictureTel\LiveWare or the drive in which you installed the PictureTel LiveWare application. If you want to create and name a folder in which to store the address list, click the New Folder button.

4. **In the File name box, type a descriptive name for your Address Book list.**

   The name can be up to 255 characters long.

5. **Click Save.**

   A *Creating. . .* message appears in the dialog box. Then the new Address Book list appears in the Address Book window, with the descriptive name in the title bar.

Adding an entry

To add a new entry to an Address Book list

1. **In the Address Book window, click New person.**

   The Name tab in the New Person dialog box appears (Figure 14-10).

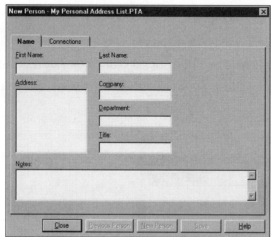

Figure 14-10: Using the Name tab in the New Person dialog box lets you enter a video conference partner's name and address.

2. **In the First Name box, type your calling partner's first name. Then press tab to move to the Last Name box.**

   Your calling partner's first name appears in the upper left side of the window.

3. **In the Last Name box, type your calling partner's last name.**

   Your calling partner's full name appears in the upper-left side of the window.

4. **Enter information in the remaining fields, as needed.**

5. **Click the Connections tab.**

   The Connections tab appears (Figure 14-11).

6. **In the Connection Name box, type the description for the connection. Press tab to confirm your entry.**

   This entry is required. The type of connection that you specified appears in the Connection Names box. If you make a mistake, you can re-enter the type of connection.

7. **In the 1st Phone Number and 2nd Phone Number boxes, type your calling partner's ISDN phone number.**

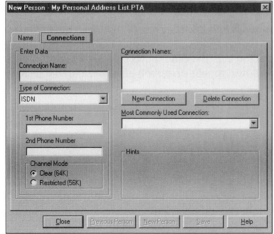

Figure 14-11:
Use the
Connections
tab in the
New Person
dialog box to
enter the
information
for making
the
connection.

8. **Choose a different channel mode, if necessary.**

   The default setting is Clear (64K).

9. **Click Save to save your entry.**

10. **Click New Person or Close when you are finished.**

    If you click New Person, the Name tab appears and you can add another person to the address list. If you click Close, you are returned to the Address Book window.

You can edit any Address Book entry by selecting the entry and then clicking Edit. You can delete an entry by selecting it and then clicking Remove.

Making a video call from the Address Book

To make a video call automatically using an Address Book list, do the following:

1. **Click the Address Book button in the Main toolbar, or choose Call⊏>Address Book.**

   PictureTel LiveWare displays the Address Book list you last accessed.

2. **Open a different Address Book list, if necessary, by choosing File⊏>Open.**

3. **Click the name of the person you want to call.**

   If you want to see more information about a person, click the + sign that appears to the left of the entry to expand the list or click the Details button.

4. **Click the Make Call button to dial the video call.**

   A dialog box appears and informs you of the progress of your call by highlighting the words *Dialing, Ringing,* and *Connecting.* When your calling partner answers the call, the dialog box closes. The Remote Video and Local Video windows appear onscreen after the video call is received by your calling partner.

HotList Speed-Dialing

A hotlist is a menu on your PictureTel LiveWare screen that lets you speed dial video calls. You can customize this menu to include the name and ISDN numbers of your most frequently dialed calling partners. To add a video-conference number to your HotList menu, do the following:

1. **Choose HotList⇨Add to HotList.**

   The Address Book window appears.

2. **Open an Address Book list, if necessary.**

3. **Click the name that you want to add to the HotList menu.**

4. **Click the Add to HotList button.**

5. **Close the Address Book window.**

   The name you selected appears in the HotList menu.

To remove an entry from the HotList menu, choose HotList⇨Remove from HotList. The Remove from HotList dialog box appears. Click the name you want to delete and then click Remove.

The hotlist lets you make a speed-dial call to a calling partner who is entered in your Address Book list. To make a speed call using the HotList menu, choose HotList and then choose the ISDN number you want to call. The call is made for you automatically.

It's Better to Share

During a video call, you and your calling partner can share one or more applications by using the options in the Remote Video window. Figure 14-12 shows what your screen might look like when sharing an application during a video conference. When you share an application, it appears on the screens of both participants, even if the application is not installed on one of the computers.

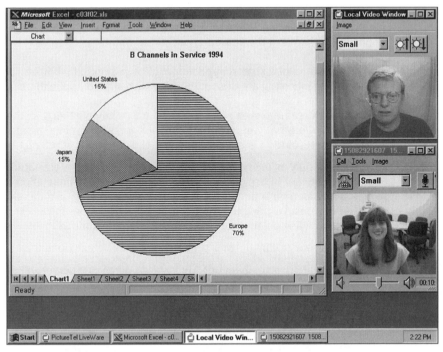

Figure 14-12:
Sharing an
application
during a
video
conference.

To share an application during a video call

1. Open an application on your desktop.

Make sure that the shared application is not covered with an unshared
application or icon, because this would obscure your calling partner's
view.

**2. Click the Share Application button or choose Tools⇨Share Application
in the Remote Video window.**

Your cursor changes to a pointing hand.

**3. Pass the pointing hand over the application or file that you want to
share.**

The unavailable symbol attached to the hand disappears.

**4. Click the application that you want to share with your calling partner
and click OK.**

You can also click on a blank area of your desktop to display a dialog box
with a list of currently open applications or files.

When you are sharing, the application you selected appears on your
calling partner's screen. A tab with your site name appears at the top right
corner of the shared application on your screen and your calling partner's
screen. All files that are modified are saved on the originating computer.

Sharing an application lets you take control over your calling partner's computer and vice versa. When you are not in control, you are viewing your calling partner's actions in the shared application.

To take control of a shared application, click or press any key on your keyboard. The following are tips for working with shared applications:

✔ Use the same screen resolution as your calling partner. Use the highest resolution that your graphics card supports for optimal results. If using the same resolution is not possible, use the automatic scrolling feature.

✔ Share only as many application windows as necessary. Shared windows that are not in use can be distracting, and it can become difficult to tell which person is in control. Also clear your desktop of unneeded windows and icons. Working together on shared applications is easiest if you and your calling partner can see only the shared windows.

✔ Give your calling partner time to see the changes you make.

✔ Alternate control in an orderly fashion. When one person takes control, the other person loses control of the entire desktop. Tell your calling partner when you are taking control, and invite your calling partner to take control when you are finished.

✔ Turn off the Remote Video Window Always on Top check box in the Video Window Preferences tab. If the Remote Video window is on top, it can block your calling partner's view of a shared window.

✔ You can use the Whiteboard before a call to prepare word-processing files or a presentation, or you can use it during a call with your calling partner.

Collaborating with the Whiteboard

The Whiteboard application lets you share and annotate documents, presentations, and graphics during a video conference call. You can capture documents and import graphics into the Whiteboard and superimpose edit marks on the page. Editing is accomplished using markup tools in the Whiteboard application.

To open the Whiteboard application, click the Whiteboard button or choose Tools➪Whiteboard. The Whiteboard window appears on your screen and also on your calling partner's screen. Figure 14-13 shows the Whiteboard application screen and identifies its key tool buttons.

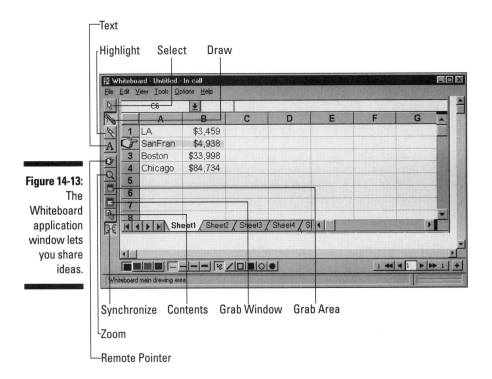

Figure 14-13:
The
Whiteboard
application
window lets
you share
ideas.

The Whiteboard toolbar provides access to all Whiteboard tool functions. The following describes the functions of the Whiteboard toolbar:

- ✔ The Select tool lets you select an object in the Whiteboard to move, copy, cut, delete, or paste.

- ✔ The Draw tool lets you create geometric shapes on top of an object using a choice of lines, widths, and colors.

- ✔ The Highlight tool lets you draw translucent lines on top of an object in the Whiteboard.

- ✔ The Text tool lets you superimpose text on a captured document or an imported graphic file.

- ✔ The Remote Pointer tool lets you and your calling partner point to an object in the Whiteboard. Your pointer is blue if you made the video call, or yellow if you are receiving an incoming video call.

- ✔ The Zoom tool lets you magnify your screen for closer scrutiny of an object.

- ✔ The Grab Area tool lets you capture a selected area on the Windows 95 desktop for copying onto the Whiteboard.

✔ The Grab Window tool lets you capture any window on your Windows 95 desktop for copying onto the Whiteboard. You can even capture the entire desktop.

✔ The Lock Contents tool lets you prevent your calling partner from making any changes to the Whiteboard.

✔ The Synchronize tool lets you refresh your calling partner's screen to make sure you are both working with the same screen at the same time.

You can access the Whiteboard toolbar functions from a pop-up menu. To use the menu, move your cursor into the editing area of the Whiteboard and *right-click*. The pop-up menu appears. Click the left mouse button over the menu item that you want to use.

Doing File Transfers

The File Transfer window lets you and your calling partner send files to or receive files from the other's computer. To open the File Transfer window, choose Tools⇨File Transfer in the Remote Video window. The File Transfer window appears (Figure 14-14). You can send one or more files to your calling partner's computer using the File Transfer window.

To send a file using the Windows 95 Explorer, drag and drop the desired file from the Explorer window to the Files Sent list in the File Transfer window. The filename appears in the Files Sent list on your computer and in the Files Received list on your calling partner's computer.

Figure 14-14: Use the File Transfer window to specify one or more files to transfer and to manage your file transfers.

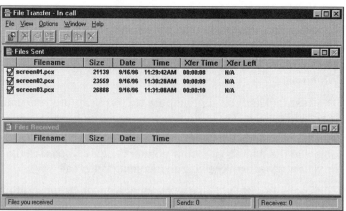

A progress bar appears in the Files Sent list. The progress bar decreases in length as the file is transferred to your calling partner's computer. When the transfer is complete, the progress bar disappears and a check mark appears in the File icon.

Chapter 15

Videum Video Vistas with CU-SeeMe

- -

In This Chapter

▶ Setting up the VideumConf Pro system

▶ Setting up and using CU-SeeMe video-conferencing software

- -

*T*he VideumConf Pro with the Enhanced CU-SeeMe video-conferencing system is an affordable, easy-to-use LAN and Internet DVC system. This chapter takes you on a hands-on tour of working with the VideumConf Pro and CU-SeeMe video-conferencing system.

About the VideumConf Pro

WINNOV's VideumConf Pro package includes an ISA video/audio adapter card, a video camera, and the Enhanced CU-SeeMe software program — all for an affordable price of $499. You can use the VideumConf Pro over a POTS modem, a LAN, or the Internet via ISDN.

You cannot use the VideumConf Pro to make a dial-up video-conferencing call over the ISDN system to another video conference user.

The Videum card includes ports for a composite format video camera, an S-Video format camera, or a Multimedia Extension Connector (MXC) format video camera. The VideumCam color video camera included in the VideumConf Pro package is an MXC format video camera. It has an integrated microphone, and the power comes from your PC so no external power supply is required. The VideumCam along with included software allows you to capture audio and video directly into your computer. For sophisticated conferencing, the VideumConf Pro supports up to three video sources — people, documents, and overhead displays — and you can control each source remotely.

Videum audio supports multimedia, AVI-compatible and WAV-compatible audio formats. Stereo line level inputs using minijacks and stereo microphone inputs are included on the video/audio card, and output is supported by amplified stereo minijacks for your favorite speakers. Videum supports full-duplex audio to allow desktop video conferencing and Internet telephone applications.

The Videum software includes several useful applications for manipulating audio and video input, controlling video images and audio levels, viewing live video, and capturing multimedia clips. The software also includes audio drivers compatible with Windows Sound System and video drivers compatible with Video for Windows. As a result, any audio, video, or still-image clip can be dragged to any Windows video-capable application for viewing and incorporation. The Videum applications follow:

- ✔ The WNTV program allows you to view high-performance video from the video recorder, from TV inputs, or live from the attached camera. You also use this program to configure the video camera capabilities of the VideumConf Pro.

- ✔ The Audio Control Panel program allows you to control the output mix and the recording source. It also operates the controls for the microphone built into the VideumCam.

- ✔ The Vid Control program allows you to pan and zoom the video image, set video tone controls, and connect to remote systems for control of remote cameras and Videum boards. This feature is handy for video conferencing, where you may want to control a second remote camera so that you can view individuals or an entire group of people. Vid Control can support up to three remote cameras.

- ✔ The Clicker program allows you to control the tuner for the source connected to the MXC port. If you have WINNOV's VideumTV installed and your cable input connected, you would use Clicker to change the channel you are viewing on the WNTV application.

- ✔ The VidClip program allows you to quickly capture video clips, audio clips, and still images and then drop them into your documents.

The Videum system uses a half-height ISA video and audio bus card, which you install in a 16-bit ISA AT-bus slot. You should be using a Pentium 90 or higher with a Super VGA adapter and display capable of a minimum of 256 colors. A 16-bit display with 65,536 color capability or higher is recommended. Your PC should have a minimum of 16MB of memory, and you need a set of external speakers or a headset. The Videum board is compatible with Windows 95 and Windows NT version 4.0.

Videum does not work with other video capture cards installed in the same computer.

Installing the VideumConf Pro Hardware

The following steps explain how to install all the VideumConf Pro hardware:

1. **Turn off the computer and all peripheral devices. Unplug the computer and peripherals from the wall outlet.**

2. **Remove the cover of the computer to access the ISA slots, and then ground yourself by touching the power supply.**

3. **Find an available ISA slot inside your computer, and remove its protective slot cover from the back of the computer using a Phillips screwdriver.**

4. **Install the Videum board into the available slot, and then reinstall the cover of the computer.**

5. **Set the camera base unit in a place where you will be able to see yourself, which is usually on top of your monitor.**

   Place the camera on the base unit so that the power light is on the right and the microphone is on the left.

6. **Connect the camera cable to the Multimedia Extension Connector (MXC).**

7. **Turn VideumCam on using the Power switch on the back of the camera.**

Additional controls on the back of the camera are described in Table 15-1.

Table 15-1	VideumCam Settings	
Switch	*Default Setting*	*Description*
BLC	On	Sets backlight compensation to prevent underexposed or overexposed images.
WB	Fixed (Freeze mode)	Sets the white balance for color reproduction. Use Fixed mode when you have a colored scene and stable lighting conditions.
Image	Pos	Shows the image normally; Neg displays the photographic negative of the image.

Installing the Videum Software

The Videum software includes the drivers and applications you need to get started. The installation software automatically determines whether you have Windows 95 or Windows NT and configures your system accordingly.

After you install the Videum software, you need to install the CU-SeeMe software for desktop video conferencing. Before you install CU-SeeMe, however, you need to make sure your video camera is configured properly using the WNTV program.

Check the WINNOV Web site at `http://wwwWINNOV.com` for any new updates to the software, which you can download.

To install the software, follow these steps:

1. **Insert the Videum Disk 1 into your floppy drive. Choose Start⇨Run, type A:\SETUP, and then click OK.**

   A welcome screen appears.

2. **Click Next.**

   The Choose Destination Location dialog box appears.

3. **Select the directory where you want the software installed or use the default, and then click Next.**

   The Setup Type dialog box appears.

4. **Select the type of installation you want, which is usually the default Typical option. Click Next.**

   All the files needed to run the Videum applications are installed. After the files are installed, a dialog box is displayed allowing you to read the ReadMe file.

5. **Click Yes if you want to read the file or No if you don't.**

   After the ReadMe file is closed or you have clicked the No button, the Restart dialog box appears.

6. **Click Next.**

   Your computer is restarted and the Videum applications are now available.

7. **Choose Start⇨Programs⇨Videum⇨WNTV.**

   The WNTV window appears.

8. **If your video image appears in the window, you're ready to install the CU-SeeMe software, which is described in the next section.**

9. **If the window is black, you need to set up the Videum card for the camera you're using.**

   a. Choose Video⇨Properties.

      The Video Control Panel window appears, as shown in Figure 15-1.

   b. Click the MXC radio button in the Input group.

      A video image from your camera will appear in the Active Video Area.

   c. Adjust the Brightness, Contrast, Hue, and Saturation settings in the Tone Balance group, if necessary.

   d. Click OK.

Figure 15-1:
The Video Control Panel window controls the source of your video and other video settings.

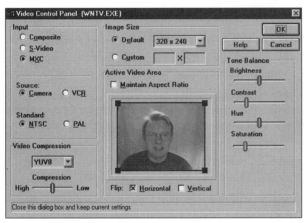

Internet DVC with CU-SeeMe

CU-SeeMe was developed as a result of a research project led by Cornell University. CU-SeeMe is designed for video conferencing over any TCP/IP network. White Pine Software is the master licensee of CU-SeeMe desktop video-conferencing technology and markets the enhanced versions of the CU-SeeMe software, which is included in VideumConf Pro.

You can use the CU-SeeMe video-conferencing software to connect to servers, called *reflectors,* or directly to a specific IP address via the Internet. Reflector sites allow group conferences, and a number of these sites exist on the Internet. You cannot use CU-SeeMe to dial up another video conference user over the ISDN WAN.

The Enhanced CU-SeeMe video-conferencing program has the following features:

- ✔ A Whiteboard application, called WhitePineBoard, for text- and graphics-based collaboration during conferences.

- ✔ Web Browser Support for launching Enhanced CU-SeeMe from any Internet Web page.

- ✔ A PhoneBook for managing your collection of conference addresses and for direct dialing your favorite conferences.

- ✔ A Listener program to alert you to incoming calls. The program gives you the option of accepting or rejecting incoming calls.

- ✔ A conference management facility that lets you control which participants you view and speak with.

- ✔ A Participants List that lets you view participants who are visible, hidden, or lurkers at a reflector site.

- ✔ Easy-to-use video controls that let you find out the status of your connection and configure transmission settings, reception settings, and camera settings.

- ✔ Audio controls that let you adjust the volume, turn on and off the speaker and microphone, and select either voice-activated communications or a push-to-talk option.

- ✔ 32-bit Enhanced CU-SeeMe takes advantage of the full capabilities of Windows 95 and Windows NT.

- ✔ Fully compatible with the freeware version of CU-SeeMe, so you can video conference with thousands of existing CU-SeeMe users.

- ✔ A text-based chat facility for exchanging typed messages with other users.

- ✔ Preference settings to allow you to easily change preferences at a reflector site or video, audio, and other settings.

Installing CU-SeeMe

Installing the CU-SeeMe program is straightforward. Before you install Enhanced CU-SeeMe, make sure you have your serial number, which is printed on your registration card. You'll need to enter the serial number during the installation process. To install Enhanced CU-SeeMe on Windows 95

1. **Insert the Enhanced CU-SeeMe CD into your computer's CD-ROM drive, and double-click the My Computer icon on the desktop.**

2. **Double-click the CD-ROM drive titled CU-SeeMe.**

   The contents of the CD appear.

3. **Double-click the folder titled Disk1.**

   The contents of the Disk1 folder appear.

4. **Double-click the icon titled Setup.exe, and then follow the instructions on your screen.**

Getting Started with CU-SeeMe

To start CU-SeeMe, choose Start➪Programs➪Enhanced CU-SeeMe. Then click the Enhanced CU-SeeMe icon. When Enhanced CU-SeeMe successfully starts, the local video window — with your picture in it — and the Enhanced CU-SeeMe window (Figure 15-2) appear on your desktop. If your local video window does not appear, press Ctrl-L.

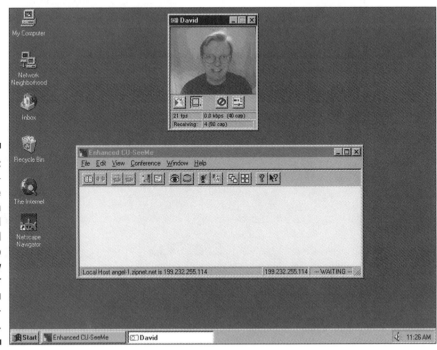

Figure 15-2: The CU-SeeMe program window and the local video window appear when you start CU-SeeMe.

The toolbar in the Enhanced CU-SeeMe window includes buttons for performing the most common functions. Moving the pointer over any of these buttons displays the button label. Figure 15-3 identifies the buttons.

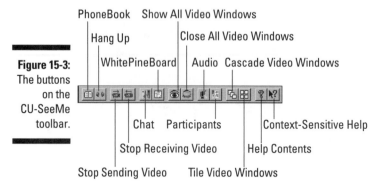

Figure 15-3:
The buttons on the CU-SeeMe toolbar.

Most of your configuration settings for CU-SeeMe are made in the Preferences dialog box (Figure 15-4), which you can access by choosing Edit⇨Preferences or by clicking the Preferences button on the local video window.

Figure 15-4:
The Preferences dialog box includes all the settings to customize CU-SeeMe.

Changing your name

The first thing you may want to do is change the name of your local video window. The default name was derived from your registration information, so you may want to change it to a less-formal name. To change the name, do the following:

1. **Choose Edit⇨Preferences in the Enhanced CU-SeeMe window, or click on the Preferences button in your local video window.**

   The Preferences dialog box appears.

2. **Select the Conferencing tab.**

3. **In the Title box, type the name you want to appear in the title bar of the local video window.**

   This is the name other users will see in your video window.

4. **Click OK.**

Entering a text message in your video window

Another thing you may want to do before you connect to a video conference is add text overlay to your local video window. This lets other users see additional information, such as your location or company name. Figure 15-5 shows an example of a text overlay in the local video window.

Figure 15-5:
A local video window with a text overlay.

To enter a text overlay, simply click the local video window and begin typing. Your message appears in the window. To delete the text, select the window and press Enter. You can choose a specific font by pressing F8 to display the Windows Font dialog box.

Setting transmission and reception rates

One final setting to check before making your video debut is the rate at which you send and receive video and audio data. Enhanced CU-SeeMe selects 80 Kbps as the default transmission rate. Using a two B channel ISDN line means you can set a higher rate. Some CU-SeeMe reflector sites, however, don't support higher rates, in which case you may get a message to adjust the transmit and receive rates. To change these rates

1. **Choose Edit⇨Preferences or click the Preferences icon in your local video window.**

2. **Click the Communications tab.**

3. **Set the minimum and maximum values for transmitting and receiving by clicking the arrows or by typing values.**

4. **Click OK.**

Making a Video Conference Connection

For your first conference, try connecting to White Pine Software's dedicated reflector set up for Enhanced CU-SeeMe users. To make a connection and view other users

1. **Choose Conference⇨Select Phone Book or click the Phone Book button on the toolbar.**

   The Phone Book dialog box appears (Figure 15-6).

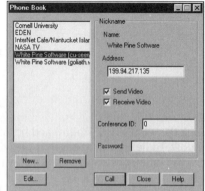

Figure 15-6: The Phone Book dialog box includes entries for making speed-dial connections.

2. **Select the White Pine Software [cu-seeme] item from the list, or type 199.94.217.135 in the Address field.**

3. **Click the Call button.**

   The status changes to `Connecting` in the local video window or in the Windows main application window.

4. **When a Message of the Day appears from the reflector, read it and then click OK.**

5. **If you get a list of available conferences from which to choose, do so.**

   You're placed in a video conference, with each person sending video to the White Pine Software reflector (up to eight users) and their images appearing in separate remote video windows. You can change the number of remote video windows that appear on your screen, as explained in the "Arranging windows for a clearer view" section in this chapter. Figure 15-7 shows a typical video conference as it appears on the screen.

6. **Any time you want to bail out of a video conference, click the Hang Up button on the Enhanced CU-SeeMe window toolbar.**

Figure 15-7:
A CU-SeeMe video conference as it appears on the screen.

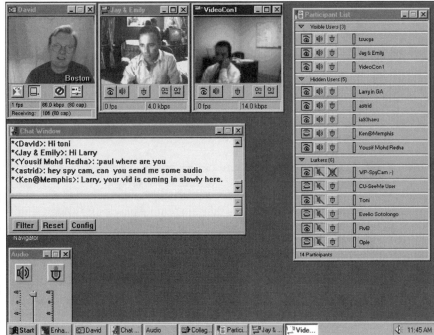

Checking out participants

To check out all the participants at a specific reflector conference, choose Windows⇨Participants or click the Participants button on the CU-SeeMe window toolbar. The Participant List window appears (Figure 15-8).

Figure 15-8:
The
Participant
List window
displays a
list of
conference
participants
and the
status of
their
connection.

Participants are classified as visible, hidden, or lurkers. Using the Participant List window, you can select which users you can view and speak to. Click the arrow to the left of Visible Users, Hidden Users, or Lurkers to display the full list of participants in the category.

The eye, speaker, and microphone icons to the left of the participants' names indicate the status of their connection, as follows:

✔ An open eye indicates that the remote user's local video window is displayed, and a closed eye indicates that the local video window is not displayed. In other words, you can't see the participant.

✔ A speaker indicates that the participants can receive audio, and a line through it means their audio speakers are turned off.

✔ A microphone indicates that the participants can send audio, and a line through it means their microphone is shut off.

You can get information about each user in the Participant List window. *Right-click* the name of a participant, and the Show Info button appears. Click the Show Info button, and a pop-up window appears displaying the user's IP address and transmission setting and the version of CU-SeeMe that the user is using.

Chatting with other participants

The CU-SeeMe program provides a Chat window, which allows you to exchange text messages with other video conference participants. Using text messages instead of audio saves bandwidth.

To use chat during a conference, choose Conference⇨Chat or click the Chat button on the toolbar. The Chat Window appears (Figure 15-9). Type text in the lower portion of the Chat window and press Return to send the text. Your text now appears in the top portion of the window with your name. Anyone who has a Chat Window open will see your text, and you will see the text that other users are typing.

Figure 15-9:
The Chat Window lets you easily exchange messages to specific participants or the entire conference.

Chat Window

*<David>: Goodbye ! bh
*<David>: Hello All
*<Ken@Memphis>: hello David
*<panda>: hi all
*<Elvis>: hi panda

Filter | Reset | Config

Doing voice communications

To communicate by voice, you can use the headset with a built-in microphone and speaker. You can also use the microphone built into the Videum camera and PC speakers connected to the Videum audio/video card. The Audio window (Figure 15-10) controls the sound coming into and going out of your computer. Using the Audio window, you can turn your speaker and microphone on and off, and filter incoming noise when receiving audio and background noise when transmitting audio.

If the audio indicator bar turns yellow, this means your computer is having trouble compressing your audio signal. As a result, your audio signal is not sent.

Figure 15-10:
The Audio window controls the audio portion of your video conference.

To communicate by voice, do the following:

1. **Open the Audio window by choosing Window⇨Audio or by clicking the Audio button on the toolbar.**

2. **Type a message in the Chat window asking another participant to talk.**

   Other participants who have their Chat windows open will see your message.

3. **Watch the indicator under the speaker in the Audio window.**

   You'll see the audio level indicator rise as a person talks. If your audio is set up correctly, you should hear sounds when the indicator rises above the diamond marker. You can easily identify the person speaking by watching for a highlighted bar in the Participants List window. You may need to adjust the speaker levels.

4. **To talk to another participant, click and hold the Push to Talk button in the Audio window.**

   The button changes to Transmitting so that you can talk to the other users.

5. **Click the microphone icon in a particular user's window to talk directly to that user only.**

   You may need to adjust the audio levels in the Audio window.

Adjusting CU-SeeMe to Your Needs

Enhanced CU-SeeMe includes a number of features that you can adjust to your needs. These include choosing color versus grayscale video images, selecting different audio compression schemes, and arranging windows.

Changing from color to gray

Enhanced CU-SeeMe supports color and grayscale video. Sending color video uses less CPU power and up to ten times less bandwidth. The color option also displays video at up to ten times the frame rate compared to grayscale. However, the color option uses more memory. In addition, if you use color, freeware CU-SeeMe users can't see your video image.

The grayscale option uses more CPU power and bandwidth, and displays video at a slower frame rate than color. However, grayscale uses less memory and lets all CU-SeeMe users see your video image.

To change between color and grayscale, choose Edit⇨Preferences⇨Video tab (Figure 15-11). Then select either the WhitePine Color or CU-SeeMe Gray in the Compression Codec drop-down list. Click the Configure button to display settings for the selected codec. *Codec* (coder-decoder) refers to software used to compress and decompress digitized audio and video.

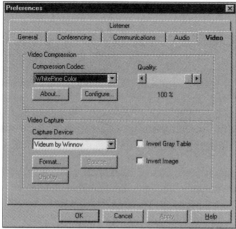

Figure 15-11: The Video Preferences properties page includes settings for defining video compression and the video capture card you're using with CU-SeeMe.

Changing your audio compression

Enhanced CU-SeeMe provides several audio codecs, offering different audio compression options. Your choice will depend on your computer and networking environment.

For ISDN, you can use any of the settings in the Audio Compression Codec drop-down list by first choosing Preferences⇨Audio (Figure 15-12). Each audio codec provides additional configuration options. The Delta-Mod (16 Kbps) and Intel DVI (32 Kbps) codecs work best for either ISDN or LAN connections.

Figure 15-12:
The Audio preferences properties page lets you define the audio compression codec and the audio devices you're using with Cu-SeeMe.

Arranging windows for a clearer view

With the audio, chat, participant, and video windows displayed, your desktop may appear cluttered at times. In addition, each window you have open on your screen requires memory. Video windows take up the most memory. Open video windows also use bandwidth, which can cause sluggish performance. CU-SeeMe lets you organize these windows in a number of arrangements and sizes. The following are CU-SeeMe window options:

✔ To arrange video windows in a cascade fashion, choose Windows⇨Select Cascade Video Windows, or click the Cascade Video Windows button on the toolbar. This stacks the windows on top of each other, starting in the upper left corner of your display.

✔ To arrange video windows in a tiled fashion, choose Windows⇨Tile Video Windows, or click the Tile Video Windows button on the toolbar. This arranges the windows in a grid, starting at the upper left corner of your display.

✔ To change the size of a video window, click the Zoom button on the Video window to make the window small (160 x 120) or large (320 x 240).

✔ To save window positions, choose Edit⇨Preferences⇨General tab. Select the Save Windows Positions on Exit option, and then click OK.

✔ To display or close all remote video windows on your desktop, choose Windows⇨Show All or Windows⇨Close All. Choose Windows⇨Close All Except Front to close all windows in the background. To redisplay them, choose Show All. Show All displays the number of video windows specified in the Conferencing Preferences (the default is 8).

✔ To display a single participant's window, click the participant's name from the list of users in the Participants window.

✔ To limit the number of windows that appear on your desktop, choose Edit⇨Preferences⇨Conferencing tab. Then select the number of windows in the Maximum Video Windows box by clicking the arrows.

Using the Phone Book for Speed Dialing

The CU-SeeMe Phone Book provides a means of storing video-conferencing addresses with nicknames that you can choose. To display the Phone Book window, press Ctrl-B or click the Phone Book button on the toolbar. The Phone Book window appears (see Figure 15-6).

Using the Phone Book, you can add nicknames to the Call submenu in the Conference menu to make calls directly. The following explains how to create and manage Phone Book entries as well as how to make a call from the Phone Book.

✔ **Adding a Phone Book entry:** In the Phone Book window, click New to create a new entry. Enter a name in the Nickname dialog box, and then click OK. Click Close in the Phone Book window.

✔ **Changing a Phone Book entry:** In the Phone Book window, select a name from the list of nicknames and then click Edit. Make your changes, click OK, and then click Close.

✔ **Deleting a Phone Book entry:** In the Phone Book window, select the entry to delete from the list of nicknames, click Remove, and then click Close.

✔ **Making a call from the Phone Book:** In the Phone Book window, select the name of the person or conference to which you want to connect. Specify the conference ID for the conference you want to join. Most group conferences use the default, 0. If a private conference has been set up, obtain the conference ID from the Conference Administrator. If you're connecting to an individual, use the default 0. Click Call.

Making CU-SeeMe Listen for Incoming Calls

It's not practical to leave Enhanced CU-SeeMe running at all times because it uses your system resources. You can, however, run the CU-SeeMe Listener to alert you to an incoming call.

For the Listener to operate, your computer must be connected to the Internet.

The Listener listens for anyone who may try to connect to your computer. It notifies you by displaying an alert message, playing a system sound, or both. You can accept or deny the connection. If you accept the connection, the Listener automatically starts Enhanced CU-SeeMe so that you can begin conferencing with the caller.

To activate the Listener, choose Start➪Programs➪Enhanced CU-SeeMe➪ Enhanced CU-SeeMe Listener. The Enhanced CU-SeeMe Listener window appears. You can choose a method of alert by choosing Edit➪Preferences. You can also minimize the Listener window to the Windows 95 taskbar to keep the Listener running in the background while you do your work.

Collaborating with WhitePineBoard

Using the WhitePineBoard, you can share drawings and documents with other participants in a video conference. You can use a WhitePineBoard document to create graphics using the WhitePineBoard tools or to import documents from presentation, word-processing, spreadsheet, or graphic applications.

WhitePineBoard tools allow dynamic editing of graphics during the conference session. When you are connected with another person using WhitePineBoard, documents you create, open, or import are automatically displayed on the other computers. Other users can easily mark up, print, and save documents from their own computers.

Starting the WhitePineBoard

The WhitePineBoard is a separate application and can be used only with other Enhanced CU-SeeMe users. To start the WhitePineBoard

1. **Choose Conference⊅WhitePineBoard or click the WhitePineBoard button on the toolbar.**

   The WhitePineBoard window appears.

2. **Choose File⊅New to create a new document.**

   A blank WhitePineBoard document appears on your computer and all other computers connected to WhitePineBoard (Figure 15-13).

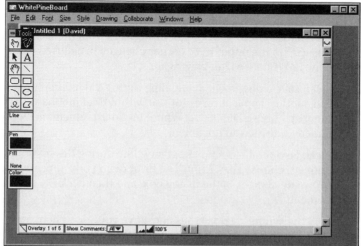

Figure 15-13:
The
WhitePine-
Board with
a new
document.

3. **To import an existing document, choose File⊅Open and select the document you want to open.**

4. **Instruct other conference participants to start WhitePineBoard.**

   The WhitePineBoard originator receives a message stating who is connecting to the conference. The other participants receive a message specifying the name of the document originator.

5. **Edit the WhitePineBoard document.**

   From the WhitePineBoard tool bar, you can select the pencil to draw freehand, the text tool (letter A) to type text, the hand to point at objects, or the pointer to select objects.

Managing documents

After a document has been created or imported, you are ready to begin reviewing it with the other users. With an open connection, the document appears on all computers simultaneously. As you view the document, scroll through it, and mark it up, all windows change appropriately.

The following explains how to perform basic tasks in the WhitePineBoard:

- ✔ Unlinking your document temporarily disables your updates from the other windows. To unlink your view of the document, choose Collaborate⇨Link View. The check mark disappears from the menu and the View Status icon in the upper right corner changes to a closed eye. To reestablish the link, choose Link View again.

- ✔ You can save a document at any time during a WhitePineBoard session for use in another application or for use with WhitePineBoard later. To save a document, choose File⇨Save. WhitePineBoard remembers who made each comment in the saved document.

- ✔ You can also print a document at any time during the session. To print a document, choose File⇨Print. The Print dialog box appears. Select the appropriate choices in the dialog box, and then click OK to print the document.

- ✔ To end the WhitePineBoard session, save your document and then choose File⇨Exit. To disconnect from other users, choose Collaborate⇨ Disconnect.

- ✔ To change WhitePineBoard preferences, choose Edit⇨Preferences. You can change your connection name, the pointer, and the pointer color. To admit users to a conference without requiring authorization, click to clear the Ask Before Admitting New Users option.

Part IV
The Part of Tens

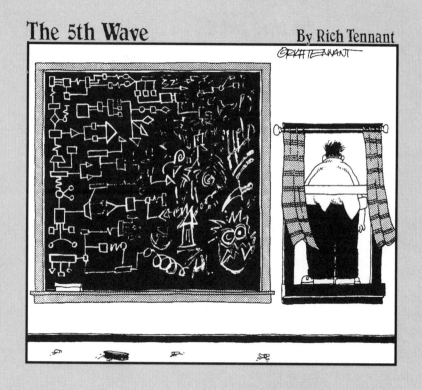

In this part . . .

As its name implies, the "Part of Tens" provides you with tens upon tens of valuable tips and resources to enhance your ISDN experience. The following chapters include tips for saving money on your ISDN service charges, a ten-step program for ISDN enlightenment, sources for more ISDN help, and ten things to check out before choosing an ISDN ISP.

Chapter 16
Ten Ways to Save Money Getting ISDN

In This Chapter

▶ Being a smart consumer when ordering your ISDN service from the telephone company

▶ Preserving your CPE investment in a constantly changing environment

▶ Doing your own ISDN wiring to save a bundle

▶ Asking for promotional prices before you buy

*I*SDN can be expensive by the time you put all the pieces together. To help, here are ten ways to avoid spending money unnecessarily.

Use the Caveat Emptor Defense

ISDN is a new technology, and there is a shortage of people who know what ISDN options are available and which ones are best for you. Even fewer people understand the needs of individuals and small businesses that are trying to get up and running with ISDN. Your only defense is to educate yourself as a consumer, even if you plan to have other people do the implementation. What you don't know can cost you time and money.

Know What You Need before Ordering ISDN Service

Get all the ISDN line-provisioning information for all the devices you plan to use on your ISDN line *before* you order service. Telephone companies typically charge $15 to $40 for each change to an ISDN line configuration after you place the initial order. Do it correctly from the start and you save.

Do Your Own Wiring

ISDN wiring is the same as POTS wiring. Your local telephone company brings the ISDN line to your premises. From there, the wiring is your responsibility. If you have a simple inside wiring job, in many cases you can do it yourself and save the cost of telephone company or independent installers. A typical telephone company installer costs $50 to $75 per hour.

Don't Get an RJ-45 U-Interface Jack

You don't need an RJ-45 jack to terminate your U interface, but most telephone companies and their installers don't tell you this fact. As a result, you don't know to tell them not to install one. They charge about $15 for the RJ-45 jack — plus installation. Instead, buy an RJ-11 wall jack for $2 and install it yourself.

Shop Around for Your ISDN CPE

Many ISDN CPE vendors sell their products through Internet service providers and telephone companies at a reduced price. Check with your telephone company or Internet service provider before buying directly from a CPE vendor. Typically, CPE manufacturers sell to the public at list price only.

Compare ISDN and Analog for Voice

Some telephone companies charge you the lower standard POTS rates for analog calls over an ISDN line. If your telephone company does this, use an ISDN device that can initiate data calls as analog calls to save on usage charges. Most telephone companies charge you the single higher rates for analog and digital traffic over ISDN. In these areas, you may find that it's cheaper to keep your analog line for analog communications.

Shop for ISDN Internet Service Providers

ISDN service for connecting to the Internet is new, and prices for service vary. The most progressive Internet service providers offer basic ISDN service for around $29 per month. For that, you typically receive 20 to 30 hours of free connect time. Keep in mind that these charges don't include any ISDN toll charges from your local telephone company. Try to find an Internet service provider that offers a telephone access number that is a local call.

Internet service providers offering ISDN service often sell a package that includes the hardware for your end of the connection. Check out these packages, because they typically offer a better deal than buying the product from a reseller or the manufacturer.

Buy ISDN Products with a 30-Day Return Policy

ISDN is a complex realm where things don't always work out as you expect. When you buy a product, use your credit card and make sure that the vendor offers a 30-day return policy. The last thing you want is an expensive piece of ISDN equipment that doesn't fit your needs.

Ask about Telco Promotional Programs

Local and long-distance telephone companies are known to run promotional programs and not tell anyone. You need to ask. For example, AT&T ran a promotional program in which it offered 50 percent off its basic long distance ISDN service charges. NYNEX offered a promotion in which it waived the $190 installation charge for ISDN service. Even after the promotional program expired, if it took you time just to get your service, you could demand the promotional price.

Don't Get Locked into Restrictive CPE

Don't get locked into ISDN CPE products that restrict your options. An example is buying an ISDN adapter card with built-in NT1 for remote access without any S/T-interface ports that restricts you from using your PC for other applications, such as video conferencing. Always try to get ISDN CPE options that allow you the most flexibility so that you can add other ISDN applications later.

Chapter 17

Ten Steps to Digital Enlightenment via ISDN

● ●

In This Chapter

▶ Checking availability and the CO switch type

▶ Determining your BRI configuration options and what your ISDN service will cost

▶ Getting wired for ISDN

▶ Developing your CPE game plan and equipping yourself with the right CPE

▶ Assembling your ISDN line-provisioning information and ordering ISDN service

▶ Setting up your ISDN devices

● ●

*G*etting up and running with ISDN is a journey through a maze of inter-related steps. This chapter paints in broad brush strokes the steps needed to attain true digital enlightenment via ISDN.

These steps provide an overview of the key elements involved in getting up and running with ISDN. Each of the ten steps references where you can find further information in this book.

Check Availability

The first order of business is to check the availability of ISDN service for your specific location. Most telephone companies offer automated systems for checking ISDN availability based on your area code and your prefix or ex-change number (the first three numbers after your area code). Even if the automated system tells you ISDN service is available, confirm this with a telephone company representative. There may be a limitation of 18,000 feet from the central office to your premises for ISDN service.

Chapter 3 covers how to check availability from your local telephone company.

Find Out the CO Switch Type

If ISDN service is available in your area, find out the type of switch used by the telephone company for your ISDN service. Different switches have different capabilities for handling multiple ISDN devices and for other configuration options. Two main switch platforms are used by telephone companies: the AT&T 5ESS and NT DMS-100. These may use any of the following software options: AT&T 5ESS Custom, AT&T 5ESS NI-1 (National ISDN), and NT DMS 100 (National ISDN). Determining the type of switch at the CO helps you plan which ISDN applications and CPE configurations you can use.

Chapter 2 explains the function of telephone company switches in ISDN. Chapter 3 provides specific information about the role that telephone company switches play in establishing your ISDN service.

Determine Your BRI Configuration Options

Although the standard for a BRI connection is two B channels and one D channel, telephone companies offer a number of configuration options. For example, you can get only one B channel or just two B channels without a D channel. In most cases, however, you want the standard two B channels and one D channel, or a D channel for signaling only. This latter service is referred to as 2B+0D.

You also must determine the channel configuration options that are available for your BRI line's B channels. The available channel configuration options are *circuit-switched voice* (CSV) only, *circuit-switched data* (CSD) only, *alternate voice/circuit-switched data* (CSV/CSD), and packet data only. Some telephone companies, however, don't allow you to configure the B channels any way you want. For example, NYNEX doesn't allow you to configure both B channels as alternate voice/data.

Beyond figuring out channel configurations, you need to check a few other important pieces of information with your telephone company. Make sure that your BRI connection supports multipoint configurations so that you can work with more than one ISDN device at the same time. If you plan to use an analog telephone or ISDN telephone, find out what supplementary services for call management are available from your telephone company.

Chapter 2 explains the fundamentals of the *basic rate interface* (BRI) and Chapter 3 covers specific BRI configuration issues.

Figure Out What ISDN Will Cost

Get the total cost from your telephone company to install ISDN and the monthly recurring costs. ISDN service costs include a one-time installation charge, recurring monthly charges, and usage charges. Your installation and recurring charges are affected by the configuration of your BRI line. Usage charges also vary, depending on whether the call is voice or data.

Chapter 3 explains the breakdown of ISDN service costs. Appendix A provides a summary of ISDN tariffs for the seven regional telephone companies.

Get Wired for ISDN

One of the first ISDN wiring issues to consider is whether you want to convert an existing POTS line for ISDN service or to add a new line. The location of the premises and whether yours is a business site or a residence affect which options you can choose. You can bring in a new line for ISDN, use an unused wire pair, or replace an existing analog line with ISDN service. If the telephone company can add a new line to your premises, you may want to do so. It takes time to climb the ISDN learning curve, so you may not want to hold your primary analog communications line hostage as you make the transition to ISDN. Additionally, you may want to use your ISDN line exclusively for data transmission and not tie it up with incoming voice calls.

Because ISDN uses the same wiring as POTS, you can do your own premises wiring from the demarcation point. If you don't want to do your own wiring, the telephone company installer can do it for $55 to $75 per hour. Remember, ISDN uses the same RJ-11 jack and connector as analog for the U interface. However, ISDN devices use RJ-45 cabling and connectors to connect to the NT1 device.

Chapter 4 explains what is involved in doing your own wiring for ISDN. Chapter 16 provides tips for saving money in getting wired for ISDN.

Develop Your CPE Game Plan

Understanding the pieces is one thing, understanding how to assemble them into a CPE package to use your ISDN connection to its fullest is another. Assembling all the pieces for an effective ISDN connection requires some visualization of the layout options as defined by different applications. You want the flexibility to work with multiple applications on your ISDN line. Typically, however, you use ISDN for remote access and video conferencing.

The key element to getting the most from your ISDN connection is the placement of the NT1 function. If you plan to connect more than one ISDN-ready device to your ISDN line, use an NT1 or an NT1 Plus device. An ISDN-ready device can be your PC with an ISDN adapter card to prepare it for remote access or video conferencing. Some routers offer S/T-interface ports. If you want to connect an analog device to the line, you need an RJ-11 port in a remote-access or NT1 Plus device.

Chapter 4 explains factors to include in developing your ISDN equipment implementation plan, and Appendix B includes resources for getting the equipment.

Equip Yourself with the Right ISDN CPE

ISDN equipment comes in two flavors, U and S/T, and CPE vendors typically sell their products in both flavors. ISDN equipment made for the U-reference point means the NT1 functional device is built in.

The significance of these two reference points is pivotal to getting the most from your ISDN connection. The bottom line is that you can't use multiple U-interface devices on the same ISDN line because they include the NT1 function. ISDN equipment made for the S/T interface requires the NT1 function to connect to ISDN. You can use multiple S/T-interface devices on an ISDN line because they don't include built-in NT1s.

Chapter 4 helps you determine what equipment is right for you. From there, Parts II and III explain the specifics of working with ISDN CPE for remote access and video conferencing.

Assemble Your CPE Provisioning Information

Each application and its associated device require special configurations that you need to convey to the telephone company when ordering ISDN service. Most CPE products include that provisioning information in their documentation. To prepare to order ISDN service, you need to pull together the ISDN provisioning information for all devices you plan to connect to your ISDN line. The telephone company will take this information to program its switch at the CO to work with your equipment at the time you order ISDN service.

Chapter 3 covers the essentials for provisioning your ISDN connection, and Chapter 4 goes into specifics about provisioning your ISDN line for particular applications.

Order Your ISDN Service

Ordering your ISDN line connection involves exchanging information with the telephone company. This information includes specifically what you need for your BRI line and CPE. In turn, from the telephone company you receive information to configure your CPE to work with the ISDN connection.

Your telephone company may assign you SPIDs for each device connected to the ISDN line, depending on the type of switch at the CO. If the telephone company assigns you SPIDs, you need it to configure your ISDN devices. The telephone company also assigns you one or more directory numbers, depending on your ISDN configuration.

After you establish ISDN service from your local telephone company, you establish an account with a long-distance telephone company for circuit-switched data. Unlike analog service, the local telephone company doesn't automatically establish your long-distance service for circuit-switched data at the time you order your local service. After you establish an account from a long-distance telephone company, you'll receive a separate monthly bill for circuit-switched data from that company.

Chapter 3 explains the factors involved in ordering your ISDN service, and Chapter 4 builds on these fundamentals by telling you how your choice of applications affects your choice of service.

Set Up Your ISDN Devices

At last you're beginning to see light at the end of the digital tunnel! The final step is to decide where you install your ISDN hardware and software. To set up your ISDN devices, you need the information from your telephone company, such as SPIDs, directory numbers, and switch type. Typically, the first device to get up and running is your NT1 or NT1 Plus device. Then you can set up your other ISDN devices. Getting all your devices to work takes time and patience — stay cool and calm. The results are well worth all your effort!

Parts II and III cover the details about setting up specific CPE for ISDN in Windows 95.

Chapter 18

Ten Sources of ISDN Help

In This Chapter
▶ Checking ISDN CPE Web sites
▶ Joining ISDN user groups
▶ Checking out the ISDN World Conference

As an ISDN user, you need all the help you can get. Here is a collection of resources available to help you on your journey toward ISDN enlightenment.

ISDN CPE Vendor Web Sites

Most ISDN CPE vendors use their Web sites for product support. They include pages maintained by their technical support groups. These sites typically offer the latest software drivers for their products, which you can usually download for free. Most product documentation includes the Web addresses, or you can simply do a Web search to find them.

ISDN Line-Ordering Help from ISDN CPE Vendors

A growing number of ISDN CPE vendors offer customer service groups to help customers get up and running with ISDN service. These services typically provide information on setting up ISDN service for your locality. They list contact information, installation charges, and ISDN provisioning information for their (and other vendors') products. These groups work with the local telephone and long-distance companies on a routine basis.

The following is a sample of vendor ISDN support services. You can check any vendor's Web site to find out whether it offers similar services.

- ✔ **U.S. Robotics's I-Team.** Call the I-Team's toll-free number, 888-USR-ISDN (888-877-4736), to have ISDN service ordered for you through the local telephone company and to arrange the scheduling and installation of ISDN service. U.S. Robotics doesn't charge for this service, as is the case for most other vendors.

- ✔ **Motorola's ISDN LifeGUARD.** If you have any questions about ISDN line ordering or configuration for the BitSURFR Pro, call Motorola's ISDN LifeGUARD service at 800-894-ISDN (4736). These folks can help you make sure that you get the right ISDN service.

- ✔ **Farallon's Up & Running Guaranteed.** This fee-based service is available for $99 for Netopia ISDN Modem customers and $499 for Netopia Internet router customers. Call 510-814-5000 for more information.

- ✔ **Diamond's ISDN Support Center.** This service assists Supra NetCommander customers with ordering ISDN service. The ISDN Support Center number is 408-325-7110.

Dan Kegel's ISDN Page

The most comprehensive links to ISDN resources on the Internet are at a Web site maintained by Dan Kegel. This site, which is updated constantly, provides links to all kinds of ISDN information, including equipment vendors and service providers offering ISDN connections. This is truly a one-stop shopping site for any resources on the Internet that pertain to ISDN. The online address for this site is

```
http://alumni.caltech.edu/~dank/isdn/
```

Dan Kegel's ISDN Page includes more than 30 main headings and several hundred links.

ISDN User Groups

Currently, there are only a few ISDN user groups. As ISDN becomes mainstream, however, more user groups should be forming. User groups can provide a powerful consumer voice to the ISDN industry equation. The following are the leading ISDN user groups in the United States:

California ISDN User's Group

P.O. Box 27901-318
San Francisco, CA 94127
Voice: 415-241-9943
Fax: 415-753-6942
World Wide Web: http://www.ciug.org

This is by far the most active ISDN user group in the country. It publishes a newsletter and regularly holds events for ISDN users to sample ISDN CPE products and services. It's also the sponsor of the ISDN World Conference.

New York ISDN User's Group

1140 Avenue of the Americas
New York, NY 10036
Voice: 212-944-5400
Fax: 212-944-5410
World Wide Web: http://www.isdn.org

This ISDN user group holds meetings on every second Wednesday of the month at 6:30 p.m. It also offers a mailing list.

Texas ISDN User's Group

Voice: 915-646-2116
Fax: 915-643-9668
E-mail: info@tiug.org
World Wide Web: http://www.crimson.com/isdn

This ISDN user group doesn't offer much information on its Web site. For more information, send e-mail to Gene Chesser, the current President.

North American ISDN User's Forum (NIUF)

National Institute of Standards and Technology
Building 223, Room B364
Gaithersburg, MD 20899
Voice: 301-975-2937
World Wide Web: http://www.niuf.nist.gov/misc/niuf.html

This is a government-sponsored organization made up mostly of ISDN telecommunication companies. It does offer some useful publications, such as an ISDN wiring guide.

ISDN World Conference

The California ISDN User's Group hosts the ISDN World Conference in the fall and spring, usually in Los Angeles or San Francisco. The conference includes dozens of sessions with ISDN technology experts where you can learn about ISDN applications, attend seminars by ISDN CPE vendors, and visit a trade show exhibit with more than 40 vendors showing their ISDN wares. For more information on attending this conference, contact

California ISDN User's Group
c/o Trade Show Solutions
960 San Antonio Road
Palo Alto, CA 94303
Voice: 800-850-CIUG
Fax: 415-857-9200
World Wide Web: `http://www.ciug.org`

Internet Service Providers

Most ISDN Internet service providers (ISPs) will also provide help in setting up your ISDN service. Many also sell ISDN CPE, sometimes at discounted prices. One of the advantages of going the ISP route is that the provider will get your ISDN line established and also set up your Internet account.

ISDN Newsgroup

USENET news — the Internet's giant distributed bulletin board system — includes an ISDN newsgroup at `comp.dcom.isdn` that's a good source of information, with several ISDN gurus who participate regularly. It's a great resource for troubleshooting problems and keeping abreast of what's happening in the ISDN realm.

Microsoft Technical Support

Your ISDN connections involve Windows 95. If you have a Windows 95-related question, contact Microsoft's technical support. You can get help also through Windows 95 forums on all the major commerical online services, or by checking the Microsoft Web site at `http://www.microsoft.com`.

Technical support for Windows 95 can be obtained from Microsoft at no charge for the first 90 days that you use the product. The technical support number is 206-637-7098. The 90-day clock doesn't start ticking until you make your first call. Call-in hours are weekdays 6:00 a.m. to 6:00 p.m. (Pacific Standard Time).

Microsoft does not include support for TCP/IP for Windows 95 through its normal support channels. For information on TCP/IP support, you need to call 800-227-4679.

After the 90-day free support expires, you can obtain support from Microsoft on a per-session basis. Calling 900-555-2000 costs $2 per minute, with a $35 maximum. You are not charged for the time spent on hold. The charges are added to your telephone bill.

ISDN Periodicals

The mainstream PC industry publications, such as *PC Magazine, PC Week,* and *InfoWorld,* are covering ISDN products with increasing regularity. Other publications to check out include the following:

- ✔ *LAN Times.* 1900 O'Farrell Street, Suite 200, San Mateo, CA 94403; 800-525-5003 or 609-426-5570. This biweekly publication provides the most comprehensive coverage of ISDN topics.

- ✔ *Communications Week.* 600 Community Drive, Manhasset, NY 11030; 708-647-6834. This weekly publication covers the telecommunications and networking industries. It routinely covers ISDN topics.

- ✔ *Interactive Week.* 100 Quentin Roosevelt Boulevard, Garden City, NY 11530; 609-829-9313. This biweekly publication routinely covers Internet and ISDN topics.

Telephone Companies

Most telephone companies now have separate ISDN ordering centers staffed with ISDN-literate representatives. One of the best places to start your quest for ISDN service is to check out your telephone company's Web site. However, consider telephone companies as the last resort in getting help with specific CPE provisioning; most telephone companies know little about ISDN CPE except by ordering codes.

Chapter 19

Ten Things to Check before Choosing an ISDN ISP

• •

In This Chapter

▶ Know your true connection costs

▶ Find out whether your ISP is overloaded

▶ Check out what ISDN CPE the ISP supports

▶ Ask about compression support

• •

*I*SDN ISPs come in all shapes and sizes. The criteria you should consider when selecting an Internet service provider are performance, price, and responsive technical support. This chapter provides general guidelines to keep in mind as you shop for an ISDN ISP.

Check Out All of Your ISP Options

Internet access via ISDN is available from national, regional, and local Internet service providers (ISPs). You may prefer regional or local ISPs to the larger national providers. Local ISPs are more likely to offer better services and rates equal to or slightly lower than those of the nationals. Regional or local ISPs may also be more willing to tailor their service to specialized requirements, and are usually in a better position to adapt more quickly to new ISDN solutions. On the other hand, national ISPs often offer better security, and in some areas the national ISPs are the only available option. Check them all out before making your decision.

A comprehensive listing of Internet service providers is available at Dan Kegel's ISDN Page at

```
http://alumni.caltech.edu/~dank/isdn/isp.html
```

Know Your True Connection Costs

When you shop around for the best price for your total ISDN package, take the following factors into account:

- Figure out how much time you spend online and compare charges based on that. Two kinds of ISDN-based Internet access service are available: dial-up and dedicated service. *Dial-up service,* which is the most common and least expensive, is similar to the way a dial-up modem account works. *Dedicated service* is a connection that generally stays open 24 hours a day, 7 days a week. Dedicated ISDN is sold in most regions as a configured service called Centrex. As you can guess, this service is more expensive.

- Compare pricing plans that have a higher set-up fee but a lower monthly fee with plans that have a lower setup fee but a higher monthly fee.

- If you're connecting a LAN via an ISDN router and anticipate more than several hours of use per day, a dedicated ISDN connection may be cheaper than a dial-up connection because telephone usage charges can quickly add up.

Determine the Type of Call

Make sure that you don't have to pay any telephone usage charges beyond a local call. Most ISDN service is metered even for local calls, but you don't want to pay any additional charges due to having an ISP that is out of your local calling area. Check the ISP's point-of-presence (POP) numbers to see whether they service your exchange area.

Another factor that may come into play for your ISDN Internet connection is what type of call can be made to your ISP. Telephone company tariffs are usually cheaper for analog calls than for digital data calls. In some telephone company service areas, you may be charged a flat rate for analog local calls but billed by usage at a higher metered rate for digital calls.

Some ISDN remote-access devices let you initiate a call as a voice signal instead of a data signal; in that way, the telephone company switch thinks the call is a voice call even though it's a data call. The result is you're charged the lower analog flat rate instead of the higher digital rates. This can save money because in most cases your Internet service provider is a local call. As such, the cost of connecting to your ISP falls within the flat monthly rate. If you connect to your Internet provider for more than a few hours, the savings can add up.

Keep in mind that this works only where there are two separate tariffs for analog and ISDN. Pacific Telesis, for example, charges one metered rate for all calls over ISDN regardless of the type of call. NYNEX, on the other hand, charges a lower analog rate, so initiating a call as voice will get you the lower rate. NYNEX reduces the value of initiating a data call as a voice call, however, by allowing only one B channel to be configured for both voice/data. (You must have a B channel configured for both data and voice for this feature to work.)

Check Throughput, Latency, and Reliability

The speed of an ISDN connection does not always match the speed at which the Internet responds. The ultimate speed you realize will be affected by the current amount of traffic on the Internet plus the size of the communications link and type of equipment at the location from which the data is being accessed. Examine an ISP's network setup for the following:

- ✔ **Backbone speed.** T-3 offers the highest throughput, but bottlenecks can occur unless the entire backbone is T-3. Some providers claim that their backbone is T-3, but it is T-3 up to several connection points and then hits lower T-1 bandwidth connection points.

- ✔ **Connections into the backbone.** Look for a provider with a direct and fast connection to the national backbone. The more router hops away you are from the backbone, the greater the chance of delays.

- ✔ **Network access points (NAPs).** NAPs, which connect different ISP customers, can be a huge bottleneck. Seek an ISP that avoids NAPs by providing direct bilateral connections to other ISPs.

- ✔ **Redundant equipment and redundant backbone links.** The use of redundant equipment on all hubs and links ensures reliability of service.

Is the ISP Overloaded?

Getting a busy signal is one of the biggest complaints from customers. Ask ISPs about their port-to-user ratio, which typically ranges from 10-to-1 to 20-to-1. A range of 8-to-1 to 12-to-1 is best. You may not get an accurate answer, but it's worth trying. Ask other Internet customers about what service providers are the best in your area.

Ask about Technical Support

Make sure that an ISP offers telephone support with a staff that knows about ISDN and different ISDN devices. Check the ISP's Web site to see whether it provides an online reference. Ideally, find an ISP that provides 24-hour, 7-day technical support.

Check What ISDN CPE the ISP Supports

Find out what ISDN remote-access devices the ISP supports or has experience working with. An ISDN ISP may support only one or two ISDN remote-access devices or may support several. Regardless of what type of ISDN remote-access device is used for an Internet access connection, the remote-access devices used at both ends of the connection must be able to communicate with each other.

In spite of PPP/MP, you can still have problems with connections between CPE devices from one vendor and another. As such, you must know what an ISP has successfully worked with. ISPs like to find solutions that work with their individual network architecture. Check what equipment an ISP supports before you buy.

Ask for ISDN CPE Deals

Many ISPs offer hardware and access packages that enable you to buy your ISDN remote-access devices at discounted prices. ISPs offer the discounted hardware as a service to their customers. This is usually a good deal for customers not only because they save money but also because it makes for easier, coordinated technical support from the CPE vendor and ISP.

Check for Compression Support

Compression can speed up file transfers by a 4-to-1 ratio, which can mean data transfer rates up to 512 Kbps. If an ISP supports any compression scheme that your ISDN remote-access device supports, you can dramatically improve your download times. Unfortunately, many ISPs don't offer compression support. Economics is the reason they don't: Adding compression capability involves spending money for the enhancement. And if ISPs spend the extra money to add compression, the faster speeds mean Internet users spend less time using their service. The result for their dial-up business is less connection time and lower revenues.

Ask about Security

Be sure that your ISP provides security in the form of a firewall, encryption, authentication, or a combination of these. This is particularly important if you're using a router to connect your entire LAN to the Internet. You also need security implementation at your end of the connection. Typically, national ISPs are the most experienced in the security area because they have the resources to hire security experts.

Ask your ISP whether it uses CHAP (*Challenge Handshake Authentication Protocol*) to verify your name and password when you dial in. CHAP offers more security for logging on to the Internet. CHAP arranges an exchange of random numbers between machines. The machine receiving a number from the first machine performs arithmetic on that number using a previously agreed secret. (A *secret* is a string of up to 16 characters used as an encryption key.) If your ISP uses CHAP, make sure that your ISDN remote-access device supports this feature.

Appendix A
Into the ISDN Tariff Maze

● ●

In This Appendix

▶ Understanding the Zen of ISDN service tariffs

▶ Surveying ISDN tariffs for the regional telephone companies as well as other smaller telcos

▶ Contacting long-distance telephone companies

▶ Surveying international telcos

● ●

*T*his appendix provides you with basic ISDN tariff information for the seven regional telephone companies. This is a starting point for compiling an estimate of what ISDN may cost you.

Tariff Terrorism

In the real world, determining the price of a product or service is typically as easy as looking or asking. But the telephone companies have operated in a regulated, monopolistic environment that hasn't been consumer driven. ISDN pricing, called *tariffs* in telephone company lingo, comes together through the application of complex cost allocation and recovery rules established by both federal and state regulators. Thus, ISDN pricing varies from one telephone company to another and from one state to another.

The 1996 Telecommunications Act may open up competition for ISDN service at some point. For now, however, ISDN rates are unrealistically high in most areas.

Determining the total cost of ISDN service from your local telephone company can become the search for the Holy Grail. Installation charges, recurring monthly charges, usage charges for each B channel, voice versus data traffic considerations, and a cornucopia of add-on charges can make figuring out what ISDN is going to cost difficult. Fortunately, most telephone companies are now providing more pricing information via toll-free numbers or Web sites.

When you contact your telephone company to find out about ISDN service and costs, ask for any ISDN promotional programs that can save you money.

Although most telcos use a metered rate for ISDN communications, a growing number are offering flat-rate packages that include blocks of connection time in the monthly bill. This block of time typically ranges from 20 to 100 hours. In some cases, you may be able to get unlimited connection time. Compare these packages with metered rates; in many cases, flat-rate packages are the better deal.

Don't take any pricing information in this appendix as gospel. ISDN prices and services are constantly changing, so you need to contact your local telephone company for the current prices.

Ameritech

Ameritech services Illinois, Indiana, Michigan, Ohio, and Wisconsin. Table A-1 lists estimated costs for a 2B+D ISDN configuration with two B alternate voice/circuit-switched data channels and a D channel for both residential and business services. These rates do not include usage charges or any other additional charges, such as taxes or other configuration options.

For more information, call 800-419-5400 for residential service or 800-417-9888 for business service, or check out Ameritech's Web site at www.ameritech.com.

Table A-1 Ameritech's Residential and Business ISDN Service Tariffs

State	*Installation Charges*	*Monthly Charges*
Illinois	$135.00 (R)	$28.05 – $34.50 (R)
	$132.35 (B)	$36.04 – $43.41 (B)
Indiana	$127.00 (R)	$94.83 (R)
	$139.00 (B)	$94.41 (B)
Michigan	$122.00 (R)	$33.51 (R)
	$147.00 (B)	$37.46 (B)
Ohio	$116.15 (R)	$31.20 (R)
	$129.35 (B)	$40.60 (B)
Wisconsin	$113.05 (R)	$30.90 (R)
	$100.65 (B)	$37.00 (B)

R = Residential

B = Business

Bell Atlantic

Bell Atlantic services Delaware, Maryland, New Jersey, Pennsylvania, Virginia, Washington, D.C., and West Virginia. Table A-2 lists the tariffs for 2B+D configurations for residential and business service. These rates do not include usage charges or any other additional charges, such as taxes or other configuration options.

For more information on ISDN service, call Bell Atlantic at 800-204-7332 or check out its Web site at www.bell-atl.com.

Table A-2 Bell Atlantic Residential and Business ISDN Service Tariffs

State	Installation	Monthly Service
Delaware	$125 – $160.96 (R) $154.65 (B)	$28.90 (R) $46.89 – $49.39 (B)
Maryland	$125 – $173 (R) $132.50 (B)	$32.52 – $34.07 (R) $36.34 – $40.75 (B)
New Jersey	$125 – $167 (R) $123.25 (B)	$26.75 – $28.93 (R) $35.49 – $37.78 (B)
Pennsylvania	$125 – $165 (R) $169.75 (B)	$26.50 – $30.50 (R) $31.33 – $39.00(B)
Virginia	$125 – $163.50 (R) $100.00 (B)	$29.89 – $31.63 (R) $34.00 – $38.43 (B)
Washington, DC	$120.25 (B)	$34.16 (B)
West Virginia	$125 – $169 (R) $135.90 (B)	$34.00 (R) $47.50 – $50.00 (B)

R = Residential

B = Business

Bell Atlantic recently merged with NYNEX, which services the northeastern states. As of this writing, however, their tariffs remain separate.

Bell South

Bell South services Alabama, Florida, Georgia, Kentucky, Louisiana, Mississippi, North Carolina, South Carolina, and Tennessee. Bell South has some of the most expensive ISDN tariffs in the United States. The price range for Table A-3 is based on four 2B+D configuration options, which Bell South refers to as Capability Packages. These rates do not include usage charges or any other additional charges, such as taxes or added configuration options.

Table A-3 Bell South Residential and Business ISDN Tariffs

State	Installation Charges	Monthly Charges
Alabama	$221.75 – $228.75 (R) $253.75 – $267.75 (B)	$72.35 – $79.35 (R) $111.50 – $125.50 (B)
Florida	$211.00 – $218.00 (R) $230.00 – $244.00 (B)	$60.65 – $67.65 (R) $111.50 – $125.50 (B)
Georgia	$202.50 – $209.50 (R) $229.25 – $243.25 (B)	$66.90 – $73.90 (R) $111.50 – $125.50 (B)
Kentucky	$254.10 – $261.10 (R) $274.11 – $288.10 (B)	$64.55 – $71.55 (R) $111.50 – $125.50 (B)
Louisiana	$267.11 – $274.11 (R) $270.11 – $284.11 (B)	$75.00 – $82.00 (R) $112.50 – $126.50 (B)
Mississippi	$238.75 – $245.75 (R) $267.75 – $281.75 (B)	$70.01 – $77.01 (R) $112.50 – $126.50 (B)
North Carolina	$241.75 – $248.75 (R) $264.50 – $278.50 (B)	$79.51 – $86.51 (R) $111.50 – $125.50 (B)
South Carolina	$230.50 – $237.50 (R) $253.50 – $267.50 (B)	$66.90 – $73.90 (R) $111.50 – $125.50 (B)
Tennessee	$24.40 – $31.40 (R) $85.90 – $99.90 (B)	$33.00 – $40.00 (R) $111.50 – $125.50 (B)

R = Residential

B = Business

The following describes the four Capability Packages:

- ✔ Capability Package N includes alternate voice/circuit-switched data on one B channel, circuit-switched data on the other B channel, and basic D channel packet-switched data. This package provides non-EKTS voice features including Flexible Calling, Additional Call Offering, and Calling Number Identification. Data capabilities include Calling Number Identification.

- ✔ Capability Package O is equivalent to Capability Package N, but with CACH EKTS voice service. This package provides more Call Offering functionality.

- ✔ Capability Package P includes alternate voice/circuit-switched data on two B channels and basic D channel packet-switched data. This package includes the same non-EKTS voice features as Capability Package N.

- ✔ Capability Package Q is equivalent to Capability Package P, but with CACH EKTS voice service. This package provides more Call Offering functionality.

For more information or to order ISDN service, call Bell South's ISDN Hotline at 800-428-4736 or check out its Web site at www.bell.bellsouth.com.

NYNEX

NYNEX services Massachusetts, Maine, New Hampshire, New York, Rhode Island, and Vermont. Table A-4 shows pricing (residential and business) for a 2B+D configuration with one B channel alternate voice/circuit-switched data and one B channel circuit-switched data. These rates do not include usage charges or any other additional charges, such as taxes or other configuration options. If your premises uses a central office that doesn't support ISDN, NYNEX can still deliver ISDN using a service called Virtual ISDN Service. Unfortunately, NYNEX charges a lot more for this service.

Table A-4	NYNEX Residential and Business ISDN Tariffs	
State	*Installation Charges*	*Monthly Charges*
Massachusetts	$67.07 (R)	$31.41 (R)
	$123.02 (B)	$37.00 (B)
Maine	$129.75 (R)	$34.40 (R)
	$141.00 (B)	$53.36 (B)
New Hampshire	$125.00 (R)	$28.00 (R)
	$125.00 (B)	$44.88 (B)
New York	$234.00 (R)	$24.10 (R)
	$325.00 (B)	$36.23 (B)
Rhode Island	$118.83 (R)	$28.04 (R)
	$129.61 (B)	$41.91 (B)
Vermont	$93.00 (R)	$60.05 (R)
	$106.00 (B)	$90.92 (B)

R = Residential

B = Business

NYNEX recently merged with Bell Atlantic, which services the mid-Atlantic states. As of this writing, however, their tariffs remain separate.

For more information on ISDN service or to order service, call the NYNEX ISDN Service Center at 800-650-4736 or check out the its Web site at www.nynex.com.

Pacific Bell

Pacific Bell services California, which by itself accounts for the largest number of ISDN users. Pacific Bell was one of the pioneers in low-cost ISDN service for both residential and business accounts. Table A-5 lists the relatively simple pricing structure for Pacific Bell ISDN service.

Table A-5 Pacific Bell Residential and Business ISDN Service Tariffs		
ISDN Service	**Installation Charges**	**Monthly Charges**
Centrex ISDN	$270.00	$31.75
Business ISDN	$195.75	$28.82
Home ISDN	$159.75	$24.50

For more information or to order ISDN service, call Pacific Bell's ISDN Service Center at 800-472-4736 or check out its Web site at www.pacbell.com.

Southwestern Bell

Southwestern Bell services Arkansas, Kansas, Missouri, Oklahoma, and Texas. SWBell has only recently made a commitment to ISDN. The Southwestern Bell Web site lists tariffs for only 913 and 316 area codes in Kansas and the 816 and 417 area codes in Missouri. The tariff for these areas has three options:

- Unlimited usage per month: $104.30 plus an installation charge of $452.25–$457.49

- 10 hours per month: $57.30 plus an installation charge of $452.25–$457.49

- 80 hours per month: $63.50 plus an installation charge of $452.25–$457.49

For more information, start with 800-792-4736. The automated system routes you to service centers for specific areas.

US West

US West services Arizona, Colorado, Idaho, Iowa, Minnesota, Montana, Nebraska, New Mexico, North Dakota, Oregon, South Dakota, Utah, Washington, and Wyoming. Table A-6 lists ISDN tariffs for states in which US West offers ISDN service.

Table A-6	US West ISDN Service Tariffs	
State	*Installation*	*Monthly*
Arizona	$140.00	$69.00
Colorado	$67.00	$60.00
Idaho	$100-$210	$39 – $68
Iowa	$100 – $210	$48 – $73
Minnesota	$100 – $210	$39 – $104
Nebraska	$110 – $210	$39 – $68
New Mexico	No rate published	No rate published
North Dakota	$100 – $210	$41 – $68
Oregon	$110.00	$69.00
South Dakota	$80.00	$84.00
Utah	$110 – $210	$39 – $84
Washington	$85.00	$35 – $50
Wyoming	$110 – $210	$47 – $88

For more information on ISDN service or to place an order, call 800-898-9675 for residential service and 800-246-5226 for business service, or check out the US West Web site at www.uswest.com.

GTE

GTE provides telephone service in the following states: Alabama, California, Florida, Hawaii, Illinois, Idaho, Indiana, Kentucky, Michigan, Missouri, Nebraska, North Carolina, Ohio, Oregon, Pennsylvania, South Carolina, Texas, Virginia, and Washington. For information on availability, call 800-483-4736 or check out the GTE Web site at www.get.com.

Other Telcos

In the United States, there are several smaller telephone companies, including Cincinnati Bell, Nevada Bell, Rochester Telephone, and SNET (Connecticut). The following sections provide ISDN service information for these telcos.

Cincinnati Bell

Cincinnati Bell provides service in Ohio and Kentucky. For more information, contact the Cincinnati Bell ISDN Service Center at 513-566-3282 or check out the Cincinnati Bell Web site at www.cinbelltel.com.

Nevada Bell

Nevada Bell sells ISDN centrex services-based volume pricing. For a single ISDN, it's expensive at around $80 a month. For more information call 702-333-4811 (small business) or 702-688-7100 (large business).

Rochester Telephone

For more information on ISDN service from Rochester Telephone, call 716-777-1234.

SNET (Connecticut)

For more information on ISDN service from SNET, call the SNET ISDN Sales & Technical Support Center at 800-430-4736 or check out the SNET Web site at www.snet.com.

ISDN Long-Distance Telcos

As is the case for POTS calls, you typically use a long-distance carrier for handling calls outside your area. Following are the telephone numbers and Web sites for finding out more about long-distance ISDN service:

AT&T: 800-820-6464 or www.att.com

LDDS: 201-804-6970 or www.wcom.com

MCI: 800-624-4736 or www.mci.com

Sprint: 708-768-6043 or www.sprint.com

Many local telephone companies will let you specify your long-distance carrier when you get local ISDN service.

AT&T domestic ISDN rates are based on mileage, total bandwidth, and time of day. Table A-7 shows the per-minute charges for long-distance service (day rate) for a single B channel. If you're using both B channels, as is the case for video conferencing, double these rates.

Table A-7	AT&T's Day Rate for Each B Channel	
Mileage	*First Minute*	*Each Additional Minute*
0–55	$.2790	$.1990
56–124	$.3090	$.2290
125–292	$.3310	$.2510
293–430	$.3530	$.2730
431–925	$.3790	$.2990
926–1910	$.3880	$.3080
1911–3000	$.4000	$.3200
3001+	$1.1470	$1.0670

AT&T is also a global telephone company offering ISDN service to many countries. International ISDN service, however, can be expensive. For example, a one-hour, two B channel connection to Japan or Australia during peak hours will set you back $597.60.

Survey of International Telephone Companies

Although ISDN service in the United States is just beginning to get off the ground in a big way, other countries have been deploying ISDN for years. Most notably, Europe (particularly Germany) is the leader in delivering ISDN service. Table A-8 provides a sampling of international ISDN service broken down by countries.

Table A-8		International ISDN Service Providers
Country	*Telephone Company*	*Information Contact*
Australia	Telstra	World Wide Web: www.telstra.com.au
Canada	Stentor	Fax: 800-578-4736 World Wide Web: www.stentor.ca
France	France Telecom	Fax: 33-1-43-42-97-77 World Wide Web: www.francetelecom.com
Germany	Deutsche Telecom	Fax: 49-651-130-2305 World Wide Web: www.dtag.de/dtag/telekom_.html
Japan	NTT	Fax: 44-171-496-0390 World Wide Web: www.ntt.jp
United Kingdom	British Telecom	Fax: 44-117-927-4218 World Wide Web: www.bt.net

The 5th Wave — **By Rich Tennant**

"I SUPPOSE THIS ALL HAS SOMETHING TO DO WITH THE NEW MATH."

Appendix B
ISDN Products, Services, and Resources

• •

In This Appendix

▶ NT1 and NT1 Plus devices

▶ ISDN remote-access products

▶ Internet service providers

▶ Desktop video-conferencing systems

▶ ISDN user groups

▶ TCP/IP software

• •

NT1 and NT1 Plus Devices

NT1 Ace

ADTRAN
901 Explorer Boulevard
Huntsville, AL 35806
Voice: 800-827-0807
Fax: 205-971-8699
World Wide Web: http://www.adtran.com

NT1D

Motorola
500 Bradford Drive
Huntsville, AL 35805
Voice: 800-451-2369
Fax: 205-830-5657
World Wide Web: http://www.motorola.com

NT1U-100TC
NT1U-220TC

Tone Commander Systems, Inc.
11609 49th Place West
Mulilteo, WA 98275
Voice: 800-524-0024
Fax: 206-349-1010
World Wide Web: http://www.halcyon.com/tcs/

NT1U700 Series
ISDN-TA710

E-Tech Research, Inc.
1800 Wyatt Drive, Suite 2
Santa Clara, CA 95054
Voice: 408-988-8108
Fax: 408-988-8109
World Wide Web: http://www.e-tech.com

UT620
Super NT1

Alpha Telecom, Inc.
7501 South Memorial Parkway, Suite 212
Huntsville, AL 35802
Voice: 205-881-8743
Fax: 205-880-9720
World Wide Web: http://iquest.com/~ati_usa

ISDN Remote-Access Products

External serial ISDN modems

3ComImpactIQ

3Com Corporation
5400 Bayfront Plaza
Santa Clara, CA 95052
Voice: 800-638-3266 or 408-764-5000
Fax: 408-764-5000
World Wide Web: http://www.3com.com

BitSURFR Pro

Motorola
500 Bradford Drive
Huntsville, AL 35805
Voice: 800-451-2369
Fax: 205-830-5657
World Wide Web: http://www.motorola.com

Courier I-Modem ISDN/V.34

U.S. Robotics
8100 N. McCormick Boulevard
Skokie, IL 60076
Voice: 847-982-5010
World Wide Web: http://www.usr.com

Express XRT
Express XR

ADTRAN
901 Explorer Boulevard
Huntsville, AL 35806
Voice: 800-827-0807
Fax: 205-971-8699
World Wide Web: http://www.adtran.com

Lava Link-650 (serial port accelerator card)

Lava Computer Manufacturing, Inc.
28A Dansk Court
Rexdale, Ontario, Canada M9W 5V8
Voice: 800-241-5282 or 416-674-5942
World Wide Web: http://www.lavalink.com

Netopia ISDN Modem

Farallon Computing, Inc.
2470 Mariner Square Loop
Alameda, CA 94501
Voice: 510-814-5000
Fax: 510-814-5023
World Wide Web: http://www.farallon.com

ISDN adapter cards

BitSURFR Pro ISA

Motorola
500 Bradford Drive
Huntsville, AL 35805
Voice: 800-451-2369
Fax: 205-830-5657
World Wide Web: http://www.motorola.com

Cardinal IDC100i

Cardinal Technologies
1827 Freedom Road
Lancaster, PA 17601
Voice: 800-775-0899
World Wide Web: http://www.cardtech.com

CyberJet

Alpha Telecom, Inc.
7501 South Memorial Parkway, Suite 212
Huntsville, AL 35802
Voice: 205-881-8743
Fax: 205-880-9720
World Wide Web: http://iquest.com/~ati_usa

Cyberspace Internet Plus

ISDN*tek
P.O. Box 3000
San Gregorio, CA 94074
Voice: 415-712-3000
Fax: 415-712-3003
World Wide Web: http://www.isdntek.com

DIVA PCMCIA
DIVA Pro

Eicon Technology, Inc.
14755 Preston Road, Suite 620
Dallas, TX 75240
Voice: 214-239-3200
Fax: 214-239-3304
World Wide Web: http://www.eicon.com

I-bahn ISDN+Fax/Modem (PCMCIA Card)

Angia Communications
441 East Bay Boulevard
Provo, UT 84606
Voice: 801-371-0488
Fax: 801-373-9847
World Wide Web: http://www.angia.com

Sportster ISDN 128K

U.S. Robotics
8100 N. McCormick Boulevard
Skokie, IL 60076
Voice: 847-982-5010
World Wide Web: http://www.usr.com

Supra NetCommander

Diamond Multimedia Systems, Inc.
2880 Junction Avenue
San Jose, CA 95134
Voice: 408-325-7000
Fax: 408-325-7070
World Wide Web: http://www.diamondmm.com

ISDN bridges and routers

Cisco 760 Series
Cisco 750 Series

Cisco Systems, Inc.
170 West Tasman Drive
San Jose, CA 95134
Voice: 408-526-4000
Fax: 408-526-4100
World Wide Web: http://www.cisco.com

CyberSwitch 100

Cabletron
35 Industrial Way
Rochester, NH 03867
Voice: 603-332-9400
World Wide Web: http://www.cabletron.com

NetGear ISDN Router RT210/211

NetGear, Inc.
A Bay Networks Company
48105 Warm Springs Boulevard
Fremont, CA 94539
Voice: 800-211-2069 or 510-490-4774
World Wide Web: http://www.netgear.baynetworks.com

Office Connect 510
3Com AccessBuilder Internet/400

3Com Corporation
5400 Bayfront Plaza
Santa Clara, CA 95052
Voice: 800-638-3266 or 408-764-5000
Fax: 408-764-5000
World Wide Web: http://www.3com.com

Pipeline 25-Fx
Pipeline 25-Px
Pipeline 25
Pipeline 50
Pipeline 75
Pipeline 100

Ascend Communications, Inc.
1275 Harbor Bay Parkway
Alameda, CA 94502
Voice: 800-621-9578 or 510-769-6001
Fax: 510-814-2300
World Wide Web: http://www.ascend.com

WebRamp

Trancell Systems, Inc.
3180 De La Cruz Boulevard, Suite 200
Santa Clara, CA 95054
Voice: 408-988-5353
Fax: 408-988-6363
World Wide Web: http://www.trancell.com

XpressConnect Series

Gandalf Technologies
130 Colonnade Road South
Nepean, Ontario, Canada K2E 7M4
Voice: 800-426-3253 or 613-723-6500
Fax: 613-226-1717
World Wide Web: http://www.gandalf.com

ISDN Internet Service Providers

A comprehensive listing of Internet service providers offering ISDN service is available at Dan Kegel's ISDN Page. The following World Wide Web page provides a constantly updated list of ISDN Internet service providers:

```
http://alumni.caltech.edu/~dank/isdn/isp.html
```

At last count, there were over 175 ISDN Internet service providers in the United States. Kegel lists these as well as ISDN service providers for Canada, Asia, Australia, and Europe.

Another good source that lists over 75 ISDN ISPs is

```
http://www.cybertoday.com/cybertoday/ISPsProducts.html#ISDN
```

Desktop Video-Conferencing Systems

Connectix VideoPhone

Connectix Corporation
2655 Campus Drive
San Mateo, CA 94403
Voice: 800-950-5880 or 415-571-5100
Fax: 415-571-5195
World Wide Web: http://www.connectix.com

Enhanced CU-SeeMe
CU-SeeMe

White Pine Software
40 Simon Street
Nashua, NH 03060
Voice: 603-886-9050
Fax: 603-886-9051
World Wide Web: http://www.wpine.com

White Pine Software provides the leading video-conferencing software for the Internet.

PicturePhone Direct

200 Commerce Drive
Rochester, NY 14623
Voice: 800-521-5454
Fax: 716-359-4999
World Wide Web: `http://picturephone.com`

PicturePhone Direct provides a one-stop solution for video-conferencing systems and a host of related products through mail order. Its product line includes camcorders, slide-to-video systems, headsets, tripods, NT1s, and books.

PictureTel Live 100

PictureTel Corporation
222 Rosewood Drive
Danvers, MA 01923
Voice: 508-762-5000
Fax: 508-762-5245
World Wide Web: `http://www.picturetel.com`

ProShare Personal Video Conferencing System 200

Intel Corporation
2200 Mission College Boulevard
Santa Clara, CA 95052
Voice: 800-538-3373 or 503-629-7354
Fax: 800-525-3019
World Wide Web: `http://www.intel.com`

Videum Conference Pro

WINNOV
1150 Kifer Road, Suite 201
Sunnyvale, CA 94086
Voice: 408-733-5922
Fax: 408-733-5922
World Wide Web: `http://www.winnov.com`

ISDN User Groups

California ISDN User's Group

P.O. Box 27901-318
San Francisco, CA 94127
Voice: 415-241-9943
Fax: 415-753-6942
World Wide Web: http://www.ciug.org

This is the leading ISDN user group in the United States. It sponsors the ISDN World Conference, publishes a newsletter, and regularly holds events for ISDN users to sample ISDN CPE as well as for ISDN CPE vendors to meet with users.

New York ISDN User's Group

Advanced Digital Networks, Inc.
1140 Avenue of the Americas
New York, NY 10036
Voice: 212-944-5400
Fax: 212-944-5410
World Wide Web: http://www.isdn.org

North American ISDN User's Forum (NIUF)

National Institute of Standards and Technology
Building 223, Room B364
Gaithersburg, MD 20899
Voice: 301-975-2937
World Wide Web: http://www.niuf.nist.gov/misc/niuf.html

This is a government-sponsored organization made up mostly of ISDN industry groups. It acts as a standards organization and offers several useful publications.

Texas ISDN User's Group

Voice: 915-646-2116
Fax: 915-643-9668
World Wide Web: http://www.crimson.com/isdn

TCP/IP Software

Internet Chameleon

NetManage, Inc.
10725 N. De Anza Blvd.
Cupertino, CA 95014
Voice: 408-973-7171
Fax: 408-257-6405
World Wide Web: http://www.netmanage.com

OnNet

FTP Software
2 High Street
North Andover, MA 01845
Voice: 508-685-4000
Fax: 508-659-6557
World Wide Web: http://www.ftp.com

SuperTCP Suite

Frontier Technologies Corporation
10201 N. Port Washington Road
Mequon, WI 53092
Voice: 414-241-4555
Fax: 414-241-7084
World Wide Web: http://www.frontiertech.com

Windows 95
Windows NT 4.0
Internet Explorer

Microsoft Corporation
One Microsoft Way
Redmond, WA 98052
Voice: 800-426-9400 or 206-882-8080
Fax: 206-936-7329
World Wide Web: http://www.microsoft.com

Glossary

ADSL *Asymmetric digital subscriber line.* A form of digital communications delivered via telephone lines that can support up to 6 Mbps for downloading. It may become a significant factor for future data communications.

analog communications The method of voice transmission used in today's telephone system. This method converts voice to electrical signals and amplifies them so that the voice can be sent over long distances. Using analog for data transmission is at the bottom of the telecommunications bandwidth food chain.

ANSI *American National Standards Institute.* The primary standards organization for the U.S., ANSI plays a significant role in defining ISDN standards.

asynchronous communications The form of data communications that transmits data one character at a time with start and stop bits. The method used for data communications over POTS using modems.

ATM *Asynchronous transfer mode.* A form of fast packet switching that allows for data transmission via broadband ISDN, a faster form of digital communications than ISDN.

AT&T 5ESS The leading telephone switch platform, made by AT&T. For ISDN, these switches use Custom (proprietary) or NI-1 software.

B channel *Bearer* channel. A 64 Kbps bearer channel used for delivering data or voice communications over ISDN. The standard BRI connection includes two B channels, for a total uncompressed capacity of 128 Kbps.

bandwidth The amount of data that can flow through a channel. The greater the bandwidth, the more data that can travel at one time.

bearer services A communication connection's capability to carry voice, circuit, or packet data. The two B channels in a BRI connection are bearer channels.

Bellcore Bell Communications Research. The research arm of the regional telephone companies. Bellcore was part of Bell Laboratories before the breakup of AT&T. Bellcore plays a leading role in developing ISDN standards and other ISDN activities among its member telephone companies.

BONDING *Bandwidth on demand interoperability group.* The concatenating of two or more B channels to form a single channel with a bandwidth greater than 64 Kbps. For applications such as desktop video conferencing, bonding combines the two B channels for a total of 128 Kbps to transmit video and audio.

bps *Bits per second.* The unit of measurement for data transmission speed over a data communications line.

BRI *Basic rate interface.* A defined interface to ISDN that includes two B (bearer) channels and one D (data) channel. Commonly referred to as 2B+D. Other configuration options are available in the BRI interface, depending on your telephone company. For example, you can get only one B channel, or two B channels and no D channel.

bridge A device that connects two networks of the same type.

BISDN *Broadband ISDN.* A type of ISDN service that uses fiber-optic lines and ATM to deliver bearer services with data transmission rates of more than 150 Mbps. This is the next generation of ISDN service that will replace ISDN delivered via the copper wiring used today.

cable modem A device for using cable TV links to transfer data at speeds of up to 10 Mbps for downloading. Cable offers a potential high bandwidth connection option in the future.

CACH EKTS *Call appearance call handling electronic key telephone set.* Supplements EKTS to allow more than one directory number and multiple call appearances on each directory number.

call appearances A supplementary ISDN service that allows multiple incoming calls. Each directory number can have multiple call appearances, depending on the switch type.

caller ID *Calling Number Identification.* A telephone company service that delivers the calling party's telephone number to the called party. The number can appear on an ISDN telephone, an LCD screen, a computer screen, or another device.

CAPI *Common ISDN API.* A collection of functions for handling ISDN communications at the messaging level. It's a more powerful set of functions than WinISDN.

CCITT *Comité Consultatif International de Télégraphie,* or International Telephone and Telegraph Consultative Committee. This organization is now called ITU, which stands for International Telephone Union. A United Nations organization that produces recommendations for standards for international ISDN.

central office (CO) The site where the local telephone switches reside for all the telephone system's call routing and other functions. This is the telephone company side of the local loop.

Centrex A service offering by telephone companies for flat-rate service via local switching features similar to those provided by an on-site PBX.

CHAP *Challenge Handshake Authentication Protocol.* CHAP is a security protocol that arranges an exchange of random numbers between computers. The machine receiving a number from the first computer performs calculations on that number using a previously agreed-upon string of characters as a secret encryption key.

circuit switching A form of communications in which an information transmission path between two devices is routed through one or more switches. The path is assigned for the duration of a call.

client/server computing The foundation for networking, in which one computer acts as the host or server and the other computer acts as a client. In the case of remote access, your PC acts as the client computer that connects to a server.

cloud A commonly used term that defines any large network, such as ISDN.

CODEC COder/DECoder. Transforms analog data into a digital data form and converts digital data back to analog form.

common carrier Telephone companies that provide long-distance telecommunication services, such as AT&T and MCI.

compatibility packages A standardized method used for ordering ISDN service. Not all telephone companies use this service.

compression A process for reducing the number of bits required to transmit information. For ISDN, the result of compression is data transmission speeds up to four times faster than without compression, or about 512 Kbps.

COS *Corporation for Open Systems,* a member-based organization that promotes open systems and connectivity. COS is instrumental in developing ISDN Ordering Codes for streamlining the acquisition of ISDN service from the telephone companies. COS is also instrumental in getting industry support for ISDN-1 standards.

CPE *Customer premises equipment.* The equipment after the point at which the telephone company terminates the line to the premises. In the United States, CPE includes the NT1 device. End users must purchase (or lease), install, and maintain their own CPE. In many other parts of the world, end-user equipment is part of the service provided by the telephone company.

CSD *Circuit-switched data.* An ISDN circuit-switched call for data in which a transmission path between two users is assigned for the duration of a call at a constant, fixed rate.

CSV *Circuit-switched voice.* An ISDN circuit-switched call for voice in which the transmission path between two users is assigned for the duration of a call at a constant, fixed rate.

CSV/CSD *Alternate circuit-switched voice/circuit-switched data.* A B channel configuration that allows either circuit-switched voice or circuit-switched data communication.

D channel *Data* channel. The separate channel for out-of-band signaling between the user and the ISDN network. The D channel can also be used to deliver X.25 data packets at up to 16 Kbps.

demarcation point The point at the customer premises where the line from the telephone company meets the premises wiring. From the demarcation point, the end user is responsible for the wiring. The physical device that provides the means to connect the telephone company's wire to the premises wiring is called a network interface box.

desktop video conferencing A PC-based video-conferencing system that allows people to conduct video conferencing in real time from their desks. The basic desktop video-conferencing system includes a video camera, a video card, and an ISDN adapter card.

Dial-Up Networking A Windows 95 and Windows NT 4.0 facility for connecting computers via modems and ISDN remote-access devices.

DMS-100 A telephone switch made by Nortel. For ISDN, these switches use proprietary or NI-1 software.

DN *Directory number.* Directory numbers are telephone numbers for ISDN. A BRI line can have up to eight directory numbers, depending on the switch type used by the telephone company.

DSS1 *Digital Subscriber Signaling System No. 1.* The network access signaling protocol for users connecting to ISDN. It includes the CCITT Q.931 and Q.932 standards.

DTE *Data Terminal Equipment.* Any device that converts information into digital signals for transmission or reconverts digital information into another form.

dynamic bandwidth allocation A key feature of ISDN remote-access devices that allows automatic adjustment of the number of B channels in use depending on the volume of data being sent or received. This feature saves you money because each B channel is billed as a separate charge. Automatically adjusting bandwidth up or down depending on your data volume means you use only what you need.

dynamic IP addressing An IP address is assigned to the client for the current session only. After the session ends, the IP address returns to a pool of IP addresses.

EKTS *Electronic key telephone set.* The National ISDN-1 standard for working with supplementary services on an ISDN telephone or analog telephone connected to an NT1 Plus device.

Ethernet The local area network protocol used in most PC networks. Typically, most Ethernet networks support data transmission speeds up to 10 Mbps.

exchange area A geographical area in which a single, uniform set of tariffs for telephone service is in place. A call between any two points in an exchange area is considered a local call.

EZ-ISDN A standardized set of ISDN line configurations developed by the North American ISDN User's Forum (NIUF). Designed to make ordering of ISDN service easier.

FCC *Federal Communications Commission.* The United States government agency responsible for regulating the telephone industry.

fiber optics A new generation of telecommunication wiring that uses light beams sent through thin strands of glass or other transparent materials. Fiber optics can transmit large amounts of data and form the physical transmission foundation for broadband ISDN.

full duplex The bidirectional communication capability in which transmissions travel in both directions simultaneously.

functional devices A classification of ISDN operational functions used to describe what tasks different components of an ISDN configuration perform. For example, the Network Termination 1 function defines the NT1 device that presents your premises as a node on the ISDN network. Another functional device is the terminal adapter, which defines the role of an adapter to convert some other form of communication to ISDN. For example, a TA (terminal adapter) allows an analog telephone to communicate over an ISDN device.

Group 3 Fax Currently, the most widely used facsimile protocol, which operates over analog telephone lines or with a terminal adapter over ISDN.

Group 4 Fax A facsimile protocol that allows high-speed, digital fax machines to operate over ISDN.

half duplex Data transmission that takes place in only one direction at a time.

IEC *InterExchange Carrier.* The telephone company that provides telephone service outside the local telephone companies. For example, AT&T and MCI are InterExchange Carriers. InterExchange Carriers are also referred to as common carriers.

IEEE 803.2 The protocol that defines an Ethernet network at the physical layer of network signaling and cabling.

in-band signaling Network signaling that is carried in the same channel as the bearer traffic. In analog telephone communications, the same circuits used to carry voice are used to transmit the signal for the telephone network. Touch-tone signals are an example of in-band signaling.

interface A specification that defines the protocols used at a particular reference point in a network. The *basic rate interface* (BRI) refers to an access interface to ISDN.

Internet The huge global network of networks based on the TCP/IP suite of protocols. The Internet, which is growing rapidly, currently encompasses more than 15,000 networks connecting more than 30 million users.

inter-networking Data communications across different network operating systems.

interoperable Two pieces of equipment are interoperable when they work together. Standards make devices from different vendors work with each other. For example, the H.320 standard for video conferencing allows you to use an Intel ProShare system to connect to a Vivo320 system.

IP *Internet Protocol.* The internetworking protocol that forms the basis of the Internet.

IPX *Internet Packet Exchange.* Novell's NetWare internetworking protocols.

ISDN *Integrated Services Digital Network.* The next generation of telecommunications services offered by telephone companies. ISDN delivers digital communications via standard POTS lines at a speed of 128 Kbps without compression.

ISDN address The address of a specific ISDN device. It consists of an ISDN number plus additional digits that identify a specific terminal at a user's interface. An ISDN number is the network address associated with a user's ISDN connection.

ISDN telephone A telephone designed for ISDN service. It typically includes programmable buttons for managing call features and an LCD display for viewing caller information.

ISP *Internet service provider.* A company offering connections to the Internet. ISPs come in all sizes, from national providers to regional and local providers.

ITC *Independent telephone company.* In the United States, a telephone company that was not owned by AT&T before divestiture.

ITU *International Telephone Union.* An organization under the United Nations that prepares telecommunications recommendations or standards, including many related to ISDN. The ITU was formally the CCITT.

Kbps *Kilobits per second.* The unit of measurement in thousands of bits per second for data transmission. ISDN has a data transmission capacity of 128 Kbps for the two B channels, or 64 Kbps for each B channel.

key systems Telephone equipment with extra buttons that provide users with more functionality than regular telephones. ISDN phones and NT1 Plus devices that support analog telephones include key systems. A key system is a protocol invoked when you press a sequence of keys on the analog or ISDN telephone's dialing pad.

LAN *Local area network.* A group of computers and other devices linked via a network operating system. LANs vary in size but are restricted to a single location because of cabling limitations. The leading protocol for LANs is Ethernet. Leading PC LANs include Novell's NetWare, Windows for Workgroups, and Windows NT.

LATA *Local access and transport area.* Local exchange carriers (RBOCs) provide service within a LATA. Typically, a LATA comprises multiple area codes. In most cases RBOCs are prohibited from offering telecommunication services between LATAs.

LEC *Local exchange carrier.* The local telephone company. An LEC is also called an RBOC (*Regional Bell Operating Company*).

local loop The pair of copper wires that connects the end user to the telephone company's central office, which is the gateway to the global telephone network. These wires, originally installed for analog communications, are the same wires used for ISDN service but require new equipment at the end user's premises and at the telephone company.

local loop qualification The process of checking the local loop distance, which is the distance between the customer's CPE and the central office switch. If the distance exceeds 18,000 feet, repeaters are required to boost the signal.

logical channels The three channels of a BRI connection, which are defined not as three physically separate wires but as three separate ISDN system channels.

LT *Line termination.* Defines the local loop at the telephone company side of an ISDN connection to match the NT1 function at the customer end of the local loop.

Mbps *Million bits per second.* A measurement for high-speed data transmission used in LANs and other digital communication links.

modem *Mod*ulator/*dem*odulator. A device used to send data over analog telephone lines. It converts digital signals to analog signals at the sending end and converts analog signals to digital signals at the receiving end.

NANP *North American Numbering Plan.* The familiar ten-digit numbering system used today in the United States, Canada, and Mexico, which includes the three-digit area code followed by the seven-digit local telephone number.

National ISDN Defined by Bellcore, National ISDN 1 *(NI-1)* is an agreement among telephone companies and CPE vendors to jointly provide the first phase of standards-based ISDN. NI-1 is a collection of standards to allow CPE to work across different telephone company switches using the basic rate interface.

NDIS *Network driver interface specification.* Developed by Microsoft, NDIS provides a common set of rules for network adapter manufacturers and network operating system (NOS) developers to use for communications between the network adapter and the NOS. Most network adapters now ship with an NDIS driver. If the NOS you use supports NDIS, which most do, you can use any network adapter that has an NDIS driver.

NetBEUI *NetBIOS Extended User Interface.* Microsoft's implementation of NetBIOS used in Windows for Workgroups, Windows 95, NT, and OS/2.

NetBIOS Developed by IBM and used as the basis for DOS and NT networks.

network interface box The point where the lines from the telephone company meet the wiring for your premises.

NIUF *North American ISDN User's Forum.* The National Institute for Standards and Technology formed the NIUF with ISDN industry players to identify ISDN applications and to encourage ISDN equipment vendors to develop CPE to meet end-user needs.

NT1 *Network Termination 1.* Located at the end-user side of the ISDN connection, this functional device represents the termination of the ISDN system at the end user's location. The NT1 function is embedded in NT1 and NT1 Plus devices.

NT1 Plus device A device that includes a built-in NT1 as well as ports to connect other devices (analog, ISDN, or X.25) to an ISDN line.

NT2 *Network Termination 2.* A device that handles network termination and switching functions, typically embodied in PBXs (private branch exchanges). An NT2 device performs intelligent operations such as switching and concentrating traffic across multiple B channels in a PRI line.

ODI *Open Datalink Interface.* The specification developed by Novell for supporting different adapters and *network operating systems* (NOS).

out-of-band signaling Allows telephone network management signaling functions and other services to be sent over a separate channel rather than the bearer channel. ISDN uses out-of-band signaling via the D channel. Out-of-band signaling used in ISDN consists of messages rather than audio signals, as is the case with the touch-tone analog telephone system.

packet switching A data transmission method in which data is transferred by packets, or blocks of data. Packets are sent using a store-and-forward method across nodes in a network.

PAP *Password Authentication Protocol.* A security protocol that establishes a two-way handshake to verify the identity of the two computers. Using PAP, passwords are sent in text format, so it offers little protection from hackers.

passband The frequency spectrum that determines the amount of data that can be transmitted through a channel. The passband is what determines the bandwidth of a channel.

passive bus Refers to the capability to connect multiple devices to a single BRI connection without repeaters to boost the signal. The configuration of the passive bus combines the terminating resistance for all the devices connected to your ISDN line to add up to 100 ohms.

PBX *Private branch exchange.* A telecommunications switch at a customer's premises that handles call management. The PBX connects to the telephone company via a dedicated, high-speed communications link to transport a large volume of traffic. Typically, PBX systems handle the internal telecommunications needs of large organizations.

PCM *Pulse code modulation.* The method used to convert analog audio to digitized audio.

phantom power The capability of the NT1 to provide power to the Terminal Equipment 1 or terminal adapters via two wires in an eight-wire cable.

Plug and Play A system for simplifying installation of hardware devices on a Windows 95 computer. Automates hardware recognition and driver installation and management.

point-to-multipoint configuration A physical connection in which a single network termination supports multiple terminal equipment devices. This configuration is supported by the S/T interface.

point-to-multipoint connection A connection established between one device on one end and more than one device on the other end.

point-to-point configuration A physical connection in which a single NT1 functional device supports only one device.

point-to-point connection A connection established between two devices through ISDN.

POP *Point of presence.* A local access point for connecting to an Internet service provider. Your telecommunications charges are affected by your proximity to a POP.

POS *Point of sale.* Any device used for handling transactions, such as card readers for credit card or debit card transactions.

POTS *Plain Old Telephone Service.* A term used for standard analog telecommunication.

powering The powering of the NT1 and CPE equipment. The NT1 and any CPE connected to it must be powered locally. Usually, these powering capabilities are built into the NT1 or NT1 Plus device.

PPP *Point-to-Point Protocol.* A communications protocol that allows a computer using TCP/IP to connect directly to the Internet. The new PPP/MP protocol is an improved version of this protocol for ISDN connection to the Internet.

PPP/MP Point-to-Point Protocol/Multilink Protocol. The new Point-to-Point Protocol for ISDN connection that allows use of both B channels for remote access to the Internet. PPP/MP also allows different remote-access devices to communicate with each other.

PRI *Primary Rate Interface.* An ISDN interface designed for high-volume data communications. PRI consists of 23 B channels at 64 Kbps each and 1 D channel at 64 Kbps.

protector block The point where the lines from the telephone company meet the lines from premises wiring before the network interface box.

protocol A set of rules that defines how different computer systems and other devices interoperate with each other.

PS/2 Powering for any ISDN device that doesn't have a local power source but is connected to an NT1 or an NT1 Plus device.

PSC Public Service Commission. See PUC.

PSTN *Public Switched Telephone Networks.* A POTS-based system that uses analog signals between the branch exchange and each end device, such as a telephone or a modem.

PUC *Public Utilities Commission.* Also called Public Service Commission (PSC). A government agency, usually at the state level, that regulates telephone companies and other utilities. PUCs define how you're charged for telephone services (charges are called tariffs). The FCC deals with some similar functions at the federal level.

R interface See R reference point.

R reference point The ISDN reference point that sits between the non-ISDN device and the *terminal adapter* (TA) functional device.

rate adaptation A system that allows two pieces of data equipment operating at different data transmission rates to interoperate.

RBOC *Regional Bell Operating Company.* One of the local exchange carriers that were created during the breakup of AT&T. RBOCs provide telephone service in a region of the United States. They currently can't offer long-distance telephone service between LATAs or manufacture equipment.

reference point A specific point in the model of how ISDN works. Each component of this model is identified using a reference point. For example, the U reference point defines the local loop of an ISDN connection. These reference points are also called interfaces, such as the U interface or the S/T interface.

repeater Equipment used to amplify a signal to boost the range of the signal over longer distances.

RJ-11 connector A modular connector used for four- or six-wire analog devices.

RJ-45 connector A modular jack that can hold up to four pairs of wires. It looks similar to an RJ-11 but is larger. ISDN connections use RJ-45 jacks at the S/T interface.

RS-232 An industry standard for serial communications connections. The current version of this standard is RS-232C. Most PCs include one or more RS-232 ports for connecting devices such as a modem and a mouse.

router A hardware device that acts as a gateway among different types of networks to route data packets based on their protocols and addresses.

serial communication The transmission of data one bit at a time over a single line. Serial communications can be synchronous or asynchronous.

S reference point The ISDN reference point that represents where a CPE connects to a customer switching device, such as a PBX system. This type of device is called an NT2 functional device.

S/T interface *See* S/T reference point.

S/T reference point Combines the ISDN reference points where a device connects to either an NT1 or an NT2 functional device.

SPID *Service profile identifier.* An alphanumeric string that uniquely identifies the service capabilities of an ISDN terminal. This is an identifier that points to a particular location in the telephone company's central office switch memory where relevant details about the device are stored.

SS#7 *Signaling System Number 7.* A common channel signaling system that performs network signaling functions. Used to establish ISDN call functions.

standard A set of technical specifications used to establish uniformity in hardware and in software.

static IP addressing An assigned IP address used to connect to a TCP/IP network. The same IP number is used every time the connection is made.

subscriber loop The pair of copper wires that connects the end user to the telephone network. These same wires are used to provide ISDN service but need the addition of the NT1 at the end-user location and the line termination at the central office.

supplementary services The collection of voice communications services available via ISDN. These services include call-management features such as call appearances, conference calling, and call forwarding.

switch The equipment that connects users of the telecommunications network. Each subscriber has a dedicated loop to the nearest telephone switch. All of these switches have access to trunk lines for making calls beyond the local exchange area. A call from one user to another consists of a loop at each end of the connection, with switches and trunk lines used to route the connection between them.

synchronous communications A data transmission method in which data is transmitted in blocks separated by equal time intervals. This is a faster method of data communications than asynchronous, but both are serial communications.

T interface *See* T reference point.

T reference point The ISDN reference point that represents where an ISDN device connects to an NT1 functional device.

TA *Terminal adapter.* The ISDN functional device that allows non-ISDN devices to work with ISDN. Any device that adapts a non-ISDN terminal for an ISDN interface. A TA gives a TE2 device the functionality of a TE1 device.

TAPI *Telephony Application Programming Interface.* A Windows standard for controlling any kind of telephone interaction. TAPI also arbitrates conflicts between applications requesting use of communications ports, modems, and so on.

tariff A rate and availability schedule for telecommunications services that is filed with and approved by a regulatory body to become effective. Tariffs also include general terms and conditions of service.

TCP/IP *Transmission Control Protocol and Internet Protocol.* The suite of networking protocols that lets disparate types of computers communicate over the Internet.

TCP/IP stack The software that allows a computer to communicate via TCP/IP.

TE *Terminal equipment.* A term for any device connected to an ISDN line.

TE1 *Terminal Equipment 1.* Any ISDN-ready device that connects directly to ISDN. An ISDN telephone is an example of a TE1 device.

TE2 *Terminal Equipment 2.* Any non-ISDN device that must be used with a terminal adapter to work with ISDN. An analog telephone is an example of a TE2 device. The combination of a TE2 and a TA has the same functionally as a TE1.

Telecommunications Act of 1996 Recent legislation passed by the U.S. Congress to open up competition in the telecommunications and cable industries.

telephony The marriage of computers and telecommunications.

UART *Universal asynchronous receiver/transmitter.* UART chips are the part of your PC's COM port that handles the communications between the CPU and the device attached to the COM port. Windows 95 supports the 16550A UART chip for higher bps rates.

U interface *See* U reference point.

U reference point The reference point of an ISDN connection that includes the local loop wiring up to the NT1 functional device.

(VIA) *Vendors ISDN Association* is an industry trade group of ISDN CPE vendors that is working with the telecommunications industry to streamline and improve ISDN provisioning.

usage sensitive The cost of a service, such as ISDN or analog telephone service, that is based on the time you actually use the service.

UPS *Uninterruptible power supply.* A device that ensures a backup power supply for electrical devices in the event of a power outage. For ISDN, NT1 Plus devices can include UPS for maintaining power for analog voice communications during a power outage.

WAN *Wide area network.* A communication network that connects geographically dispersed sites.

whiteboard Collaboration software typically bundled with desktop video-conferencing systems. It allows two users to share a computer screen just as people share a whiteboard in a meeting room.

WinISDN An ISDN communications API designed for Windows. It is incorporated in most third-party TCP/IP products for supporting ISDN adapter cards. The Windows 95 TCP/IP stack does not support WinISDN.

WinSock A program that conforms to a set of standards called the Windows Socket API *(Application Programming Interface)*. A WinSock program controls the link between Microsoft Windows software and a TCP/IP program.

World Wide Web A hypertext multimedia-based system for accessing Internet resources. Commonly referred to as the Web or WWW, it lets users download files, listen to audio, and view images and videos. Users can jump around the Web using hyperlinks embedded in documents. The leading Web browsers are Netscape and Mosaic.

X.25 The protocol for packet-mode services as defined by CCITT. A CCITT interface standard that lets computing devices communicate via wide area packet-switched data networks.

Index

Notes

Notes

ALPHA TELECOM, INC.
YOUR ISDN CONNECTION

CyberJet Series Internal ISDN PC Terminal Adapters

Provides instant ISDN connections and delivers digital high speed Internet access and lightning fast file transfer. CyberJet-U features a built-in NT1.

Super NT1

An integrated TA/NT1 that allows analog devices and ISDN Terminal Equipment to simultaneously access BRI services. The Super NT1 provides one U-interface, two S/T-interfaces and two "ISDN ready" analog ports for connecting analog phones, modems, fax and answering machines to ISDN.

UT620 NT1

Provides the link between ISDN CPE and the central office. Easy-to-install, affordable and compact. The UT620 is available with a power adapter (PA) or with a PS2 switching power supply (SPS).

ALPHA TELECOM, INC.
PANVEST GROUP

7501 S. Memorial Parkway, Suite 212, Huntsville, Alabama 35802
Tel: 205.881.8743; Fax: 205.880.9720
E-mail: sales@alpha-tele.com; Home Page:http://www.alpha-tele.com

NO FINES FOR TRAVELING TWICE AS FAST!

$14.95 ISDN
Internet Access Only 14.95/month

ZipLink Internet is a Full-Service ISP With a State-of-the-Art Nationwide Network

- **ZipLink** offers standard modem accounts at $16.95/month: ISDN is no extra charge

- ISDN access available from all of our local numbers

- Free licensed copy of Netscape Navigator

- 7 day free trial; money-back guarantee

- Nationwide access in 36 major metropolitan areas

- Unlimited free technical support

- Support for LAN connections, including router purchase, configuration, and installation

ZipLink Network: Technical Specs For Our Network

- Ascend MAX 4000 communications servers

- Dial tone delivered on fiber optic T1s, PRIs, and T3s

- Cisco 7000 and 4700 series routers

- WorldCom multi-megabit national backbone

- Internet feeds on T3

- Redundant feeds on T1

- Peering agreements in place over T3 to MAE-East

- Pentium and Alpha Unix servers

- 24 x 7 Network Operations Center

It's About Freedom - It's About Service - It's About Time

1-888-ZIPLINK
or
1-888-948-5465

ZIPLINK
INTERNET

ZipLink provides dial-up services, ISDN, dedicated lines, and full web site hosting and design services.

http://www.ziplink.net

get hooked

isdn isdn isdn isdn isdn isdn isdn isdn isdn isdn isdn isdn upsi upsi isdn isdn upsi upsi upsi isdn upsi upsi isdn upsi upsi isdn

i s d n

Tired of waiting all day for those really neato images to download off the web? A 64kbps ISDN line from TIAC reduces wasted time on the web. Our ISDN accounts offer 100 or 300 hours of access; award winning service; excellent software and a user kit; a subscription to Hotlist, TIAC's monthly magazine; free access to Email; access to over 28,000 USENET newsgroups including TIAC's; local phone calls for access and customer service; hold times of under one minute; 15 minute Email response from customer service; 10M of storage on our web servers; and discounts at dozens of retail outlets.

212.748.5360 ext 706 • 617.276.7422 ext 409
202.463.5107 ext 1003

TIAC
WHERE IT'S @!

175 the great road • bedford, ma • 01730 • www.tiac.net • info@tiac.ne

The High Quality, Low Cost Internet Videoconferencing Solution for Your PC!

VideumConf Pro™

VideumConf Pro has been specially designed for Internet videoconferencing. Videum technology lies at the heart of current products from PictureTel, Vivo Software, and Netscape. Full-duplex audio gives you true desktop videoconferencing and Internet telephone. Color video images appear clearer than ever. Videum also supports up to three video cameras for sophisticated conferencing involving people, documents, and overhead displays — each easily controlled locally or remotely through Videum software. With award-winning Enhanced CU-SeeMe, you can use your existing communications device, or one of your choice, and communicate across the Internet with a modem, ISDN or LAN.

Includes
- VideumAV ISA audio/video capture add-on card
- VideumCam color video camera
- Videum Software for Windows 3.11, 95 and NT 4.0
  - Video/audio/image capture application
  - Local and remote camera control application
- White Pine Software Enhanced CU-SeeMe desktop videoconferencing software

Features
- NO-DMA, NO-INTERRUPT installation
- Support for up to three cameras
- Windows 3.11, Windows 95, Windows NT 4.0
- Full-duplex audio — for hands-free operation
- Communication device-independent (modem, LAN, ISDN, ATM)
- Local and remote video camera control for controlling pan, tilt, zoom, color, brightness & more

20% Discount for ISDN For Dummies Readers
Just Mention This Ad

To order, call
1-888-4-WINNOV

To order outside the US, call +1 408-733-9500

"Four stars! All the options you need for videoconferencing and video capture."
PC Computing, 10/96

Winnov
1150 Kifer Rd., Suite 201 Sunnyvale, CA 94086
Tel: (408) 733-9500
Fax: (408) 733-5922
E-mail: info@winnov.com

www.winnov.com

IDG BOOKS WORLDWIDE REGISTRATION CARD

Title of this book: **ISDN For Dummies®, 2E**

My overall rating of this book: ❑ Very good [1] ❑ Good [2] ❑ Satisfactory [3] ❑ Fair [4] ❑ Poor [5]

How I first heard about this book:

❑ Found in bookstore; name: [6] _____

❑ Advertisement: [8] _____

❑ Word of mouth; heard about book from friend, co-worker, etc.: [10] _____

❑ Book review: [7] _____

❑ Catalog: [9] _____

❑ Other: [11] _____

What I liked most about this book:

_____

_____

What I would change, add, delete, etc., in future editions of this book:

_____

_____

Other comments: _____

Number of computer books I purchase in a year: ❑ 1 [12] ❑ 2-5 [13] ❑ 6-10 [14] ❑ More than 10 [15]

I would characterize my computer skills as: ❑ Beginner [16] ❑ Intermediate [17] ❑ Advanced [18] ❑ Professional [19]

I use ❑ DOS [20] ❑ Windows [21] ❑ OS/2 [22] ❑ Unix [23] ❑ Macintosh [24] ❑ Other: [25]_____
(please specify)

I would be interested in new books on the following subjects:
(please check all that apply, and use the spaces provided to identify specific software)

❑ Word processing: [26] _____

❑ Data bases: [28] _____

❑ File Utilities: [30] _____

❑ Networking: [32] _____

❑ Other: [34] _____

❑ Spreadsheets: [27] _____

❑ Desktop publishing: [29] _____

❑ Money management: [31] _____

❑ Programming languages: [33] _____

I use a PC at (please check all that apply): ❑ home [35] ❑ work [36] ❑ school [37] ❑ other: [38] _____

The disks I prefer to use are ❑ 5.25 [39] ❑ 3.5 [40] ❑ other: [41]_____

I have a CD ROM: ❑ yes [42] ❑ no [43]

I plan to buy or upgrade computer hardware this year: ❑ yes [44] ❑ no [45]

I plan to buy or upgrade computer software this year: ❑ yes [46] ❑ no [47]

Name: _____ Business title: [48] _____ Type of Business: [49] _____

Address (❑ home [50] ❑ work [51]/Company name: _____)

Street/Suite# _____

City [52]/State [53]/Zipcode [54]: _____ Country [55] _____

❑ **I liked this book!** You may quote me by name in future
IDG Books Worldwide promotional materials.

My daytime phone number is _____

IDG BOOKS

THE WORLD OF
COMPUTER
KNOWLEDGE

❏ YES!

Please keep me informed about IDG's World of Computer Knowledge.
Send me the latest IDG Books catalog.

COMPUTER
BOOK SERIES
FROM IDG